EXISTENCE
and LOGIC

EXISTENCE
and LOGIC

Milton K. Munitz

New York: NEW YORK UNIVERSITY PRESS
1974

Copyright © by New York University Press
Library of Congress Catalog Card Number: 74-10417
ISBN: 8147-5366-3

Manufactured in the United States of America

To

WILLIAM BARRETT

Contents

II   *Logic and Existence: Some Current Theories*

Preface

What to make of existence (or, as some would prefer to say, of Being) has been a major preoccupation of Western philosophers ever since the days of the Pre-Socratics. It lies at the heart of that area of philosophy called 'metaphysics' or 'ontology'. A major traditional solution to this problem had been that of theism and its attendant doctrine of Creation. However, for many this solution is no longer a viable one. For such persons as well as others the philosophic problem of existence persists in one form or another, and is the central matter calling for attention if a satisfactory philosophy is to be found at all.

The search for such a philosophy, when looked at in very broad terms, dominates the history of philosophy during the entire modern era, ever since the long-standing prevalence of the medieval world view succumbed under repeated and varied assaults. However, the lineaments of a philosophy that would prove to be as satisfying and therefore as widely accepted as the one it would replace have not yet come into sufficiently full view. What form a theory of existence or Being will have to assume in order to achieve soundness and acceptability is the fundamental philosophic question, still under active debate, and one to which all other questions are in a sense subordinate. For until it is solved, the solutions to all other philosophic problems, even where available, will continue to lack a unifying framework.

The search for a promising path on which to pursue this goal of formulating a satisfactory ontology is what has animated my own philosophic efforts, both in two previous works—*Space, Time, and Creation* [1] and *The Mystery of Existence* [2]—and in the present book.

I recall with what excitement and hope I began, in the late

thirties, to read the literature of the recently revived science of cosmology, as represented by the writings of Einstein, Tolman, Robertson, Hubble, Bondi, Hoyle, McVittie, Milne, and others. For here was the promise, it seemed to me at the time, that now, at last, with the refined conceptual tools of relativity-theory joined to the powerful telescopes of the astronomer, one might develop a theory of the space-time properties of the universe as a whole that would give us what we are looking for. It is true that no satisfactory model of the physical universe as a whole was then available (in the thirties and forties), nor has one been settled on by the specialists even now. But this was not the important consideration, for surely with persistent inquiry some relative success of this sort ought, at some point, be forthcoming.

But even if this should happen, I soon began to ask myself, would it really solve the problem of existence? As a philosophic observer and outsider with respect to this scientific bustle, I came to realize (what a more perspicacious philosopher might have seen from the very beginning) that even if found, this, by itself, would not provide the philosophic answer to the philosophic problem I or others were enmeshed in. For a theory of the universe, in the way the cosmologist construes what this amounts to, could not, _as such,_ provide an analysis of the ontologic problem of existence. However important and intellectually exciting it is to develop a cosmology, or even (as I attempted in _Space, Time, and Creation_) to examine the methodological features, aims, and limits of what is involved in the construction of cosmological theories, this could not give us a theory of existence. A theory of the universe, like any scientific theory, is surely relevant to one's conception of existence, but a theory of existence, I came to realize, cannot be replaced by, or reduced to, a cosmological theory. While not exactly a false scent, the philosophic discussion of cosmology could not take the place of, or solve, the problems of ontology proper, that is to say, of that part of philosophy that deals specifically with _the problem of existence._

But what _is_ the problem? Is the 'problem' of existence perhaps only another way of conveying a sense of the _mystery_ of existence? And is not this sense of mystery, as some skeptic might suggest, nothing more than the mental cramp induced by the hangover of a pseudo-problem with which theism itself had grappled and to which it had its own answer? Was it not the case, in other words, that the 'problem' of existence was nothing more than the persistence of the question "Why is there Something rather than Nothing?" (that is, "Why is there a World at all?"). And should we not try to *get rid* of that 'problem'? Is not the so-called 'mystery of existence' a cloak for a meaningless question for which a thoroughgoing course of philosophic therapy might prove effective by eliminating it once and for all from the sphere of our intellectual preoccupations?

I turned, next, in *The Mystery of Existence,* to explore this theme, and found that far from being either eliminable or a question to which only theism is allied, the mystery of existence can be framed as a question both meaningful and yet unanswerable, even after one has discarded theistic or other 'solutions' to the question. The agnosticism which I there defended, the acknowledgment of the fact that *there is* an uneliminable mystery at the heart of existence, is a position I continue to believe we must retain in any satisfactory theory of existence.

However, the mystery of existence is *only one side*—though a crucial one—of the general character of existence. The *problem* of working out a theory of existence is not exhausted by, or reducible to, the matter of recognizing the *mystery* of existence. A satisfactory theory of existence would have to leave room for both the intelligibility *and* the unknowability of existence. But how, precisely, is this to be done? To answer this question requires a systematic analysis of the *meaning of 'existence',* and *this,* it seems to me, is genuinely *the problem of existence* for philosophy.

In short, an examination of the philosophic *problem* of existence is to be distinguished from a discussion of the *mystery* of existence. Both the problem and the mystery may be put in the form of questions, but the questions, though related, are nevertheless different. To speak of 'the mystery of existence' is to focus on the question of how to *explain* the existence of the world. It is to ask for the reason for the existence of the world. In the present inquiry, however, I shall not be concerned principally with the matter of the mystery of existence, although at the very end of our inquiry, in discussing what it is to speak of the existence of the world as a whole, I shall link our discussion of this topic with the question of the mystery of existence. The question, rather, that I am principally interested in examining here is what I call 'the philosophical *problem* of existence'. This problem is one of analyzing what is *meant* by using the terms 'exist' or 'existence'. As a philosophical problem, I believe it *can* be answered, although the answer consists essentially in giving a *clarification* of how these terms are to be understood, *not an explanation* in the sense of giving reasons for the existence of the world or for any of its parts.

In recent philosophic literature the logicians have undertaken a vigorous and many-sided series of attacks on the problem of existence as *they* understand it. Might it not be, after all, that here, in the carefully formulated aseptic language of the logician (whether formal or 'informal'), one will find a way of dealing with the problem of existence (in the sense of giving an analysis of the concept of existence) that will be responsible and successful? Russell, for one, and more recently Quine, for example, have been fairly clear and firm in their claims that it is to quantificational logic to which we must turn in order to understand how to deal with the meaning of 'existence'. And other voices, too, have arisen—not always belonging to followers of the traditional orthodoxy of *Principia Mathematica*—who would offer us their own improvements upon and alternatives to that orthodoxy. The present book, while not an exhaustive or technical survey of all these recent tendencies, selects some examples of these trends and seeks to come to terms with them.

To approach the question of existence from the side of logic brings to the fore such matters as the analysis of the general *form of propositions,* the use of *quantifiers* and *variables,* the nature of *reference* and of *predication.* I shall argue that attention to these matters (where the question of existence is concerned, and however relevant and important they are), proves to be insufficient. Ontology, as a theory of existence, cannot abdicate its responsibility to logic. Logic, where it concerns existence, needs to be subordinated to an *ontology* of existence, not the other way around. It is the task of ontology, not of logic, to develop a theory of existence. And this is not a mere question of terminology. The stress and direction of interest, the orientation, are altogether different. For ontology it is existence —what is 'out there'—that is of controlling interest; for logic it is the form of statements and the kind of linguistic devices we use that are of controlling interest. What can be captured by starting with one orientation rather than the other is likely, therefore, to be different even though the results, for some particular account, may overlap. My own approach would restore and preserve priority for ontology when it comes to studying the meaning of 'existence', rather than cede this interest or acknowledge it as belonging primarily to logic.

To put it briefly, the primary orientation I shall adopt in dealing with the ontology of existence is one based on a cosmologic concern with the Universe rather than one based primarily on a study of logic, on a theory of meaning, or on a philosophy of language. By 'cosmology' here I understand, in its broader usage, whatever has to do with the Universe and all that it contains. This will include, of course, the Universe as studied in astronomy, that is, as an all-inclusive system of galaxies; but it will include much else besides since it will have to do with whatever is to be found within the Universe, and as located in space and time, regardless of its scale of magnitude or evolutionary development. It is cosmology in this broad sense which gives us, in my opinion, a proper and fundamental orientation for discussing the meaning of 'existence'. Other disciplines such as logic and philosophy of language, are to be appealed to for giving us the *tools* for dealing with existence in this primary cosmologic sense.

One immediate consequence of taking cosmology rather than language as our guide is that the mereological distinctions between 'whole' and 'part' will be of primary interest. While to be sure a study of 'quantification', 'instantiation', 'predication', 'singular term', 'object', 'sentence', 'truth and falsity', and related matters will—as the stock-in-trade of students of logic and language—make their important contributions to the study of 'existence', we shall turn not to these primarily but to the notions of 'whole' and 'part', as connected with the Universe and its constituents, in order to obtain the crucial and guiding concepts for our analysis.

I emerge with some results, accordingly, and especially in Part III, that, while not overlooking the contributions of logic, point to the direction in which, it seems to me, one should look for a satisfactory discussion of the nature of existence as a primary ontologic concept. The point of view I argue for is an ontology that would do justice to two dimensions of existence, or to two directions in which the meaning of this term can be explicated. One has to do with what is involved in speaking of individual existents, that, as parts of the world, are in space and time, and are qualitied, structured, and determinate. The other has to do with what is involved in speaking of the world as the totality of individual existents, or with Existence as such. To work out such a theory would require that we not only deal with what we mean when we speak of individual existents and proceed to formulate sentences about them, but with that sense of 'existence' that lies beyond language and conceptualization altogether (an awareness of which is for the most part, therefore, wholly outside the ken and concern of the logician).

It is the task of ontology, as I conceive it, to work out the special character of each of these dimensions of existence and the relations between them. The ontology I propose is one in which both the contributions of logic, empirical science, and cosmology on the one hand, and the legitimate and important claims of mystical experience and a religious response to existence, on the other, are acknowledged and seen to cohere in perfect harmony with, and as complements to, one another. In connection with this latter aspect (the 'religious' one), the view of existence I accept is one that has ample room for a recognition of the 'transcendent' and for an exercise of a type of spirituality that is no longer tied exclusively to a theistic philosophy, but that finds a natural home and scope here. (The present book only lays the groundwork for, and points in the direction of, how to characterize such an exercise of spirituality and a religious response to existence; it does not pursue the details on this occasion.)

What the reader will find, then, in the following pages, is one more attempt to work out a theory of existence. It is an attempt that will not be so novel that it will not show marked affinities to what other writers or older traditions have called attention to. At the same time it claims some novelty for itself in the way it arrives at those results, and through considerations that have some special interest and relevance for our own day.

I am indebted to the Rockefeller Foundation for the opportunity to do some of the writing of this book while a resident scholar at the Villa Serbelloni (Bellagio, Italy) during the early months of 1972. I have had the benefit, too, of many discussions with my friend Professor William Barrett of New York University. Finally, I wish to record my indebtedness to my wife for many helpful comments and suggestions.

Introduction

Chapter 1

The Philosophical Problem of Existence

1.1   *The Concept of Existence*

Consider the following sentences:

1. This table exists.
2. I exist.
3. The Temple of Solomon no longer exists.
4. Pegasus does not exist.
5. The World (the Universe) exists.

It would normally be accepted, I shall assume, that not only is each of the foregoing sentences grammatically well formed, but true as well. These sentences might very well appear in ordinary discourse and the truth of them accepted preanalytically, that is, without benefit of the kind of reflective, critical analysis we associate with philosophy.

My purpose is to begin by considering the uses of the term 'exist(s)' in sentences such as these, for if we can utter sentences in which the word 'exist(s)' functions in such a way that the entire sentence is true, then clearly the use of the term has some value or importance for us. We are able, apparently, to convey *something* by the use of the term in this grammatical position that evokes our assent to the entire sentence in which it appears. And of course the philosophical question is precisely how to bring out what that 'something' is. To admit this much is not to commit ourselves in advance to any one philosophical position; for example, neither to the view that 'exists' is a predicate applicable to individuals, nor to any other. Nor does it prohibit us from transforming the original grammatical sentence by rephrasing, by the substitution of other expressions, or by the introduction of specially devised technical terms and symbols. These are all matters to be investigated and the merits of this or that analysis or philosophic proposal considered.

One task, for example, would be to examine what it means to say that some individual object, person, or occurrence (for example, this table, I, The Temple of Solomon, Socrates, that lightning flash) exists (or existed). And another task is to examine what it means to say that the world exists. Further, in this connection, we should need to inquire whether the use of the term 'exists' in both types of sentence has the same use, or whether on the contrary there are distinguishable senses of 'exist' involved. Also, of course, as part of such an inquiry, there is the question of how the two types of sentences, or, better, that which they are about—the extralinguistic situation or facts they describe or point to—are related to each other. What is the connection between what is conveyed by a true sentence such as 'This table exists' and what is conveyed by the sentence 'The world exists'?

One way, then, in which one might formulate the philosophical problem with respect to existence is to say it is a matter of giving a clear, coherent, and cogent analysis of what it means to say that an individual, say this table, exists, and what it means to say that the world as a whole itself exists. In starting with sentences such as 'This table exists' or 'The world exists', we are starting, as I have said, with what everyone knows and accepts. The call for conceptual analysis, in this case, does not arise, as it does in the case of some other philosophic inquiries, because we are troubled by some paradox, puzzle, or antinomy. We are not trying—in connection with the problem of existence we have just briefly formulated—to somehow dissolve a puzzle, or to rid ourselves of one or another beliefs that are in conflict with one another. Our goal is simply one of trying to *deepen* our insight, not one of looking to remove or disabuse ourselves of the belief in the truth of the sentences we started with.

I have started with examples of sentences in which the term 'exists' is used in ordinary language and in which the use of this term as it occurs in these sentences is generally regarded as being non-controversial. To this extent we may say that the term thus used or the concept it expresses belongs to 'common sense'. But if the task of philosophy is to deepen or analyze this concept, what we shall emerge with is something we may call a *philosophic* concept of existence. It is to be hoped, of course, that the philosophic concept (or, better, the entire set of sentences which explicates the term 'exists' and thereby constitutes a philosophic *theory* of its meaning) will not only preserve a genuine continuity with the commonsense concept with which we started, but will be accepted as a philosophic account that does in fact give us a better (because deeper) grasp of what we should want to say about the term 'exist'. Yet of course each philosophic theory that starts out in the same way—that is, by trying to clarify a concept already in ordinary use (rather than by trying to fashion a concept *de novo* and therefore as having no previous commitment to clarifying a term in current usage)—will share the same hope. However, we know that philosophic theories differ, and this is to be expected since they represent acts of *creative* analysis, they constitute at bottom a set of *proposals* as to how we should, if called upon, offer to 'bring out' the meaning of the concept with which we started. Far from having a single course of analysis we are constrained to follow, we are presented instead with a set of suggestions—what I am calling 'philosophic theories'—among which we are asked to make a choice or, if none proves satisfactory, to undertake the construction of some new set of proposals. What I shall offer in what follows, especially Part III of the present book, are some suggestions, to some extent only programmatic for further research, as to how this analysis or clarification of the concept of existence as I have sketched it ought to be carried out.

To my own account of what is to be taken as constituting 'the philosophical problem of existence' in the sense I have briefly described, it may nevertheless be objected that it is unduly restrictive. It may be legitimate, some critic might object, to begin by considering the noncontroversial sentences I began with, but the fact is that, controversial or not, some people do use the term 'exist' in connection with God, numbers, universals, and so on, and surely one cannot simply ignore or dismiss these uses without examining them and without determining whether, after all, they do have both meaning and truth. And if one does examine them (our critic continues) it might turn out that the sense of 'exist' used in them is a perfectly acceptable one. In that case one should not restrict the investigation into the concept of existence to the cases listed, namely, individual ('space-time') existents, such as material objects, events, persons, and the world as a whole as composed of these. By considering (as I indeed plan to do) the use of 'exists' only in connection with the individual existents and in connection with the world as a whole, it could be argued, I am failing to allow for the perfectly legitimate sense in which we could maintain that there are possibly still other modes of existence. Let it be granted, it might be said, that the question of the existence of God (where God is thought of as transcending and in some sense distinct from the world) is a matter of controversy; let it be granted, too, that the existence of abstract entities such as classes, universals, and propositions (as distinct from sentences) is under active debate. Should we not say, therefore, that while ontology is concerned with *existence* (or, as some prefer to say, with *being*)—precisely because there are differences of opinion—we should leave open the question of what forms, types, or modalities of existence (or being) there are, and for our *particular* ontology to declare? Why, after all, should we not leave room, for example, for an ontology that includes a belief in the existence of God as in traditional theism, or an ontology that subscribes to the existence of universals as in Platonism, or a Meinongian ontology that allows for the existence in some special sense of round squares or Pegasus? Should we not, therefore, prefer a formulation such as Quine's that at least leaves the matter open as to what types of individual entities we may wish to commit ourselves to? Or a formulation which, in using the traditional terminology of 'being', says that the study of ontology studies what it is 'to be' in general, and therefore permits us to consider various modes of being, without binding ourselves in advance as to what these are?

My reply to this objection is the following. In the first place, and at the very least, ontology—*however one defines it*—is concerned to examine the sense or senses in which we say an individual, such as a material object, event, or person exists, and also what it means to say the world exists. Since these are, we shall assume, noncontroversial cases in which we do use the term 'exists', these uses, even our critic must agree, call for philosophic analysis. In the second place, however, and this is where the difference with my critic sets in, I should want to *propose* that the legitimate uses of 'exists' are in fact to be *confined* to the cases mentioned, namely, to individual existents as parts of the world and the world itself. The disagreement with anyone who would dispute this restriction is in part a terminological one, but also in part a disagreement over what our ontology needs to be in order to be adequate. As a terminological matter, I should wish to restrict the term 'existence' in the way previously pointed out. In short, I prefer to use the term 'existence' as having to do exclusively with the sorts of subjects I mentioned: individual constituents of the world and the world itself. To those who would speak of the existence of God, the existence of classes, propositions, and universals, to those who might even wish to speak of the existence of round squares or Pegasus, I should say that their use of 'exists' is wholly different from mine. They might wish to allow for an extended or neutral use of 'exists' (or 'being'), and they might accordingly propose to separate out the type of existence or being which belongs to the world and its constituents, and to distinguish them from other types. This could be done, for example, by speaking of divine existence as *necessary* and the world's existence as *contingent,* or by distinguishing, with (the early) Russell and Moore, the domains of *existence* and *subsistence* as species of *being*; or, with Meinong, distinguishing the domains of the actual and the possible along with the impossible, as having *Sosein.* And so on. Let those who wish to defend one or another of these kinds of ontologies do so. Their terminology, orientation, and conclusions are not mine. What the theist calls 'the contingent existence of the world', what the early Russell calls 'existence' as distinguished from 'subsistence', what Meinong calls the domain of 'the actual', is what I call 'existence'. But I reject the wider frameworks within which they would include 'existence' so understood. Given what others would prefer to speak of as the existence (or perhaps being) of mathematical objects, universals, God, and so on, I should myself reject this use of the term 'existence' as applicable to what these terms signify.

Thus, the disagreement with someone who would disapprove of my own way of talking and thinking is not just a terminological one. The terminological choices reflect more basic conceptual choices, different ways of ordering and interpreting our experience. Here it is true I cannot appeal simply to 'common sense' or 'ordinary usage'. What I propose to work with, therefore, is an ontology—a philosophic viewpoint—which deals with 'existence' in the way I have briefly indicated. There is no reason, therefore, why I should have to accept, for example, Quine's philosophy, or the early Russell's, or the theist's, or Meinong's, and say that what I am doing, in talking about existence, is exploring one 'part', or one 'domain', or one 'dimension', of what their conception of ontology would allow. To grant this much, for me, is already to subscribe to and to submit to *their specific ontologic* or, in general, *philosophical* commitments, in terms of which they are prepared to 'accommodate' my view. I see no reason to accept this kind of hospitality. I propose to start the way I do, with my own concentration upon an analysis of existence as I have characterized it.

The philosophic problem of existence, as I have sketched it, has engaged the attention of some philosophers from the very beginnings of philosophy down to our own day. Despite all the differences in their language, background, approach, and conclusions, it is a common concern with this central problem that, for example, unites philosophies as diverse as those of Parmenides and Spinoza, among others.

To pursue the theme of the nature of existence in the sense I have specified is to focus on a matter of perennial philosophic interest, never exhausted and never to be satisfied in some final way. It is to explore an intellectual meeting ground at which various disciplines might converge—logic, linguistics, history of ideas, scientific cosmology, and metaphysics, and to which each might make its contribution. The problem of existence is a problem whose exploration furnishes the opportunity too for finding some points of contact among philosophies that might otherwise seem wholly disparate, or even hostile. We might, for example, come to recognize how writers as different as Quine, Leśniewski, or Heidegger can be seen to offer some useful suggestions for handling our problem. We, in seeking to benefit from their respective contributions, yet without being merely sentimentally ecumenical or succumbing to the pitfalls of naïve eclecticism, might even find ways of incorporating some of their insights in a comprehensive and conceptually harmonious scheme.

1.2 *'Ontology'*

How ontology is to be characterized, what its scope is, its problems, and its method, is something on which not all philosophers are agreed. Furthermore, not only is the character and range of the discipline itself not universally agreed upon, but just as notoriously the specific theories advocated by different philosophers—theories that are denominated by their authors as being 'ontological theories'—are matters on which no universal agreement prevails. Such a situation is by no means novel in philosophy and is perhaps endemic to the subject. It is necessary therefore at the outset of an inquiry such as the present one not only to take note of this fact, but in the face of this situation to say something by way of clarification of how the question we have set for ourselves concerning the meaning of 'exists' in connection with individuals and the world is related to the field of ontology, and how this fits in either by way of agreement or difference with some other widely accepted views as to the nature of ontology. This I now proceed to do, at least to a degree sufficient for the reader to know in what direction we are heading and the reasons for our choice.

It is possible, of course, to offer an account of ontology that would be sufficiently general so that it might serve up to a point as a kind of neutral formula within which all sorts of different positions might be accommodated. This, for example, could be done by saying that it is the task of ontology to consider such terms as 'exist' ('existence', 'existent', etc.), or 'being' ('to be', 'beings', 'Being', etc.). And in its own way such a brief formula is admittedly useful by way of giving some general initial clue as to the kind of topics with which one will be concerned. In this sense one could also make a perfectly accept-able use of the traditional formula, originating with Aristotle, that ontology (what Aristotle called "first philosophy") is a "study of being qua being." Or again one could appeal to the general slogan Quine has made famous and say that it is the task of ontology to establish "what there is". And if one is looking for some brief simple formula of this sort at the outset of an inquiry, one need not seriously carp at any of these formulations. It is, however, when one begins to probe more deeply into what is behind each of these formulations, in order to explain in greater detail the reasons for the choice of the terms involved in the definiens, that we come upon matters that no longer can be said to be a neutral meeting ground for diverse viewpoints in ontology. For it turns out that each of these formulas tends to cloak some specific commitments of a general philosophic sort that a particular author or school might be willing to subscribe to, but that others would not necessarily be willing to accept as presuppositions of inquiry.

For example, some philosophers agree with Quine that the central problem of ontology is to establish "what there is". On this approach to ontology, general existential sentences (as these are treated in first-order quantificational logic) are of paradigm importance. Underlying this general orientation to existence is a reading of the so-called existential quantifier as the symbolic means through which ontologic commitments are expressed. For Quine 'exists' means simply what is expressed by the existential quantifier, and such questions about existence as he would countenance have to do with the range and kind of variables we would set up for an ontology. The answer to this, he argues, defines our ontological commitments. Are we to allow only individual space-time objects, or also classes and other abstract entities such as universals or propositions? The elaboration of a particular ontology is a matter of specifying what are the types of entities it acknowledges. Such a view of ontology presupposes that the basic meaning of 'existence' is conveyed by the use of the existential quantifier. The important questions of ontology for Quine, therefore, arise only after logic has settled once and for all the correct and legitimate meaning of 'exists'—and this meaning he takes to be conveyed by the existential quantifier. What remains for legitimate differences of opinion in Quine's view has to do with the types of entities to be admitted in our ontology.

Quine's conception of ontology accordingly presupposes his interpretation of quantificational formulas. That interpretation— sometimes called the 'referential' or 'objectual' interpretation—rests on the claim that in binding a variable through the existential quantifier one is making reference to the *entities* that are the values of the variable being bound. The ontological commitment of a theory is conveyed by what the theory, when formulated in the language of quantification, recognizes as marking out the domain of values—the entities—of the bound variables it employs in its formulation. This is the substance of the famous slogan, "to be is to be the value of a variable."

I, for one, cannot accept this way of viewing ontology. It passes over, it seems to me, the major question that ontology itself must ask, namely about the use of 'exists', 'existence', and their cognates. It cannot be assumed that logic has settled this question once and for all. To examine the meaning or meanings of 'exists' remains therefore a primary task of ontology. My own approach to ontology, accordingly, diverges from Quine's. It does so, first, by placing greater stress on the need to examine what existence is, as used in singular existence sentences. It does so without seeking to reduce these to the form of allegedly more fundamental general (quantified) existential sentences. Second, it appeals to a reading of the quantifiers such that no objectual or ontological reference is involved in their use, and hence as not serving as the crucial logical means by which to convey 'ontological commitments'. (A fuller discussion of these matters will be found in Chapter 7). Whereas, too, in Quine's conception of ontology, the chief problem to settle is what kinds of entities there are—whether these include abstract entities as well as space-time entities and so on—for my own approach to ontology the central question is not one of determining *what there is* but rather of determining what it means to say *that* the world and all that it contains *exists*. The problem of abstract entities is handled not as a central problem of ontology but rather as a problem that arises from having adopted certain prior views both as to the nature of quantification and as to the role of singular terms and predicate terms in the logical analysis of sentences. In our later discussion we shall consider these alternative possibilities. We shall see in particular that for the view we shall adopt the question of 'abstract entities' as well as 'fictional entities' appears in a different light from what it does for Quine, and why for our own view the question of 'ontological commitment' need not be thought as occupying the central focus of interest. For the approach to ontology to be adopted here, it is the fact of existence of the world and what it contains which has the fundamental primacy, not "what there is" in Quine's sense.

In general, then, it would be found, I suggest, that neither Aristotle's definition of "first philosophy" as "the study of being qua being", nor Christian Wolff's use of this same formula for ontology and his inclusion of it along with rational cosmology, rational theology, and rational psychology as branches of metaphysics, nor Quine's account of ontology as a study of "what there is", nor Heidegger's conception of ontology as concerned with "the meaning of Being", nor any one else's, is or can be at bottom neutral. Each, already, in its formulation, rests on certain antecedent philosophic commitments and presuppositions of one sort or another.

Rather than stopping to offer a definition of ontology that one might hope will be acceptable to everyone, therefore, let us concentrate our attention upon dealing with the question we have set for ourselves. That it surely belongs to ontology in some loose and general sense of this term will, I take it, be readily acknowledged. It is not necessary in order to pursue our inquiry to insist that the question we propose to consider should be taken as *the* principal topic of ontology, although one might be tempted to do so. In any case, such a use of the term would at best constitute a recommendation, itself no more neutral than any other 'definition'.

What, then, is offered in what follows is a particular theory in ontology, or, better, the first steps in one, which takes existence in the sense I have previously indicated as primary. It is a particular theory, however, that, I believe, while restricted to the examination of existence in the special sense we have specified, can accommodate a great number of intellectual and spiritual needs and interests. For one thing, it can deal with the use of general terms that, for other philosophies, leads to the positing of abstract *entities*, but which for it are matters wholly of language-use. Further, it provides ample opportunity, within its own confines, for the exercise of what can be identified as the genuine sentiments of religious awe and a sense of mystery. It gives fertile field, too, and a proper target for the exercise of mystical awareness. But it does all this within the framework of a conceptual outlook that takes logic and science seriously, and as giving us the tools for discriminating the detailed intelligible structure of what exists.

The only relevant legitimate question is whether this way of thinking is an adequate one, whether it is clear, consistent, and able to satisfactorily answer and accommodate our various intellectual needs. The answer to this question is one that has to be found pragmatically, on how well the system stands up in practice under critical scrutiny. And this judgment is one that each reader would have to provide for himself, ultimately.

1.3   *The Role of Analysis*

I began by saying that it is a major task of ontology to give an *analysis of the concept of existence*. I should like to comment briefly on the use of the term 'analysis' in this connection. For there is one use of 'analysis' in which we should say that to perform an analysis of a concept is to exhibit it as made up of some more fundamental or more simple elements. Now one of the outcomes of our discussion will be to show that there is a use of the term 'existence' in which it is not possible to perform this kind of conceptual analysis, for the reason that there are not any more fundamental or more simple component conceptual elements out of which it may be said to be composed, or to which it may be reduced, or in terms of which it could be defined. To say this is to say that the concept of existence insofar as we may be said nevertheless to have it or to understand it, is such that it is ultimately simple and unanalyzable. And this is a conclusion, in one direction of our discussion, that I shall indeed argue for. However, I must introduce some words of caution at this point in order not to be misunderstood. For, first of all, even if we bear in mind the sense of the word 'analysis' according to which to analyze is to break down into simpler or more fundamental components, it need not be claimed that *all* senses of 'exist', 'existent', 'existence'—the terms that make up the core of the concept of existence—are unanalyzable. There are, in fact, for some uses of 'exist', 'existent', 'existence', analyses which exhibit them as definable in terms of other concepts.

Further, there is another sense of 'analysis', of special relevance to the kind of discussion in which philosophers engage, that is wholly appropriate to a discussion of existence, whether or not some one or none of the terms under discussion is analyzable in the sense of being reducible to more simple concepts. I mean that sense of 'analysis' in which we say that to analyze a concept is to clarify its logical geography (to use Gilbert Ryle's useful metaphor), that is, to clarify its place in, and interconnections with, other concepts in a more complex conceptual scheme. To perform this kind of analysis is to take a term such as 'exists' or some other, and by exploring its place in a network of concepts, to make it clear in a way or to an extent that it would not be without such analysis. The network of concepts in which a given concept is embedded and to whose components a philosophic analysis calls attention is a network that includes many other terms and concepts. There is no fixed constitution to this network, nor a uniquely correct way of traversing its terrain. Nor, needless to say, can one ever claim finality or 'perfect understanding' for some particular exploration of this terrain. Among the terms and concepts to which a given concept may be related, some lie fairly close; others lie further afield. It is by establishing as many relevant and fruitful links with these other terms that we become clearer about the term under investigation. And this type of analysis is possible even for a concept that we may wish to say, for various reasons, is unanalyzable in the sense of being ultimately simple.

1.4   *The Program of This Book*

To conclude, now, this introductory discussion, let me indicate how I shall organize the following investigation. There are roughly, three things I try to do. First, I shall examine the logic of singular existence statements. By a 'singular existence statement' I mean one whose general grammatical form is '*S* exists', where '*S*' is the grammatical subject expression, such as a proper name, and 'exists' is the grammatical predicate. The problem for logic and ontology is to show what type of analysis to give such a sentence in order to bring it into conformity with the requirements, in general, of an acceptable logical and ontological theory. In this connection, I shall explore, in Chapters 4-7, a number of current theories and offer some proposals of my own. Secondly, I shall explore the logic of 'world-talk', that is, what it *means* to speak of 'the world as a whole'. Here I shall consider, specifically, the use of the term 'Existence' as it applies to the world as a whole, and what relation this has to the notion of existence as used in connection with individuals. These matters will be taken up in Chapter 8. Finally, and as a preliminary to all of this, I begin in Chapters 2 and 3 with an examination of the views of two giant figures in the early history of ontology, namely

Parmenides and Aristotle. Their contributions to ontology have had, and continue to have, an influence and fascination that no student of the subject can afford to neglect. Our study (in Part II) of some current logical theories of existence, as well as the constructive remarks of my own (in Part III), will perhaps take on added meaning when seen against the background of what these earliest investigators in ontology had already worked out in their own terms.

Part I

Ancient Models

Chapter 2

Making Sense of Parmenides

2.1 *The Importance of Parmenides*

Parmenides occupies a position of unique importance, for historical as well as conceptual reasons, in the study of ontology. That
importance is out of all proportion to the brief and fragmentary
character of the literary remains that have come down to us—some
161 lines of a poem—whose title, too, if there was one, is a matter of
conjecture. The scholarly and philosophical interpretation of these
remains continues with unabated interest, indeed with renewed
vitality, to judge by the number of books and articles about him that
have continued to appear in our own day, some 2500 years after he
lived. As with other seminal thinkers, the importance of Parmenides
is precisely his power to provoke in us a wish to understand and
assess what he said, and, when we think we have succeeded, his
power to light up for us in a fresh and striking way some basic
perspective, some fundamental way of looking at things. However,
considering the extent of the differences among scholars and the
length of time these same scholars have had to resolve those
differences, we need not be rash enough to believe that we shall now,
at last, be able to come to a definitive interpretation, or that we shall
finally come to see once and for all what Parmenides 'really meant'.
It is enough if we can make out a plausible case, that we do not
outrage—on the contrary, that we take advantage of the best
available scholarship—and that we emerge with an account that
helps us to set out wherein Parmenides's philosophy is the important
thing it is generally acknowledged to be.

19

Let me first sketch then what I take to be the main reasons for assigning to Parmenides a position of unique importance in the study of ontology. For he is not only the first ontologist, he is by all odds one of the most profound. I say 'ontology', rather than use the name of some other discipline, 'cosmology', for example, and to clarify this choice perhaps is as good a point as any with which to begin. In characterizing Parmenides as the first ontologist, I mean to say he took as his principal theme the analysis of what it means 'to be', or what 'Being' is. I use these two expressions for the moment without claiming in any way that they amount to the same thing. I intend merely at this stage to point in a rough way at the topic Parmenides took as his concern. We shall come later to see the kinds of distinctions that his own analysis recommends, and why indeed we do *not* do well to lump these distinctions under the umbrella term 'Being'. Also, while we may wish to keep distinct, for various reasons, the analysis of the terms 'Being' or 'to be' from whatever extralinguistic matters they may be taken to represent, for Parmenides there is no such initial distinction between what is a matter of language (and thought), as *contrasted* with what is a matter of reality. Typically, as with many Greek philosophers, he operates with the broad assumption that thought, when adequate, mirrors or articulates what is ontological. Consequently, the philosophic analysis of being is *at once* both an analysis of how, when we think logically, we think or speak of being and what being itself is, whether thus articulated or not.

The classification of Parmenides as an ontologist is to be preferred to saying he is a cosmologist or a natural philosopher—without, of course, denying to him an interest in these other matters. For Parmenides was not *primarily* a cosmologist, nor had as his principal interest giving an account of natural phenomena after the manner of the Milesians or the Early Pythagoreans. Nevertheless, to take Parmenides as primarily a cosmologist has been a standard way of thinking of him on the part of many historians of philosophy, starting with Aristotle, and down to F. M. Cornford in our own day.[1] Not only is it a fact (which is perhaps only an accidental historical fact) that what have come down to us of the fragments of his poem contain as their principal and largest sections those that deal with questions of ontology (the 'Truth' section as contrasted with the 'Doxa' section), but this ratio of the fragments perhaps also suggests the ratio of his own philosophical and intellectual interests. Parmenides was mostly concerned with an analysis of what it means 'to be' and only secondarily with physics. As I shall argue later, we need not accept the view that, given what Parmenides says about being (*esti* and *to eon*), he cannot consistently have a cosmology. There is no *incompatibility* for Parmenides (let alone in general) between developing an ontology and a cosmology. Indeed, it is possible to discern—despite the uncertainty of interpretation of some of its parts and the extreme fragmentariness of his poem—an overall genuine unity, a philosophical integrity and coherency among its several components and sections; and it will be one of the principal aims of my own discussion to give reasons to support this claim.

I have said that Parmenides's principal interest is ontology. Without in the least retracting this, but in fact as a way of bringing out the special direction of the concern Parmenides had in this area, I should want to point to two further aspects of his thought, namely, an underlying 'religious' quality and an interest in reasoned argument. I shall argue later that in his ontology Parmenides makes a fundamental distinction between 'it is' (*esti*) and 'that-which-is' (*to eon*) (the One Reality, or Being). I should want to say, with respect to this distinction, that the analysis of *to eon* is for him the principal concern. His analysis of 'it is' (*esti*) is in the service of understanding *to eon*. As we shall see, the analysis of 'it is' is not originally or exclusively tied to the understanding of *to eon*. It provides us not only with a schema for approaching the to-be status of *to eon*, but a schema for dealing as well with the more familiar entities of ordinary experience that we take as making up the world of nature. *However, it is with* to eon—*the One Ultimate Reality or Being, and with establishing its properties that Parmenides is principally concerned.* His interest in *to eon*, and what he has to say about it, stamps him as *au fond* a *religious* thinker, and, provided we are cautious in our use of this term, a *mystic.*[2] By using the word 'cautious' here, I mean to suggest that Parmenides does not intend that one cannot say anything *at all* about *The One*, nor that reason and argument are incompetent to determine its nature. On the contrary, Parmenides is not only a religiously oriented thinker, he is, as everyone knows, the first major thinker to introduce argument into philosophy. He gives reasons for his views; he deduces conclusions from premises; he draws conceptual distinctions in the interest of giving us philosophic understanding. It is, then, because of his interest in ontology, his religious slant on Being, and his efforts at giving a reasoned defense of his views, that Parmenides occupies a strategic and seminal role in the history of Western philosophy. He is truly 'Father Parmenides'.

But there is still another reason for his importance to us in a study of ontology, and especially as the first of the great Greek ontologists. It is this. Parmenides shares with Plato and Aristotle (to go no further) a common interest in approaching being in terms of *predication*. For Parmenides the starting point and basis of ontology (though not its culmination) is the understanding of what is involved in using the term '*esti*' ('it is', 'is'). To this extent, Parmenides, Plato, and Aristotle are in agreement. While taking note of this common thread, it is equally important to acknowledge major and important differences among these thinkers that supervene upon this common basis. The differences might be briefly summed up as follows: Taking the basic predicational formula '(*S*) is (*esti*) (*P*)' as giving the basis for the analysis of 'to be'—Plato focuses his attention on the use of general terms as predicates and develops the Theory of Forms to provide the ontological correlates of these predicates. Aristotle is primarily interested in the subject and in the paradigm role and status of primary substances as such subjects. Parmenides is interested in applying the basic formula to *to eon*, Ultimate Reality, as the fundamental subject. The understanding of 'to be', as infinitive and copula, is the gateway for Parmenides to understanding the nature of *to eon*.

I mentioned earlier the underlying *unity* of Parmenides's thought. I propose to explore this aspect of his total philosophy in what follows—by considering in turn three separate yet related matters: (1) the fundamental analysis of *esti* ('it is'), (2) the analysis of *to eon* ('Being', 'what-is', 'that which is'), and (3) the analysis of the *doxa* (cosmology). The first theme gives us an introduction to Parmenides's theory of being (and knowledge) in terms of the notion of predication, truth, and knowability. It provides a schema for the treatment of anything about which knowledge might be had. The second opens up for us his principal interest in Reality, The One, Being (*to eon*), what-is. The third attempts to see how the *doxa*—the way of mortal opinion in cosmology and natural philosophy—fits into this whole picture.

The weakness of many traditional and contemporary interpretations of Parmenides, it seems to me, arises from three causes: (1) The failure to distinguish the analysis of *esti* and *to eon*—and, by running these together, to assume that Parmenides is saying the same things about both. He doesn't. (2) The failure to assess properly the various things Parmenides ascribes to *to eon*. (3) The failure to realize that the account he gives in the *doxa* is in no way incompatible with, or left hanging with respect to, the earlier treatment given to Being.

2.2 'It Is' (Esti)

The poetic and allegorical description of the chariot-journey that makes up the *Proem*, along with the theses presented in the exceedingly compressed statements presented in Fragment 2, with which the philosophic analysis proper begins, together provide us with important clues as to the framework of Parmenides's entire philosophy. In them Parmenides articulates his fundamental 'premisses', the basic 'methodological presuppositions' for his investigation; he indicates in them the controlling 'logical', 'epistemological', and 'ontological' 'axioms' to which he will make repeated appeal in the subsequent argument. Finally, he also reveals to us the goal or aim of his inquiry. I have put in scare-quotes a number of terms or concepts the majority of which, of course, are not to be found in Parmenides himself—these are terms we have become accustomed to use; they express the result of making a number of explicit and familiar distinctions and categorizations that we find helpful and important in giving an account of philosophic or other discourse. This is not to say that we are thereby falsifying anything in Parmenides; on the contrary, they are all implicitly present in what he has to say, and there is no reason why we should not take advantage of them, if in doing so we at once get a clearer insight into what our author was saying, and at the same time are not doing violence to his thought by bringing them to bear on his text.

Fragment 2 may be rendered as follows:[3]

Come, mark my words: I shall tell you what are the only ways of search there are for knowing or understanding [νοῆσαι]. The first way is *that it is and that it cannot not be*. This is the way of conviction, for conviction follows Truth.

The next is *that it is not and that it is necessary that it not be*: [that is] a way of no information, a way from which no tidings come, for you cannot know what is not, nor can you point it out.

The first point to note is that Parmenides tells us at once that he is concerned to discriminate certain 'ways of search' (or 'routes of inquiry'). Moreover, these ways of search are for the purpose of achieving knowledge or understanding.[4] And since this is not qualified in any way, we may presume that Parmenides meant his discussion to have general, unrestricted, or universal applicability. He is interested in finding out the proper way of getting (or stating) what it is to have knowledge, no matter what the subject matter is of which such knowledge is had.

To get at what Parmenides means by 'way of search' I suggest we think primarily not of a method but of a *'presupposition' that guides or underlies inquiry*. He is concerned with what can be known, with what is *knowable*. He wants to distinguish two presuppositions: one, which if made, makes inquiry possible and capable of fulfillment; the other, if made, renders any such search wholly impossible and fruitless. If we follow the first presupposition we should need to say the following: To be knowable requires that what is knowable *exist*, that there be something *there* to be known; moreover, to be knowable requires that a state of affairs, that such and such is the case, holds true of that of which we have knowledge. To be knowable, in short, requires both the *existence* of the *subject* of which knowledge is to be had, and it requires too that something or other be *true of* that subject; that one could correctly ascribe some properties or state some fact with respect to that subject. It is necessary to accept this presupposition of the twofold character of the being of what is knowable, that it *be* in both senses, 'be' in the sense of 'exist' and 'be' in the sense of 'be true of'. Such a presupposition is essential in order for there to be a meaningful search for knowledge, and for such a search to be capable of successful consummation. Without this presupposition we can neither get started nor reach our goal. Conversely, it would be wholly *futile* to proceed in the search for knowledge if we denied this presupposition—namely, by presupposing instead that there is nothing of which we are to inquire, that there is no existent to be known, and moreover that there is no state of affairs that obtains, no truths to be discovered and set out as constituting what we know. Such a presupposition would be totally senseless and self-defeating,[5] not allowing any inquiry to get off the ground much less reach its goal. If there is nothing *there* to be known (if there is nothing that exists, if there is no *subject* to be known), there cannot be any meaningful search for truth about it, since there is no 'it'. And if there is no subject at all, if it doesn't even exist, then, of course, there cannot be any search for knowledge of the truth about that subject. There is no *possibility* of truth or knowledge of what the subject has by way of properties; there is no state of affairs that holds with respect to 'it'. To have the presupposition, then, that what is knowable does not exist is a wholly self-defeating presupposition. It is a 'way' that is absolutely non-traversable and from which no 'tidings', no information, no insight, in short, no knowledge, can be brought back.

The key word in Parmenides's text on which all these ideas converge, or (to change direction), from which they all can be extracted by way of unfolding and explication, is the word '*esti*' (εστι). Scholars have expended an enormous amount of effort in seeking to get at the meaning of this word in Parmenides, and they have emerged with widely differing and conflicting interpretations, and also in some cases with different translations.[6] I shall follow, for the most part, in my own account, the analysis of this term as given by C. H. Kahn. (Some parts of this analysis also overlap with the treatments given by Mourelatos, Owen, and Furth.) [7]

The term '*esti*' in Greek can be used—was used—to serve a variety of uses. Let us discriminate three, as relevant to our purpose: (1) the *copulative-predicational* use, illustrated whenever we utter a proposition of the form '*S* is *P*'—for example, 'Socrates is wise'. The 'is' here is a *sign of predication*; it conveys the fact that something (the predicate) is being said of, or ascribed to, the subject. (2) The *existential* use; this use is conveyed by such sentences as '*S* exists' or '*There is* (in the world) something to which '*S*' (the subject-term) refers'. (3) The *veridical* use: '*It is indeed the case* that *S* is *P*'. This is sometimes conveyed by italicizing the word 'is' in the statement '*S is P*'; this has the force of saying: "What is said by '*S* is *P*' *is true, is a fact*".

Now the thing to note is that whereas we can (and should!) distinguish these three uses, since their logical roles are so different, the use of '*esti*' in Greek (as indeed that of 'is' in English) very often *combines* these uses in the single occurrence or utterance of the word '*esti*' ('is'). In saying, for example, 'Socrates *is* wise' the word 'is' sometimes does triple duty, sometimes double duty, and sometimes just one of these. Which use or uses are intended or to be understood is, of course, a matter either of the context to make clear, or the speaker's subsequent clarification of his intent, or, where these are not forthcoming satisfactorily, a matter of inference and conjecture.

Now to return to Parmenides. What does the single word '*esti*' mean in Fragment 2? The first point to be made is that this word constitutes a word-*sentence* (or, more accurately, as we shall see in a moment, a *sentence-frame*). (That single words can convey entire sentences, 'complete thoughts', is of course a common occurrence in various languages.)

The second point is that the single word '*esti*' in Parmenides's Fragment 2, in the context in which it is being used, can be best understood as combining *all three* of the functions discriminated above. But if it does, it will be asked immediately, what, on the analysis given above are the *subject* and the *predicate* that are being joined by the copula '*esti*'? Parmenides himself gives us no specific subject or specific predicate. Insofar as he incorporates in his multi-layered use of '*esti*' a predicational use, it is of a wholly *formal* sort. In other words, it would hold for whatever is our subject and whatever our predicate, provided the combination is of something *knowable*, provided, that is, it has to do with something that *can be known*. To represent this state of affairs we can adopt either of two devices: (1) we can use the place-filler pronoun 'it' in the sentence-frame "it is _____." By leaving a blank after the 'is' we signify that a predicate would still need to be specified. (2) On the other hand, since the word 'it' really doesn't help us at all here except to give us a *grammatical* subject and to serve as a place-marker for a genuine, to-be-supplied, subject, we might simply leave the place for the subject-term blank, as we had already done for the predicate. We should then have "_____ is _____." This expression is a sentence-frame in which the subject position and the predicate position are both left blank. In it the word 'is' ('*esti*') alone is retained to indicate its role. That role, an invariant logical one, is to link subject and predicate. It serves as a sign of predication. It marks the fact that a predicate is being attached to, predicated of, a subject. Let us, while retaining this sentence-frame to mark the predicational use of '*esti*', now add the two further uses, namely, the existential and the veridical.

The existential use would be conveyed by saying either

1. "_____ exists" (or, "_____ is an existent,") or
2. "There is that to which the subject term in '_____ is _____' refers."

The veridical use would be conveyed by saying:

1. "The entire sentence '_____ is _____' *is true*" or
2. "*It is the case* (it is a fact) '_____ is _____' " or
3. "*The state of affairs* represented by '_____ is _____' *obtains, holds.*"

In all these cases, the blanks in the sentence-frame would need to be filled by appropriate expressions to yield a sentence, and in which one or another of the senses of '*esti*' would function in the manner described above. The proposal I wish to make is that while Parmenides uses just the single word '*esti*', we are to read his one-word sentence as *combining all three* of the above formulas, that is, that he intends to convey at once all of the separate uses of the word '*esti*'.

To accept this conceptual analysis of '*esti*' (as I have here reconstructed it on Parmenides's behalf) is a necessary presupposition, he would say, for anyone who has a clear idea of what it is to engage in a search for knowledge and to claim to have successfully consummated that search; it would mean that we should be able to express or convey the fruits of that search in coherent, true, logically sound, and perspicuous language and that that knowledge is *of* or *about* or identical with, that is, *revelatory* of what exists.

This last point, that where knowledge is achieved, where the search is successful, there is *aletheia*, truth, disclosure, a direct revealing of what is the case, that there is in this sense an identification—an 'identity' of mind and being, is what is conveyed by Parmenides in a number of places, for example, in Fragment 3 (just following the passages we have been examining). It reads:[8]

"For knowing and being are the same"
and he repeats the same point later:

"Knowing and the goal (or aim or motive) of knowledge are the same" (8.34)

There is no need whatever to interpret these remarks of Parmenides as defending some type of 'idealistic' or 'mentalistic' metaphysics. He is *not* saying that what exists, the world or Being, is constituted of, is identical in total nature with, is pervaded by Mind (or minds), depends on, is derivative from Mind, or any thing of that sort. He is simply calling attention to the fact that when or insofar as our minds, our cognitive powers are successful they disclose what in fact is there: what is known is at once both 'in the mind' and 'in the world'. What is known is 'what it-is-to-be-such-and-such'.

Yet it is important to note that so far Parmenides *has not dealt with any specific subject matter*. In one sense, he has not made any assertions; *he has not propounded any specific knowledge claims about the world*. What he has to say about '*esti*' is a framework, a schema, a logical form for *anything* that can be known, for any particular knowable subject or subject matter, that can serve as content, filling, example, illustration or case study of this general form or schema. Those interpreters, therefore, who take this statement about '*esti*' as already giving us the essence of Parmenides's views on the nature of reality, about Being or '*to eon*', are mistaken. They confuse or run together the schema with *one* example—an important example for Parmenides, to be sure, but still an example—of the '*esti*' formula. For Parmenides, this formula is to be used for an inquiry not just into Being (*to eon*), but also, for example, into nature (or *physis*), namely, cosmology, astronomy, meteorology, psychology, and so on.

It follows, too, if the above be accepted, that the '*esti*' *formula* is not a tautology. Since it is a *sentence-frame*, it says nothing. It shows rather how the term '*esti*' is to be understood. On the other hand, if we take the *analysis*, such as we have given, as a tautology because it gives us the meaning, the definition of '*esti*'—at any rate this type of tautology is not of the same type Parmenides is usually convicted of uttering, namely "*Being* is". It is fatal to an understanding of what Parmenides is saying in the '*esti*' formula to read him as asserting "Being is". Being (*to eon*) is *not* the subject of '*esti*', for there is no special subject at all in the '*esti*' formula.

Another fruit of the foregoing analysis is that it enables us to overcome the frequently asserted complaint that Parmenides confuses the existential and copulative uses of 'is'. He does no such thing.

For, not only is the Greek verb '*esti*' as Parmenides uses it normally employed for the various purposes we have discriminated [9]—but it serves Parmenides's specific purpose well to *conjoin* (but *not confuse*) these various uses! For in saying (or rather hinting and implying) what he does about what is knowable, he needs to appeal to all three of the senses: the copulative-predicational, the existential, and the veridical. Nothing short of their combined uses would do justice to the rich content of this one-word sentence.

There is, finally, another benefit that flows from the analysis we have given of the threefold use of '*esti*'. It provides us with a way of understanding the reasons why Parmenides rejects as a wholly un-traversable 'route', or a wholly unacceptable presupposition, one which would *deny* the philosophical soundness of asserting '*esti*'. This denial consists in the affirmation of the formula *ouk esti*, "it is not." Let us see how we might interpret this formula. Our first step is to take the negation as applying to the meanings of '*esti*' we have given—the predicational, existential, and veridical. In that case the negation would need to be understood (by De Morgan's rule) as asserting *either* (1) a negative predication ("_____ is not _____"), *or* (2) as asserting the nonexistence of the subject: "*S* does not exist" ("*S* is not an exist-ent") ("There is no *S*"), *or* (3) finally, as asserting some falsity: "It is false that '_____ is _____'." It is not necessary, it should be noted, that we impute to Parmenides the claim that the denial of '*esti*' is the *conjunctive denial* of all three interpretations or meanings of '*esti*'. And yet, I think that, given the choice from among the three negated alternatives, Parmenides would have maintained the one which shows the *ouk esti* to be a wholly untraversable way is the second, the *existential* sense of '*esti*'. For what the negation of the existential sense of 'is' accomplishes, if true, is to eliminate the sentence altogether! What the denial of existence (*ouk esti*) asserts is that there is no subject of the sentence: there is no entity or existent to which we can or do refer. If this is so, then indeed there is no point in going on to ascribe something to 'it', to consider the predicate as attaching or not attaching, holding or not holding, of the subject. There is no subject! Therefore, we cannot even get started in making a meaningful assertion, because there is nothing to which the subject term refers. Hence there is no assertion at all, and this, of course, not only eliminates the predicational use of 'is', it also *a fortiori* eliminates the third or veridical use of 'is' as well, for there is no predicational statement to which it *might* apply. It is then the failure to make sense of there being a *nonexistent* subject 'about which' we could have knowledge, that, Parmenides would say, renders the '*it is not*' (*ouk esti*) formula a wholly senseless presupposition for inquiry.

If what I have said thus far is correct, we have another important clue for understanding what Parmenides may have meant by rejecting the way of *ouk esti*. Many commentators assume Parmenides is required to deny the possibility of *negative predicational statements*.[10] I do not see that this follows at all. Not only does he himself use negative statements, as all language users obviously do—there is nothing inconsistent with his philosophy for him or others to do so! For the *ouk esti* formula only applies to the presupposed possibility of making meaningful assertions (whether consisting of affirmative *or* negative predications, whether true *or* false) about a nonexistent subject, about a nonentity. But because Parmenides rejects this possibility of there being a sentence at all, much less a true sentence, in which there is *no subject*, it does not follow that he need object to there being negative *predications* as such.[11] For where the '*esti*' formula is satisfied—at least on the level of the *existence* of the subject being referred to—there is no reason why one could not have true negative predications. Thus 'Theatetus is not flying' can be a perfectly acceptable true statement. Parmenides's rejection of negation is a rejection of any formula in which we should not have an existent *subject* at all, not one in which we might have negative *predicates* about a *bona fide* subject.

Parmenides has distinguished two 'ways', two 'presuppositions' to guide inquiry. Of these, Parmenides insists, one and one only is sound and acceptable; the other is wholly to be shunned as totally futile, unsound, and completely self-defeating. These two ways, moreover, are not only exclusive; they are *exhaustive*. Parmenides makes this point quite emphatically: "These are the *only* ways of search there are for knowing" (B2.2). There is no 'third way' that 'combines the two'. Those commentators who would ascribe the acknowledgment of the possibility of such a third way to Parmenides fail to see what he is saying. If the way of 'is not' is wholly untraversable, then of course there cannot be a third way which incorporates this 'way'; such a putative 'third way' reduces to the 'second way' since it includes it, and since that second way has been proved to be unavailable and impossible, so too is any 'third way'.

Moreover, those who take Parmenides to be identifying the adoption of the 'third way' with those who undertake to develop a cosmology, a physics, a *'doxa'*—or who, on the level of everyday ordinary experience recognize plurality and change—are also in error. There is nothing in the adoption of the 'first way' which excludes either the acknowledgment of the existence of plurality, a manifold of objects and events in the world, or change with respect to these objects and events. All that Parmenides need insist on is that *if* we are to get knowledge of these, such knowledge, too, would have to satisfy the presuppositions of the 'first way'. Indeed, he himself develops a cosmology. Such an enterprise is not in any way inconsistent with what we have seen thus far to be the major argument of Fragment 2, the methodological-logical preamble about the nature of the knowable. There are those who argue that Parmenides is inconsistent in presenting such a cosmology, if it is intended as his own; and there are others who suggest that if we are to save Parmenides from inconsistency we are to think of him not as presenting his own views, but as reporting on the misguided views of other mortals. In either case the *'Doxa'* presents a problem for them, a dangling addendum. But these radical proposals are wholly unnecessary. They both flow from the shared assumption—a mistaken one—that Parmenides's conception of *esti* is at the same time a statement of what he has to say about *to eon*. But as we shall see, what he has to say about *to eon*—that it is unchanging and unique—has to do with one domain of application of the *'esti'* formula. It does not tell us anything at all about the meaning of *esti*. Moreover, the fact that these properties of unchangingness and uniqueness hold true for the *to eon* in no way makes it incorrect to say that there is a plurality of changing things and events in the world. And the *'Doxa'* which would give us an account of these things and events, the domain of plurality and change, would be but another application, another direction for exemplifying the basic pattern of the *'esti'* formula.

2.3   *'That-Which-Is'* (To Eon)

In Fragment 8, the longest and most important section of his poem, Parmenides develops his ontology proper, his theory of Being. This theory consists in a series of arguments that together specify the various properties of Being and that explicate how we are to conceive it. What I have been calling 'Being' is what Parmenides designates as το εον. It is a name formed from the participle ον, of the verb ειναι, 'to be'. (το εον is the Ionic form for το ον.) [12] It can be translated not only as 'Being', but equally well as 'what-is', 'that which is', 'what is so'. What Being is, what *to eon* is, is not to be confused with what Parmenides has to say about *esti* in Fragment 2. *Esti* and *to eon* are not the same. They are connected, of course—in the way a *logical schema* is connected with an *example of that schema*; in the way a *methodological or epistemological preamble* is connected with a *description of a specific subject matter*; in the way, finally, in which a *presupposition* of an inquiry is connected with an inquiry that falls back on and appeals to that presupposition.

To eon, like any object of knowledge, anything that is knowable, will need to satisfy the general formal requirements of the *esti* formula, namely: (1) it exists; (2) it is such-and-such (or has such-and-such properties); (3) what can be said about it is true.

It is necessary to understand how Parmenides is using the term '*to eon*', what its distinctive features are, and how he establishes these. These questions are, of course, interrelated, and the answers to them do not lie on the surface: on the contrary, the questions have been, as we know, matters for the most divergent interpretations and the topics of almost endless controversy. Nevertheless, what follows is offered as giving us a plausible solution to these questions.

The basic clue we need in order to understand what Parmenides means by *to eon*, and the various things he says about it, is that he is talking about *the existence* of the world, *that* there is a world at all. It is absolutely essential that we isolate and concentrate upon this sheer fact of the existence of the world and not bring in other matters with which it is then (mistakenly) identified. The existence of the world is not itself a body, is not itself a truth, does not have a duration or shape, is not itself located 'in' space or time, is not itself a plurality or manifold of objects or events, does not itself undergo any kind of change, is conceptually unanalyzable into more elementary or component concepts, and is therefore totally unique.

Parmenides himself summarizes the main properties of *to eon* at the beginning of Fragment 8, before he undertakes to prove them, separately. The "signs" on the road to Being that point to its properties consist, he says, in the fact "that Being is ungenerated and imperishable, whole, unique, immobile, and complete."

To arrive at the proofs of these various properties of *to eon*, Parmenides relies on two essential premisses. One is the general *esti* formula; the other is the *application* of that formula as a basis for completely rejecting the notion of *NonBeing*, or the absolute nonexistence of the world, το μη εον (*to me eon*). *To me eon* is not to be confused with the formula "is-not," *ouk esti* (ουκ εστι): it is rather an *example* of this "forbidden" way. To assume that we could meaningfully talk about or know *absolute nothing* (that is, not just the nonexistence of this or that particular thing or event) but nothing whatever—the nonexistence of the world altogether, is for Parmenides wholly unacceptable. Absolute NonBeing as the putative counterpart of Being is for Parmenides without any meaning or knowability whatsoever. "For you could never come to know what-is-not, nor could you single it out, for it cannot be consummated." [13] Once we rid ourselves of this spurious and vacuous concept, we are left not only with the *esti*-premiss, but with the awareness of the fact of Being, *that* there is a world (*to eon*). The proofs of the various properties of *to eon* now follow both from this positive awareness of the fact of the existence of the world and from the rejection of the notion of absolute NonBeing.

With respect to Parmenides's own programmatic summary (quoted above) and his subsequent proofs that correspond to these, it is possible to distinguish four basic properties of *to eon*. (I use, to begin with, Parmenides's own terminology, leaving for subsequent discussion the matter of how these terms are to be understood.) Being (*to eon*) is said to be:

1. "ungenerated" (αγενητον) (*ageneton*)
2. "simple" (indivisible) (ουδε διαιρετον) (*oude diareton*)
3. "immobile" (ακινητον) (*akineton*)
4. "complete" (τετελεσμενον) (*tetelesmenon*)

Parmenides also uses the term "unique" in his summary, and throughout uses such additional terms as "it lies by itself" (καθ εαυτο τε κειται), "inviolate" (ασυλον), as well as others.[14] These various terms, sometimes to be found in the statement of various proofs, sometimes to be found alone, without proof, are nevertheless also important as "signposts" to what he is referring and describing, and whose significance and appropriateness emerge as we see how, taken together, they represent so many converging attempts at explicating what it is to be Wholly Other, One, and Ultimately Real.

Are these several proofs of the various properties of *to eon* connected in some way? They are, though not, in any strictly serial order, where the conclusion of one proof serves as a premiss for a succeeding one. A case perhaps might be made that the first proof, which establishes that *to eon* is ungenerated, is the fundamental proof of which all the others are corollaries.[15] But another way, too, in which we may think of the relations of the proofs to one another is on the model of the spokes of a wheel radiating from the center. At the hub (in addition to the *esti* formula) is the awareness of Being and the simultaneous rejection of NonBeing; each of the properties follows directly (radiates out) from this central, common source, and in turn when so derived can be used in the reverse direction to describe that common source, that is, *to eon*. When so derived, *any one* property gives a model, a pattern for deriving the rest—for they all rest ultimately on the appeal to the same fundamental awareness of the fact that-there-is-a-world—and the simultaneous denial of the meaningfulness or knowability of absolute NonBeing. That the image of a wheel, spokes, and hub is not altogether farfetched is in accordance with Parmenides's use of the phrase "well-rounded Truth" (in the *Proem*, 1.29) and his own description (Fragment 5): "It is all one to me where I begin: for I shall come back there again in time." [16]

Let us examine now the first proof Parmenides gives. He wishes to prove it would be a mistake to think Being was generated, that it had an origin or birth. Correlated with these rejections is the denial that it can undergo accretion, that it can grow, or will perish, or that it has a past or a future. Being, in short, cannot come into being or go out of being, nor can any temporal terms apply to it. The basic proof that Parmenides appeals to in support of these claims is that if these terms were, putatively, to have applicability to Being, this could only be by appealing to the concept of absolute NonBeing *(me eon)*. For Being to come into being would require that it do so out of an absolute NonBeing, or again for Being to pass out of being would require that it pass into absolute NonBeing. But we cannot give sense to these descriptions because in using the term 'NonBeing' we are using a term that has no meaning: it cannot stand for anything knowable or existent. Hence the description collapses. Parmenides adds another reason: he argues that even if, *per impossible, to eon* did come into existence out of nothing, we should find such a situation wholly inexplicable. For, he asks, "Besides what requirement should impel it, later rather than earlier, having started from nothing, to grow?" [17] Here we find Parmenides formulating what is, historically, the earliest appeal to what came later to be called 'The Principle of Sufficient Reason'. (Parmenides's statement is in fact the basis of Leibniz's rejection, on the basis of this principle, for allowing within a Newtonian framework of absolute Time, any sense to the world's having begun at one moment of such absolute time rather than another. It was the same argument, again, to which Kant appeals for the formulation of the argument in the antithesis of the first antimony of the *Critique of Pure Reason,* against there having been a coming-into-existence of the world a finite time ago.)

The basic appeal to the unavailability of coming-into-being out of nothing because of the illegitimate reliance on the pseudo-concept of absolute NonBeing also serves Parmenides as a basis for rejecting a number of additional views. One such notion is that of accretion as thought of in connection with Being. Being, Parmenides insists, is "altogether or not at all" (8.11). Nor will it be possible that "something out of what-is-not should come to be alongside it" (8.12-13). In other words, there cannot be an 'addition' to Being, for such an 'addition', too, would require that we conceive of 'additional' Being as an accretion to what is already in existence. However, since this depends on presupposing a NonBeing out of which the additional Being is to arise, it is again disallowed.

In the same vein, Parmenides declares (though without explicitly proving) that Being cannot "perish". Yet the proof is not hard to reconstruct and supply. For 'perishing', too, if we are to try to conceive of what it would mean when thought of in connection with Being, would imply a transition to NonBeing, and this, as Parmenides keeps reminding us, is a path we cannot traverse. "The judgment on these matters depends on this: either it is or it is not. Now it has been already decided, as is necessary, to abandon the latter as unknowable and nameless, for it is no true way, but [to judge] that the former *is* and is true." [18]

Another important vantage point from which to consider *to eon* is with respect to the question of temporality. Parmenides denies that one can describe Being in tensed language; it has neither a past nor a future. It does not have a career. It does not span a durational interval, even if infinitely prolonged on either side of the present. For Being is not the sort of thing that is *in* time. Parmenides expresses this as follows: "Nor was it ever, nor will it be, since it is now, all of it together." [19] We may interpret Parmenides's use of the expression "it is now" ($\nu\nu\nu\ \varepsilon\sigma\tau\iota\nu$), not as signifying the present-tense use of 'is',[20] but rather, since there was no special technical expression he might have appealed to, to convey tenselessness, the phrase "is now" is his way of saying Being is *timeless* and that it transcends time, that it is not capable, even in principle, of receiving temporal descriptions. At 8.27 Parmenides describes *to eon* as $\alpha\nu\alpha\rho\chi\circ\nu\ \alpha\pi\alpha\upsilon\sigma\tau\circ\nu$, "without a temporal beginning and never ending." This description, too, confirms the interpretation that Parmenides wishes to say of *to eon* not merely that as a matter of fact it had no beginning nor will it have an end, but that as a matter of principle it cannot have a beginning or an end. *To eon* is not the sort of thing to which we can ascribe a beginning, or an end, or a duration, not even a specious present, much less a momentary existence in the present. It is altogether timeless, beyond time.[21]

Parmenides, as we have just seen, denies all forms of description of *to eon* that in any way involve the concepts of change or time. One way in which he sums up this fact is by using the term $\alpha\kappa\iota\nu\eta\tau\circ\nu$ (*akineton*). If this is translated 'immobile' or 'immovable' it tends to conjure up images of a body left in a static position, not undergoing locomotion. These associations, if taken literally, need, of course, to be wholly rejected. One way of freeing ourselves of any physicalization or spatialization in our conception of *to eon* is to realize that the term $\alpha\kappa\iota\nu\eta\tau\circ\nu$ is to be taken in its most general sense as meaning "not changing in any way" (not merely spatially). And what Parmenides means is that the fact of Being is not itself an object or process of any kind that undergoes or manifests change and that, in so doing, occupies a temporal duration. The fact of existence of the world transcends time and change altogether. Even in the more narrowly spatial sense, Being remains "in place", in the sense of never leaving what it is to "go elsewhere". "Constraint" keeps it forever in its "own place", "identical with itself", "inviolate", and unable to "become" or "reach" anything else.

And this account of *to eon* leads immediately, in Fragment 8, to Parmenides's description of *to eon* as "not incomplete": "It is not in need of anything"; "it is present within the bounds equally", "like a well-rounded sphere". Again, all such descriptions—being at once couched in negative terms and, in the case of the reference to a "well-rounded sphere", explicitly metaphorical—are so many ways of conveying the fact that the existence of the world (Being) is not to be understood by reference to something beyond itself, to a *telos* (goal or limit) which transcends it and in terms of which it is to be understood. It contains its *telos* within itself, it is self-contained and self-sufficient.

In his summary of the signposts on the way to truth about Being, Parmenides uses, along with other descriptions, the phrase ουλον μουνογενες (*holon mounogenes*)—which can be rendered as "only one of its kind", "*sui generis*", "unique".[22] And when he comes to develop this point (in lines 8.22-25) he argues that it is "not divisible" (ουδε διαιρετον), since it is all alike or "homogeneous" (ομοιον). To understand what he is saying here we must avoid all temptation to think of what he is referring to as some all-inclusive material body. Rather, what he is saying is that when we try to analyze the idea of the very existence of the world into something more elementary, we cannot do so. It is neither subsumable under some wider genus, nor is it to be reached by a process of combination or synthesis. The concept of the existence of the world is, in short, an *absolute simple*. Not being made up of parts in any sense, it does not have internal divisions or gradations of degree of 'more' or 'less'. It is therefore "indivisible", "homogeneous", and "the same thoughout".

If, as I have argued, Parmenides's treatment of *to eon* is an application of the *esti* formula, we must stop and ask ourselves to what extent it satisfies the conditions of the *esti* formula. In what sense is it something genuinely *knowable*? To be a genuinely knowable object something must exist and have properties that do in fact belong to it. Now surely there are important differences between the kinds of knowable objects we ordinarily encounter in our experience and the Beingness of the World? I can satisfy myself about the existence of some person or object by direct inspection, or through indirect means, by reliable inference and connectivity with what is accessible to direct inspection. I am assured of the existence of the table before me and see it is brown. I am prepared to believe there was a person called 'Socrates' and that he was wise. These individuals and an indefinitely large number of other particulars *exist*, we say, *in* the world. But it makes no sense to say the existence or Being of the world exists *in* the world. Further, we can satisfy ourselves about the brownness of the table or the wisdom of Socrates, for we know how such terms are being used and that they do apply literally and correctly to their respective subjects. But the terms used by Parmenides about *to eon* are all either negative or metaphorical. In what sense can I say that in using these to describe *to eon*, I *know* what it is?

These differences between ordinary knowable objects and 'the knowable object' which Parmenides calls *to eon* have to be admitted, indeed insisted on. Yet, for all that, there is nothing in such an admission which prevents the application of the *esti* formula to *to eon*. What Parmenides is talking about is after all wholly different in status and character from ordinary objects. Existence does not exist in the world in the way tables and persons do; but shall we for all that therefore deny existence to *to eon*, to Existence itself? This surely would be the very limit of absurdity. And again, insofar as we are dealing with something so uniquely different from ordinary individual existent objects and events, why need we suppose that the kind of knowledge we have of it should be couched in the language of ordinary description? Must not such knowledge as we do have inevitably have to be couched in terms of *negations* and *metaphors*? How else could such knowledge of what is absolutely unique be conveyed?

The fact that Parmenides uses the term translated as "signposts" (σηματα) in connection with his account of *to eon*, is significant, and no more than itself a poetic image. It may be taken as embodying the philosophic claim that *all* descriptions of Being are so many symbols or useful pointers, at best, to what Being is, but that none are literally adequate. After all, a signpost is not what is to be found at the end of the road. But once we reach the end of the road the signposts are no longer necessary. This is to say that Parmenides's ultimate ontological thesis is a variant of a mystical philosophy. Once we have come to know Ultimate Reality we no longer need signposts, or, to use the more recent Wittgensteinian metaphor, we can "throw away the ladder."

2.4 *Doxa*

Many commentators see in Parmenides's discussion of the subject matter of cosmology and natural philosophy (in the *Doxa*, "the way of mortal opinion") an inconsistency with the earlier discussion in Fragment 8, of "The Way of Truth". These commentators read Parmenides as denying plurality and change altogether; they read Parmenides in this way because they think that for him to think otherwise would be inconsistent. For example, G. E. L. Owen says: "He [Parmenides] is driven to denying the existence of some kinds of thing—change and plurality *in primus*—in order to maintain his thesis that nonexistence makes no sense." [23]

My own analysis thus far has attempted to support the view that we need to separate Parmenides's appeal to the formula *esti* and, by way of special application of that formula, what he says about *to eon*. It is *to eon* and only *to eon* that is indivisible (lacking in plurality), unique, unchanging, without temporal parts, and so on. And all of these predicates, too, I have argued, are best seen as so many symbolic pointers, "signposts" on the way of getting at Being itself. Yet nothing in what Parmenides says about Being need in any way prevent him from attempting to describe and explain the manifold variety of objects, events, and processes in Nature. To deny to Parmenides's philosophy the rudimentary awareness of plurality and change is to attribute to it sheer madness and incoherency. I see no reason what-soever to do so, especially if we can not only have Parmenides believe what we all believe—that there is a world of plurality and change—but that he can do so without in the slightest having to retract or modify what he says about Being. On the contrary, it is a mark of the great profundity and originality of his philosophy, its capacity for being able to see with two eyes and on different levels, that makes him the great philosopher he was.

In the *Proem* Parmenides has the Goddess tell the young man that it is necessary for him to learn all things, "the unshaken heart of the well-rounded truth" as much as "the opinions of mortals". The Goddess promises to instruct the youth in mortal opinions about the world (about natural phenomena), for she says—and this I take to be the sense of the passage—what these opinions are about "have genuine existence [δοκιμως ειναι], being indeed the whole of things [δια παντος παντα περ οντα]" (1.32).[24] The contrast is between the knowledge to be had of *to eon* (Being) and the knowledge to be had of the manifold domain of objects and events that make up the world of Nature—of φυσις. The one is "the way of truth"; the other, "the way of opinion". The contrast is between what we can know with certainty, with complete conviction, and what at a given time is taken as true by men, yet is open to modification and revision, since only probable. Once we isolate and study the properties of Being we know the truth about it once and for all. Not only does Being itself not change, but the knowledge we have of it, since it does not rest on fragmentary and changing evidence, or on the vagaries and contingencies of human sense-experience, can be set out with complete certainty. Those who see the truth, who get a glimpse of what transcends time and their own cultural history or personal biography, see what is eternally true. On the other hand, attempts to systematically interrelate and explain the multifarious details of natural phenomena—concerning the heavenly bodies, meteorological and biological phenomena, and human affairs—are never crowned with complete success. The theories men have may, to be sure, be "acceptable" to them, and be their best available knowledge at a given time; but they cannot merit complete and unshakable πιστις, faith, or conviction. Yet the drive to understand natural phenomena is not a delusion, and the results we get here are not to be thought of as confined to a domain of mere appearance. The goddess would have the youth learn what others have done in this area. Moreover, there is no reason why he (Parmenides) should not take a hand in this enterprise himself. There is nothing either forbidden or inconsistent with the knowledge of Being in so doing.

Such hints as we get of the cosmology in the *Doxa* section are much too fragmentary to permit us to reconstruct with any confidence what the 'system' (διακοσμος) might have been, much less any clear or adequate sense of its details. All we can surmise is that Parmenides takes the contraries "Fire" and "Night" and attempts to show how from their mixture and interaction the varied phenomena of the world arise, from the heavenly bodies at one extreme to the operations and powers of man's capacity for knowledge at the other. One might suppose that if we had the complete picture it would be no worse surely, and every bit as ingenious and representative of the then-current speculation, than any other. Parmenides would be the first to admit that our "acceptance" of it, our "faith" in it needs to be circumscribed and tentative. And if he could have foreseen the enormous development of science in our own day, he need not have been any the less ready to grant how far we have been able to supersede his own crude efforts, or those of his predecessors and contemporaries. Yet as a philosopher he would be just as careful to insist that even with the scientific advances we have been able to register, such knowledge, or any that will come to replace it of the world of nature, remain only *doxa*, informed opinion, of varying degrees of reliability and certainty, as compared with the simple yet unshakable truths we can know about *to eon*, Being itself.

Chapter 3

Aristotle and Ontology

3.1 *'Being qua Being'*

Aristotle's famous description of first philosophy as an inquiry into "being qua being" (το ον η ον) (*Metaphysics* 1003a 21) needs to be kept free of all mystical overtones, as well as of all other philosophic associations that import meanings alien to his own, those for example that might derive from a Heidegerrian preoccupation with the *Seinsfrage,* or a theistic attempt to grapple with the mystery of existence. But we need to guard ourselves, too, against other interpretations of Aristotle's meaning—some rather widely accepted ones—which, though not as obviously off the track as the ones just mentioned, are, I believe, to be classed with them as just as unhelpful in getting at his meaning. One such view, briefly put, takes the study of being qua being to consist in a study of the most commonly shared property of all things, their *being*, in contradistinction to other more restricted interests of other disciplines. Thus what first philosophy deals with, according to this interpretation, is the property of 'being', for this is what all things, whatever their differences, *do* have in common. Therefore, a knowledge of being qua being would be a knowledge of this common property. This interpretation goes hand in hand, often, with the further attempt to reconcile the rather different accounts which Aristotle gives, at separate points in the collection of his writings known as the *Metaphysics*, of what first philosophy is about. For in addition to the description of first philosophy as "a study of being qua being" which we find in Book Gamma, he also describes it in Book Alpha (982b 9) as "the science that investigates the first principles and causes" and in Book Lambda as 'Theology', that is to say, the study of God as the 'highest being', the being that is both unchanging (ἀκίνητος) and independently existing (χωριστον). There are some interpreters who would reconcile these differing accounts. They would say that the *common property of being* is to be *identified* with the 'ground' of being, with God.[1] A typical and clear example of these attempts at getting at Aristotle's meaning in using the formula 'being qua being' is to be found in the following statement by R. G. Collingwood:

The subject matter of any science is something abstract or universal. Abstractness or universality is subject to degrees. Where a generic universal A is specified into two sub-forms B and C, as number is specified into odd and even, A will be more abstract, more universal, than B or C. In such a case A is the logical ground of B and C; that is, A by its own nature gives rise to its own subordinate forms B and C. . . . This ABC pattern among universals is not merely a pattern that crystallizes out among universals here and there. It is present in all universals. All such patterns are part of one single pattern. All universals whatever are to be found somewhere in a system which, according as you look at it, may be called a system of classification or a system of division. Every universal is potentially at least the subject-matter of a science. There is potentially, therefore, a system of sciences corresponding with the system of universals. . . . The system does not go on for ever. At the top and bottom it stops. At the base of the system of universals there are universals which are *infimae species*, not giving rise to any further sub-species. At its top there are universals which are *summa genera*, not species of any higher genus. Or rather, strictly speaking, there is only one *summum genus*. The ten "categories" recognized by logic are the ten species of the genus being; they are the γενη των οντων, the forms into which being is specified. Thus there is only one pyramid of universals, and at its peak the universal of being. . . . At its top will be a single science, the science of being; being in the abstract or being as such, pure being, το ον η ον. This will be the First Science in the sense that it is logically presupposed by every other science, although from a learner's point of view it is the Last Science, to be approached only when all the others have been to some degree at least mastered. . . . Lastly, since every universal is the immediate logical ground of those immediately subordinate to it, and hence indirectly the ground of the universals which are subordinate to those, the first and last universal, pure being, is directly or indirectly the ground of all other universals, and the First and Last Science is therefore the science of that which stands as ultimate logical ground to everything that is studied by any other science. The ordinary name for that which is the logical ground of everything else is God. The most adequate, explicit, and easily intelligible name for the science which in its relation to other sciences is alternatively called First Science or Wisdom, the name which tells us what it is about, is therefore Theology.[2]

Now the above summary of Aristotle's alleged views is, I submit, a travesty of his views. When, therefore, Collingwood himself proceeds to attack the notion of a science of pure being, as he interprets Aristotle to have conceived it, he is in effect attacking a straw man, a myth-ridden conception of what ontology is about. At bottom Collingwood is in error in thinking of being in Aristotle as a 'universal', as a *summum genus*', as 'abstract', as 'pure being', or as 'God'. I shall not stop to discuss each of these errors at the moment, but in the course of our discussion we shall see the reasons for saying his account is a total misrepresentation.

I mention, finally, by way of preliminary cautionary remarks, one other false scent. W. D. Ross translates the opening sentence of Book Gamma of the *Metaphysics*, where Aristotle sets out his conception of first philosophy ('ontology') as follows:

There is a science which investigates being and the attributes which belong to this in virtue of its own nature. Now this is not the same as any of the so-called special sciences; for none of these others treats universally of being as being. They cut off a part of being and investigate the attribute of this part; this is what the mathematical sciences for instance do.

Now it would be a mistake to presume that Aristotle, in disclaiming to deal with *parts* of being, is interested instead in dealing with being *as some singular all-inclusive whole*. The fact is, the principal bent of his investigation has nothing to do with being as some alleged *whole*. What he is interested in are the various *ways* or *modes* of being, or of 'to be'. And among the several ways of being or of 'to be', he is going to show the primary role of the mode of being or 'to be' that belongs to substance. In any case substance, too, needs to be understood as pluralized, and not as Spinoza or Bradley conceive it, as some single all-inclusive totality.

3.2 The Question: 'What Is Being?'

While it may be useful in some ways to formulate the general question of ontology with which Aristotle was concerned as the question 'What is being?', this can also be misleading and unhelpful. For it suggests, through the use of the single word 'being', that there is some single Greek equivalent to which Aristotle directed his attention, and about which he tried to get clear. The fact is, however, that this single word—even in English—hides a cluster of meanings, since it cloaks a possible ambiguity as to whether it should be taken as a participle or as a noun (and even as a noun it leaves us unclear as to whether it is an 'abstract' noun or not). At any rate, when Aristotle raised the question in the Greek, he clearly had in mind a cluster of meanings that included the infinitive ειναι (*einai*) ('to be'), the verb εστι (*esti*) ('is') used as copula, the participle ον (*on*) ('existent'), the participle as nominalized and as used in the singular το ον (*to on*) ('being', 'what exists') and the plural τα οντα, (*ta onta*) ('existing things', 'entities'), and finally the noun ουσια (*ousia*) ('substance'). These terms for Aristotle, to be sure, have important interconnections—and it is the principal task of his answer to the broad question, 'What is being?', to bring out these various interconnections. But it is important at the outset, in understanding Aristotle's treatment, to realize that in order to explicate these interconnections, and to do justice to the complexity of the subject, he does not look in only one direction, or, to put it in linguistic terms, that he does not take from the mixed bag of infinitive, copula, participle, and noun, one of these only to the exclusion of the others: rather he investigates them all.

We get one kind of answer, for example, for Aristotle, when we start with the infinitive, *einai, to be*, and ask 'What does it mean '*to be*'?' And we get a somewhat different perspective on the whole matter when we begin with the participle *on*, or its nominalizations (*to on, ta onta*), and ask "What does 'being' mean?". In following through the answer to the first line of inquiry, Aristotle emerges with a theory of being that stresses the notion of *predication*. The infinitive *einai* ('to be') as well as the copula *esti* ('is') serve fundamentally as signs of predication. Thus in a normal proposition or sentence we say something (predicate) about something (subject). The analysis of being, in the sense of 'to

be', points in the direction of what can be said about the *predicate*
relation, for here 'to be' means *to be such-and-such*, as conveyed by the
predicate. Moreover, Aristotle recognizes *different* ways or types of
predicative relations or ties. This is the point of his theory of
categories, a matter also insisted on in his thesis that being is not a
genus. Also there are in this connection two further uses of 'is' that are
best seen as supplementary to the primary predicative meaning.
Thus, Aristotle calls attention to the use of 'is' as meaning 'is true',
and again to the fact that the term 'to be' is sometimes also used to
mean 'to exist'. But these are further extensions or refinements built
upon the analysis of the basic predicational meaning of 'to be', as we
shall see, more fully, below.

When we turn to the other main direction of his analysis, to the
analysis of the nominalized participle *to on* and to the associated
analysis of *ousia* (primary substance) as a principal mode of *to on*, we
turn, as it were, from the analysis of being as predicate to the
analysis of being as subject. For here we may take Aristotle to be
asking the questions: 'What are the basic types of entities there are
in the world?', 'What really exists?', 'What is that which is?' [3]
Among other things, Aristotle here wants to challenge the view of
Plato according to which we must include Forms as constituting or as
among such basic existents. Aristotle's own preferred and central
thesis is that *ousia*, in the sense of primary substances, or entities
undergoing various types of change, constitute the basic entities of
the world, and are the primary existents. Related to this central
doctrine is the attempt to work out the distinction between being *'per
se'* (το καθ αυτο ον) and being *'per accidens'* (το κατα συμβεβηκος ον) or
again the distinction between being a subject and being *in* a subject.

As we may expect, and as we have already remarked, these two
prongs of his theory, or lines of inquiry, have important interconnections; at the same time they also pose a variety of questions for
Aristotle as well as for his commentators and readers. One important
line of interconnection is pointed out by Aristotle himself when he
remarks (*Metaphysics* Δ 7) that there are as many varieties of *per se onta*
as there are categorial ways of specifying to be (*einai*). And among the
kinds of questions that are raised by carrying through this two-
pronged line of inquiry, we may mention these two (themselves
interconnected): (1) Are the *ta onta*, the basic 'entities' of the world,
'objects' or 'facts'? If we stress the approach in terms of subjects, we

seem to be led to the former; if we stress the approach in terms of predicates established or articulated through true assertions, we seem to be led to the latter. (2) Since, for Aristotle, a primary substance is never a bare particular but a 'this something', how are we to construe the relation between the *'this'* and the *'what'* it is? The question consists at bottom in trying to understand whether in any way an individual's *existence* does or does not involve a relation to a *universal*, and if so, how that relation is to be described.

In what follows, I shall turn to a brief examination of Aristotle's view of being when seen first through the fundamental perspective of predication, and second, when seen through the perspective of a study of the basic entities in the world, and in particular the existence of individual substances.

3.3 *Predication and Being*

One direct and sound approach to what Aristotle was concerned with in his theory of being is to be found by starting with his analysis of *predication*. Aristotle's treatment of being, as an ontologist, goes hand in hand with his treatment of predication as a logician. This is not surprising, for in a very profound sense reality for him is what it can be said to be when that saying is true. What the world is coincides with our account of what the world is when that account is infused with a proper awareness of the norms that make our account logical. Since language has this kind of intimate connection with being, we can study what the modes of being are, what it means to be, by attending to certain basic patterns and relationships present in our use of language, and therefore present whenever we say what is the case. Among these fundamental patterns is that of predication, present whenever we say something of the form 'A is B'. One way in which we can understand what being is, Aristotle in effect proposes, is to study the use and application of the predicative copula 'is'. He puts it thus in the *De Interpretatione*: "For neither are 'to be' and 'not to be' and the participle 'being' significant of any fact, unless something is added; for they do not themselves indicate anything, but imply a copulation, of which we cannot form a conception apart from the things coupled" (16b 22). What Aristotle is saying is very simply that neither 'being' nor 'to be' signify anything when taken by themselves;

they are not names or quasi-names that have a referential or desig-native use apart from some way of saying 'what' or 'how' something is, that is, apart from specifying through predicates the such-and-suches of things. Rather 'to be' is always *to be something or other*. Before you begin to worry about *ousia* or *to on*, Aristotle would seem to say, you had best realize that these various noun and participial forms of the verb 'to be' (*einai*, ειναι) have to be seen as arising from the more fundamental copulational or predicational use of the verb 'to be'. In such a use, that is in a typical *logos* or sentence (a 'compounding' of terms), one says something about something, one makes a predica-tion. What 'to be' is, is exhibited and made clear in the various ways in which we go about articulating such predications.

At this point, however, it is necessary to stop and say something about the use of the term 'predication', since unless we are clear about the ways in which this term can be used, and in particular about the way this term is to be understood in connection with our analysis of Aristotle's theory of being, we shall be prey to all sorts of confusions and misunderstandings. Much of the difficulty here arises from the fact that the term 'predication' can be used in various senses, and that Aristotle's understanding of what we might mean by this concept is to a large extent differently oriented from what we have become accus-tomed to understand by this term, largely as a result of post-Aristo-telian grammatical and logical investigations, especially those of our own day.

I shall distinguish [4] three different senses in which the term 'predication' may be used: namely, (1) the *syntactic*, (2) the *semantic*, and (3) the *ontologic*. The term 'predication' taken generically may be understood has having to do in *some* sense with a 'tie' between 'subject' and 'predicate'. But how we shall understand 'tie', 'subject', and 'predicate' will take on different meanings as we shift from one to another of these different senses of predication.

Syntactic predication is to be understood as the tie that holds between two sets of linguistic expressions, designated respectively as the *subject* and *predicate* of some sentence or proposition. (How to give the formal criterion by which this grammatical or linguistic separation can be accomplished is a difficult and subtle question; it is a matter that lies beyond the province of our present concern.) It should be noted that when Aristotle came, in his own fashion, to attempt these syntactic or linguistic distinctions, especially in *De Interpretatione*, he refers to what we have called 'subject' by the Greek term for noun or name (ονομα, *onoma*), and to what we have called 'predicate' by the Greek term for verb (ρημα, *rhema*). The Greek equivalent terms for 'subject' and 'predicate' (υποκειμενον, *hypokeimenon;* and κατηγορημα, *kategorema,* respectively) are *not* used by Aristotle to mark these syntactic or grammatical distinctions, although they have come to be so used generally by us. Thus in the paradigm sentences "Socrates is wise" or "Theatetus flies", Aristotle, in making these syntactic distinctions, would recognize 'Socrates' and 'Theatetus' as names (*onoma*), and 'is wise' or 'flies' under the heading of *rhema*. (The syntactic concept of *rhema* includes in its wide use not only verbs of action strictly so called and as tensed, but also adjectives and perhaps even sortal terms as well.)

By *semantic predication* we shall understand a relation or tie between an extralinguistic subject and the predicate taken as a linguistic item. A proper name such as 'Socrates', as used in the sentence "Socrates is wise", *refers* to a person about whom something is predicated or said, namely, that he is wise. The proper name 'Socrates' is a linguistic item, but what it refers to is nonlinguistic: it is the individual person who lived in Athens, was the teacher of Plato, drank the hemlock, and so on. Aristotle's term for the extralinguistic entity referred to typically by proper names (e.g., 'Socrates'), or definite descriptions (e.g., 'this man') is *hypokeimenon* (υποκειμενον). It is this extralinguistic entity that *he* means by the term 'subject'. A subject in this sense is an individual object or person to be found in the world. It is not a linguistic or grammatical item in a sentence; it is that which can be referred to by means of a *grammatical* 'subject' (e.g., proper name). A subject or *hypokeimenon* in its most fundamental sense is a primary substance and as such occupies a central role in Aristotle's philosophy. It is that about which ultimately all the various discriminations that Aristotle is interested in making about categorial modes of being have to do. In semantic predication the predicate, in contradistinction to the treatment of 'subject', is to be understood as a linguistic expression; it is an expression used to say something about, to predicate (something) of, the nonlinguistic subject. To 'predicate of' in this semantic sense is to use a linguistic expression to say something about a subject that is itself extralinguistic.

By *ontologic predication* is meant a relation or tie between subject and predicate where *both* are extralinguistic. As before, the subject is typically an individual object or person, an individual substance. And a predicate is an attribute or property, which can be *said of*, or belong to, the subject. For Aristotle, in this extralinguistic sense, a predicate is a *categoreumenon* (κατηγορευμενον), for example a genus, species, quality, action, state, and so on.

Aristotle's own most fundamental sense of predication conforms to what we are here calling 'ontological predication'.[5] Some have argued, on the contrary, that he is to be understood as using the notion of semantic predication throughout, on the ground that ontological predication is an incoherent notion.[6] And in fact it may be that much of what Aristotle has to say can be read as illustrating the structure of semantic predication. Nevertheless, I shall, in what follows, adopt as a working hypothesis that *au fond* Aristotle is working with the notion of ontologic predication.[7] In any case, there surely is no question that for him what predication has to do with in paradigm cases are subjects in the sense of extralinguistic individuals, for this sense of 'subject' is common to both the conceptions of predication as ontologic or semantic. In appealing to the notion of ontologic predication as our basic framework, we shall be able to understand in what sense Aristotle's whole approach to being is a matter of building out the details of the ontologic tie between primary substances and the such-and-suches that mark the various types of predicate that hold of them or belong to them.

3.4   *Categories of Predication*

Aristotle would further insist that not only must we turn to the context of predication to get at the meaning or meanings of 'being' as it is revealed in the predicational copula or in the use of predicates generally, but we must also be prepared to take note of the variety, the plurality of ways in which different kinds of predicates carry with them some clues to the different ways of being, of the senses of 'to be'. One way in which we may suppose Aristotle arrived at his list of categories, as marking this plurality, is by considering the ways in which we may group the answers to questions that constitute the information or descriptions given by such answers about some *individual*, especially some individual person.

Take such sentences as 'Socrates is a man', 'Socrates runs', 'Socrates is wise', 'Socrates is the husband of Xantippe', 'Socrates is made to drink the hemlock', 'Socrates is sitting', 'Socrates is five feet ten inches tall', and so on. They are examples of the basic types of sentences Aristotle has in mind in constructing his ontology. They have to do with an individual subject (in these examples, they all happen to be the same subject, an individual person), and in each case a different predicate is asserted of the subject, the person Socrates. Sentences such as these yield for Aristotle a sense of the varieties of predication and thereby important clues as to what it means 'to be'. Yet 'being' does not have as many meanings as the open-ended set of predicates taken in all its unrestricted plurality of possible cases. For, Aristotle suggests, the plurality can be simplified into basic types or sets of predicates. These he calls 'categories'. Thus, while 'is white', 'is healthy', 'is bitter', 'is smooth', 'is curved' are different from one another, they can all be said to belong to the category of *quality* and their mode of being therefore discriminated and distinguished from, say, the kinds of predicates that the category of *substance* collects, or *quantity*, and so on. Categories as classes or types of predicate have to do with the kinds of answers we should get in response to various types of interrogatives—for example, 'What like?', 'What kind?', 'Where?', 'When?', and so on. They classify the various kinds of predicates we use in answers to our questions. Since there are many predicates, the categories are the basic types, the schema within which specific instances can be grouped. Aristotle himself gives various lists of these fundamental types, although substance and some others reappear in all such lists. (There are of course various problems connected with the soundness of this whole enterprise of effectively separating categories, and the problems continue beyond Aristotle down to our own day. It is beyond the scope of my present interest to explore these difficulties.)

There is an alternate route leading to the same broad list of categories that Aristotle also employed: for we might ask concerning *anything whatever*, considered as subject, *what it* is, and the answers we should obtain may again be grouped in certain fundamental ways as we consider the kinds of predicates that specify these answers. This route for arriving at the categories might start, then, not merely by taking as our subject some individual, but for example something represented by an abstract noun, or an infinitive, or a participle, and so on. Thus we may ask not only 'What is Socrates?', meaning, thereby, 'What *kind* of individual is he (to what class of things does he belong)?', we might also ask 'What is generosity?' or 'What is a rhomboid?', or 'What is running?', or 'What is it 'to think'?', and so on. And by considering with respect to this wide range of types of subjects, the kinds of answers we should get as conveyed in the predicates (the descriptions or information), we can again group these predicates and find that they reduce to certain ultimate classes; some belong to what Aristotle would call the category of 'substance', others to 'quality', still others to 'quantity' and so on. When we follow this latter route, we note that the characteristic question which generates the answers is conveyed by the interrogative *'What?'*, whereas the first route might use any of a wide set of interrogatives (e.g., 'When?', 'Where?', 'How much?', etc). It is necessary to be clear about the fact that the term 'what' in the foregoing account is being used in a broad sense as capable of yielding *all* the categories. There is, however, a narrower use of the term 'what' in which it is specifically restricted to the category of substance, so that in asking *what* something is we wish to know to what *class of substances* it is to be assigned. It is the broad sense of 'what' that Aristotle himself employs when he points out that in response to the question "What is this?" we need not be restricted to the category of substance, and that

Someone who signifies what a thing is sometimes signifies substance, sometimes quantity, sometimes qualification, sometimes one of the other of the predicates. For when a man is under discussion and one says that what is being discussed is a man or is an animal, one is saying what it is and signifying substance; whereas when the color white is under discussion and one says that what is being discussed is white or is a color, one is saying what it is and signifying qualification; similarly, if a foot length is being discussed and one says that what is being discussed is a foot length, one will be saying what it is and signifying quantity. (*Topics* I, 103b 23-27) (Ackrill translation) [8]

Or again, " 'What-a-thing-is' may refer to a primary being (to a this-something), or it may refer to one or another of the predicates (quantity, quality, and the like)" (*Metaphysics* 1030a 20).

The importance of this analysis of the categories as types or classes of predicates is that it yields, by such a classification, an analysis of *types of being*, of the different senses of 'to be'. Aristotle makes the point as follows:

Since then, some predicates indicate what the subject is, others its quality, others quantity, others relation, others activity or passivity, others its 'where', others its 'when', 'being' has a meaning answering to each of these. (*Metaphysics*, 1017a 22; cf. *Metaphysics*, 1042b 25-28; *De Anima* 415b 12-15)

Anything that *is* in any category, for Aristotle, is a 'what' (in this broad sense), and therefore something that can be brought out in some type of predication. To be a such-and-such under some categorial heading is to manifest one or another mode of being.

While for certain purposes it may be useful or important to distinguish the *copula* from the *predicate*, there is another vantage point, philosophically a more fundamental one, in which the distinction between the two evaporates, or rather the copula is assimilated to the predicate. Aristotle himself points out "There is no difference between 'the man is recovering' and 'the man recovers', nor between 'the man is walking' or 'cutting' and 'the man walks' or 'cuts'; and similarly in all other cases" (*Metaphysics*, 1017a 22). It is not necessary therefore in every case of predication to explicitly use some form of the predicative copula. In a broad sense of 'predicate', nevertheless, every proposition has to do with a subject and predicate, and every true proposition articulates or discloses a particular case of some type of ontological predicational tie, some mode of being. However, even where in language we separate the 'copula' from the 'predicate', the point we have been making about the variety of senses of 'to be' can now be made for the copula as well as for the predicate in the narrower sense. Thus, the categorial diversity of senses of 'to be' coincides with the variety of senses of 'is' as copula, and we might therefore speak of 'modes of copulation' that correspond to the different modes of being in the predicate.[9]

Aristotle's interest in categories as a philosopher is linked with his own interests as a scientist in telling the truth about the world as we find it. The discussion of categorial predicates is at the service of our interest in getting at the true predications of things, to say how things are, to determine what their knowable or intelligible structure is. The theory of predication as a theory of being is a framework or schema whose content and details are furnished through the

predications of common sense or science. It is of course not enough
merely to have a predication, for predications after all occur in false
propositions as well. In order to know what *is* the case, the predications have to state what is in fact the case. Hence what the world is,
what being amounts to, is always a matter of detail, of specific
assertions, of specific predications, of backing up particular
statements of fact, whether these have to do with this or that individual or some class of individuals. The truth about the world is
furnished by these innumerably specific statements of fact, in which
categories are made use of, and implicitly employed. The truth
about the world is thus given not merely by a list of categories. The
truth about the world, the truth about being, is pluralized and
distributed among the vast open-ended set of statements that are
themselves exemplifications of the use of this or that category.
Therefore, in one sense, a theory of being as the philosopher's enterprise and interest, is only a facade, a ground plan or framework
for the innumerably detailed and specific disclosures of truth as
furnished by common sense and science. It is not a substitute for
them.

Just as being is a matter of true predication in its manifold
instances, so too what truth is, what 'to be' is, is what it is said to be.
For language and thought can disclose the *form* of things. For Aristotle, what is, is primarily the *form* of things as captured and
expressed in language, and thereby brought out into the open.
Thought makes actual what is the inherent structure of things; what
does not get expressed is not known. The 'to be' of veridical
predication and the 'to be' of things are one and the same 'to be'.

3.5   *'Being Is Not a Genus'*

The general analysis we have given thus far links Aristotle's
treatment of being with predication and in particular with the
various modes of predicational tie belonging to the several
categories. Wherever we have a veridical predication, there we have
an instance of what being is. We must be careful, however, not to
restrict the 'to be' relationship to any one category, for example to
the category of substance, however central and focal that category is.
Aristotle brings out the nonrestrictive predicational status of being

in the several categories by repeatedly insisting on the claim that *being is not a genus*. Let us briefly examine this thesis from this point of view and see to what extent it bears out the interpretation we have given thus far. (Incidentally, in examining Aristotle's claim that being is not a genus, we shall see at the same time why he does not need to show that it is not a *summum genus*, since if it is not a genus at all, it cannot be a *summum genus* either.) The argument he gives for this claim is stated in *Metaphysics* 998b 20ff. In the Ross translation it reads:

But it is not possible that either unity or being should be a single genus of things; for the differentiae of any genus must each of them both have being and be one, but it is not possible for the genus taken apart from its species (any more than for the species of the genus) to be predicated of its proper differentiae; so that if unity or being is a genus, no differentia will either have being or be one. (Cf. *Metaphysics* 1045b 6, 1059b 30; *Posterior Analytics* 92b 14)

The argument as stated here is compressed and somewhat obscure. But perhaps a reasonable interpretation would be the following. In the first place, we note that the general form of the argument is *reductio ad absurdum*: If being were a genus, it would have such-and-such consequences, but these cannot be allowed, therefore being is not a genus. Aristotle appeals in this argument to his general conception of how genus, species, and differentia are related to one another.[10] Thus to take a standard example: Let man (A) be defined as an animal (B) that is rational (C). Then A corresponds to a *species*, B to a *genus*, C to the *differentia*. Both the genus (B) and the differentia (C) are wider than the species. Now the genus, he argues, can only be predicated of the species, *not* of the differentia. (The differentiae too are predicated of the species.) The reason Aristotle gives as to why the genus is not predicated of the differentia is that we should then have a redundancy of predicates with respect to the species. Since the differentiae are predicated of the species, if the genus, too, were predicated of the differentiae, the genus would be predicated of the species "several times over" (*Topics* 144b). "The genus is predicated," he points out, "not of the differentia, but of the objects of which the differentia is predicated. 'Animal', for example, is predicated of 'man' or 'ox' or other walking animals, not of the actual differentia predicated of the species. For if 'animal' is to be predicated of each of its differentiae, then 'animal' would be predicated of the species several times over; for the differentiae are predicates of the species" (*Topics* 144a 32-38).[11]

Now let us apply these general considerations about the relationships between genus, species, and differentia to our present concern, the question whether being might be thought of as a genus. The fact is, Aristotle insists, if being were a genus, being—*that is to say, the predicational relation or tie of being a such-and-such*—would nevertheless still be exemplified by the differentia as well, "for the differentia of any genus must each of them both have being and be one" *(Metaphysics* 998b 22ff). The 'to be' relationship or tie, namely, *to be such-and-such*, is as much exemplified in the differentia, since it is a predicate, as it is in any other type of predicate. (In the present context, notice the 'to be' tie, which is found in predicates, is not spoken of as belonging to the species, since the species is the 'subject', that *of which* the predicates represented by the genus and the differentia are being asserted. This is not to deny, of course, that the term represented by the species may serve in turn as a predicate in another situation, where *it* is used to describe some particular object.) If 'to be' were a genus on Aristotle's rule, it could not be said that what the differentia of a species conveys, being 'outside' the genus, could have the genus predicated of *it*; it could not be, for *any* instance of the use of the differentia, an example of 'to be'. Yet it is! We *can* predicate the (putative) 'genus' ('to be') of the differentia. The differentia as predicate, when used in a statement, allows one to say that the subject (species) *is* in the 'to be' relationship to what it, as differentia, conveys. Now since the rule for the relation between a genus and its differentia—that the genus cannot be predicated of the differentia—is here being violated, therefore *being is not a genus*. The 'to be' relationship, *to be such-and-such*, is not to be modeled on the genus-species-differentia relationship exhibited in the category of substances. The 'to be' relationship not only cuts across all categories, it also holds wherever we have a predicate veridically applied, whether that predicate be a genus, differentia, or whatever.

We may, moreover, use the 'being is not a genus' thesis to support the claim about the diversity of the categorial types of 'to be', and not simply to point to the unity or commonness of their predicational role. For 'being' is not some quality or property held in common that remains invariant as we go from one category to another. What is the same is that each category represents a fundamental type of predication, although the mode of 'to be' exhibited in each case is different. For example, what it is 'to be a substance' is different from what it is 'to be a quality'; yet these do not share in the common property of 'to be'. It is because he wants to stress this aspect of the diversity of 'to be' in the several categories, that Aristotle denies that being is a genus. For if being were a genus then the predicate which the genus represents would be held in common, and be applicable to all cases falling under it. We cannot, accordingly, form a class or genus of the various predicational modes of 'to be', nor therefore of all instances or 'things' which bear these predicates. If, in the latter case, there were such a class of instances of all 'things', we might be tempted to speak of these in some *univocal* way as the class (or genus) of 'beings', or 'the all-inclusive class of beings'. If there were such a class, then 'tree', 'nine-o'clock', and 'white', as predicates would all have something in common, and similarly for what 'have' these predicates. But these types of predicates are diverse: their 'to be' is different; neither they nor the 'things' that exemplify or instantiate them can be subsumed under a single class or genus.[12]

This is to say that the several categories are irreducible and ultimate, each in its own way. A category cannot be *defined* in such a way that 'being' appears as the 'genus' of its definition, for that would allow the several categories each to include, in its own individual definition, the shared common property of the (putative) genus 'being'. But Aristotle rejects this; for each of the modes of being is distinctive—even as far as the 'being' is concerned. He makes this point as follows:

But of the things which have no matter, either intelligible or perceptible, each is by its nature essentially a kind of unity, as it is essentially a kind of being individual substance, quality, or quantity (and so neither 'existent' nor 'one' is present in their definitions), and the essence of each of them is by its very nature a kind of unity as it is a kind of being—and so none of these has any reason outside itself for being one, nor for being a kind of being; for each is by its nature a kind of being and a kind of unity, not as being in the genus 'being' or 'one' nor in the sense that being and unity can exist apart from particulars. (*Metaphysics* 1045b 1-8)

Another way of making Aristotle's point is to say being is a *formal concept* in Wittgenstein's sense.[13] Whereas, for example, a typical nonformal concept such as 'horse' has associated with it a number of determinate characteristics that serve to describe what it is to be a horse, as distinguished, say, from what it is to be a tree, the concepts of 'function' or 'property' or 'predicate' have no set of characteristics in the same sense. The term 'predicate' is a *formal concept*, a place-holder for terms such as 'runs', 'tree', 'white', and so on. A formal concept such as 'predicate' has no material, factual, or nonlogical characteristics that all predicates share by virtue of which they are predicates. We might make an analogous point now in connection with 'being' or 'to be', as this is conveyed by the use of predicate expressions of various types. 'To be' or 'being', we might say, is a *formal concept*. As such, the 'to be (such-and-such)' tie does not carry with it any list of determinate characteristics that all nonformal, actual predicates will be found to share. Each particular predicate, for example, 'white', 'runs', 'tree', and so on, will be found to have certain characteristics that all things correctly designated by one or another of these predicate terms will be found to share. While we may, further, collect terms such as 'white', 'red', 'pale', and so on and assign them to the category 'quality', and so on for each of the different categories, it will not be the case that all these predicates or predicate classes, each exemplifying some mode of 'to be', will be found to share some property with all other predicates that we could then call the property of '*being*'. Being, rather, is the formal concept of the 'to be' relationship. Thus, for Aristotle we might say (using Wittgensteinian language), to be is a formal concept represented by the predicative tie. Yet when we collect different examples of the predicative tie, we do not find that we can extract from them some one *property,* their 'being', in which they all share.

There is still another interpretation we may give for the thesis 'being is not a genus'. Let us suppose that instead of regarding 'being' as a general term for the predicational-tie (the 'to-be-such-and-such') relationship—that 'being' is to mean *instantiation* of some (any) predicate. We may then say 'to be' can be conveyed by the expression 'there is' when prefaced to some general conceptual term; 'to be' means that *there are* instances (or perhaps only one instance) of a given concept (general term). There are cows; there are squares; there are dragons; there is a prime number between 6 and 9; there is a tallest building in the world; there are fictional characters, and so on. Then, despite the fact that there are instances of each of these general terms one could give, there is nevertheless no one kind or class of things to which all these instances themselves belong, merely because they are all instances of things there are. If 'to be' means 'there are' this does not define some one *kind* of thing. There is no *genus* which would consist of all those instances of which we can say that each is an instance—for we cannot form a class or genus of things defined by such a 'property' as '*that there is* a such-and-such'. Aristotle puts this as follows: "There is nothing whose essence is that there is such a thing, for there is no such kind of things as *things that there are*." [14] In short, if being is taken as instantiation, we cannot say 'being an instance' defines a characteristic such that we can then form a class or genus based on this 'characteristic'; 'to be an instance' is not a characteristic in the way to be two-legged, brown, square, an annual wage, prime number, and so on are characteristics, hence it cannot define a genus.

3.6 *Predicational, Existential, and Veridical Uses of 'Is'*

We have concentrated thus far on the kind of answer Aristotle gives to the general question 'What is being?', where this question is taken to mean '*What does it mean 'to be'?*' or 'What are the uses of *einai*?'. And we have seen how, in a general way, Aristotle's answer to this question is one which would stress the fundamental *predicative tie* as the basic logico-ontological fact. Other ways of understanding or using 'to be' are to be seen as in some way related to or supplementing this basic meaning. Thus, *esti*, for example, can also be used—and is so used by Aristotle himself—not only as a copula, or as a general sign of predication, but as having two further uses: a special 'existential' use and a 'truth-affirming' use. In its specifically 'existential' use (in one special but fundamental meaning of that term) it signifies that *there is* (in the world, in actuality) something to which the subject term refers. There is a use of '*ειμι*' which can be translated as '*is (am) alive*' as, for example, in 'Socrates exists', 'I exist'. From the point of view of logic this *combines* the predicative and the existential use of 'is'. Aristotle points out in *De Anima* (415b 13, cf. *De Generatione et Corruptione* 318b 25, *Ethica Nicomachea* 1166a 4-5) that "for living things *to be* is to be alive." On the one hand, this is a predicative use of to be—where 'to be alive' represents a type of descriptive predicate—having its own logos or definition as compared, say, to being inanimate, or being colored. On the other hand, to be alive has an additional 'existential' sense. It means to be actual, or real, to be *located* (genuinely) *in the world.* In this latter sense, for Socrates to be alive means not simply that a certain set of characteristic features can be ascribed to him; it also means *there is* (in fact, in the world) an individual who possesses or displays those characteristics: *there is something in the world* to which the subject term does refer, that is, the 'existence condition' for its referential use is *satisfied.* The term 'existential' as *contrasted* with 'predicational' has then this second-order use. Again, by way of illustrating the appeal to the existential use of *esti*, we can consider the following two passages: in the *Posterior Analytics* (89b 32) Aristotle points out that in some inquiries we seek to establish not the reasons for certain facts, but *whether* something exists *(ei esti)*

such as whether there is or is not a centaur or a God. (By 'is or is not' I mean 'is or is not, without further qualification'; as opposed to 'is or is not (e.g.) white'). On the other hand, when we have ascertained the thing's existence, we inquire as to its nature, asking, for instance, 'what, then, is God?' or 'what is man?'.

Another passage which seems to suggest that Aristotle was on occasion conscious of the existential use of ειμι is his remark to the effect that "Neither 'Socrates is sick' nor 'Socrates is well' will be true if Socrates himself does not exist at all" (*Categories* 13b 18).

In its truth-affirming use, the term εστι serves as a kind of 'sentence-operator', affirming that what the sentence as a whole says 'is true', 'is the case'. This veridical use of 'is' is a use to which Aristotle himself calls attention in *Metaphysics* Δ 7: "The 'is' in a statement also means that the statement is true: and 'is not', that it is not true, but false. These meanings obtain for affirmative and negative forms of speech alike . . ." (1017a 31). (Cf. *Posterior Analytics* 92b 1-20.) This meaning of 'being' is best regarded as a secondary use and to be understood in connection with the primary predicational use of 'to be'. Thus in saying 'S *is* P', the 'is' does double duty: one function is to serve as a 'sentence operator', affirming *truth* of the entire sentence; the other use of 'is' is that of the normal predicational copula. 'S *is* P' becomes: "*It is true* that: S is P". The first use of *is* marks the veridical use: it says that the sentence 'S is P' is true; the other use of *is* in the sentence 'S *is* P' is predicational. In any case, of course, it is evident *the veridical use of* esti *('is') cannot be understood apart from the predicational use* of 'is' as copula, or at any rate, apart from *some* predication in an assertion, whether or not the assertion contains the use of the predicative *copula*. While these two uses are both present in the single occurrence of the term 'εστι', their logical roles and status is nevertheless different and need to be sorted out. In any case, then, both the 'existential' and 'truth-affirming' ('veridical') uses of 'εστι' are dependent on, and are secondary to, the primary predicative-copulative use. Indeed we best think of the 'existential' or 'veridical' uses as *second-order* uses, and the *predicative-copulative* use as a first-order one.

3.7 *Being and Existence*

Whatever be the basic interest that Aristotle has in the predicational tie as one way of approaching the analysis of being—in the different varieties of 'to be' in the various categories that specify such a tie—and in the related existential and veridical uses of 'is', there is nevertheless another way in which we can approach the sense of Aristotle's interest in raising the question "What is being?" For we can understand him as asking not only for an analysis of the different uses of *einai*, 'to be', but for an analysis of *to on*: What is *that which is*?', *What exists*?, What are the *actual entities* that make up the world? Aristotle's answer to this question is not to be thought of as a rival to the first line of analysis, much less as in any way incompatible with or contradictory to it. If anything, it is a parallel way of analysis, for some of the basic distinctions he makes and theses he upholds in connection with the 'predicational' analysis are duplicated or restated in terms of the analysis of *onta* (beings or existents). Suppose, for example, one were to ask whether the categories are ways of classifying types of *predicates* or ways of classifying types of *entities*. (I use the term 'entity' here as a term signifying any type of 'to be' and therefore including not only things in the narrow sense of substances, but any other mode of 'to be' as well, for example, a quantity, quality, place, and so on.) The answer, in Aristotle's philosophy, is that the two ways of regarding categories ultimately come to the same thing, since our language on the level of types of predicates we use (the categorial level) reflects the modes of being to be found in the world. For example, the point that 'being is not a genus' can now be translated from being a thesis about predicates, to being a thesis about 'things' or *onta*. It becomes the thesis that there is no single class of 'existent things'. Thus, in general, instead of taking 'categories' simply as classes of *predicates*, we can, with appropriate qualifications, also take them as representing different *classes of entities*.[15]

Aristotle's analysis of being in the sense of *to on* is dominated by a search for, and characterization of, what constitute *primary beings*. Of the various ways in which we may say what is, what exists, Aristotle takes as a basic presupposition of his inquiry that some types of 'what is' are more fundamental than others. "For, though all things 'are', they 'are' not in the same way; but some things are primarily, and the rest dependently" (*Metaphysics* 1030a 22). Or again:

Hence, one might even question whether walking, being healthy, sitting, and the like 'are' or 'are not'; for none of them is naturally self-dependent or capable of being separated from some primary being: . . . Hence, it is clear that only because there is primary being can the other ways of being be and consequently, that what is first or simply, not derivatively, is primary being. (*Metaphysics* 1028a 21, 29-30)

'More fundamental' can be specified in terms of 'being independent of', not requiring the being of something else, whereas 'less fundamental' would be the opposite of this, that is, to be dependent on something else for its own existence. From this point of view, Aristotle's whole analysis in ontology is to show the fundamental role of *individual existents* as providing the basis for all other types or modes of being. There is, first of all, the needed distinction between what is individual and what is universal or general. "What many beings have in common cannot itself be a this-something, but is a 'what'; whereas a primary being is a 'this'" (*Metaphysics* 1003a 9; cf. *Metaphysics* 1038b 8ff.) As contrasted with general forms, individuals are primary. Indeed insofar as the universal has any existence or being, it is wholly derivative from and dependent on the primary existence of individuals. For example, primary substances are more fundamental than the sorts, types, or classes of such individuals—what he calls 'secondary substances'. Further, we can speak of what it is to be an individual in *any* category, and need not be restricted to the category of substance. Thus, among individuals in this broad sense (καθ εκαστα, ατομα), we may include not only individual substances, for example 'this-man' (who may also be referred to by a proper name, e.g. 'Socrates'), but also individual quantities, qualities and the like; for example, 'this red', 'this square', 'this sitting-posture', and so on.[16] Yet among individual existents, Aristotle draws a further distinction: for while as a group, individual 'this-es' are primary and basic with respect to 'universals' or 'whats', in turn among individuals or 'this-es', those individuals that belong to the category of substance are primary or basic with respect to other individual this-es in other categories.

This distinction, in the *Categories*, is signalized by Aristotle's drawing a distinction between being a subject (an individual, primary substance) as contrasted with being *in* a subject. While both ultimately constitute *'per se'* existents (καθ αυτο ον), those which are primary substances—for example, this man, this rock—are those *in* which the individuals in other categories—for example, this red, this rough, this healthy, this-earlier-than exist as particular qualities, quantities, relations, and so on. For example, this particular state of health exists as a state (quality) of *this man*; or again, "the shape of the bronze sphere exists at just the same time as the particular bronze sphere" (*Metaphysics* 1070a 23).

3.8   *The Primacy of Primary Substances*

When confronted by the question 'What is being? (*to on*)', Aristotle says (*Metaphysics* Z, 1028a 10-1028b 7) that this question turns out to be the very question 'What is *ousia*?' (generally translated as 'substance'). We must ask what significance this interpretation of the question has for Aristotle; how did he come to give the question 'What is being?' this direction and force? At first glance, this seems to conflict with the interpretation of his views we have been examining thus far. For one of the principal theses we have seen Aristotle defending is the claim that being is a matter of being something or other, and therefore that there are as many senses of 'being' as there are modes of copulation or, otherwise put, of principal types of predicates or categories of predication. Indeed at one point (in the *Eudemian Ethics* (1217b 25-41)) in comparing the multiple senses of

'good' and the multiple senses of 'being', Aristotle suggests that since
'being' does have these multiple *different* senses, there cannot be a
single unitary science of being, any more than there can be one of
what is good. Yet in *Metaphysics* Γ he insists, virtually in direct
opposition to this claim, that despite the various senses of 'to be', "it *is*
the work of *one* science to study the things that are, *qua* being" (1003b
16). What enables Aristotle to take this new line is that when he came
to write this part of the *Metaphysics*, he no longer strictly adhered to
the strict dichotomy and exhaustive classification of terms (or, more
accurately, things) as being either homonymous or synonomous.
(When things are said to be homonymous, the same name applies to
them, although their respective definitions differ, whereas in the case
of synonymy not only the names are the same, but their definitions
are alike as well. This distinction is roughly parallel to what
nowadays would be designated as the distinction between being
multivocal and being *univocal*.) He came, in short, to recognize a *tertium
quid*, a type of 'equivocal' that is προς εν, one in which, despite
differences in meaning, there is nevertheless a common reference, a
nuclear or focal meaning. He illustrates what he means by the way in
which such terms as 'healthy' or 'medical' are used. Although they are
variously employed in connection with different sorts of things—we
speak, for example, of a medical man, a medical knife, a medical
book—nevertheless they all have a common focus of meaning, a
common primary reference. "For a treatise and a knife are called
'medical' because the former *proceeds from* medical science, while the
latter is *useful to* it. And things are called 'healthy' in a similar manner;
one because it is a *sign* of health, the other because *productive* of it"
(*Metaphysics* K, 1060b 36-1061a 7; Γ, 1003a 34-b 5).

    In precisely the same way, Aristotle proposes, there is a common
focal meaning among the otherwise disparate meanings of 'being'.
There is, in fact, a relationship among the various senses of 'to be' in
the several categories, whereby the category of substance serves as the
primary sense of 'to be' around which all the other senses of 'being' in
the nonsubstance categories cluster. Statements involving to-be
predications in the various nonsubstance categories of quantity,
quality, and the rest, depend on, and require, reference to the 'to be' of
substance in order for their own meaning ultimately to be clear. It is,
then, by virtue of this central role of the category of substance among
the other categories that there can be a unitary science of being qua

being. The science of being qua being, although including a treatment of all the different senses of 'to be', shows them all to have a focal relatedness to substance, to what it is to be in the category of substance. Being in the categories of time, place, quality, action, and the rest depend on or require the being of substance in order for them to have any applicability or role to perform. Unless therefore we are clear about the sense in which we understand the category of substance, we cannot be clear, philosophically, about the other categories. The meaning of the categoy 'substance' and hence the question of 'being' in the sense of 'to be a substance' has a philosophical priority for Aristotle. It is in this sense that the question of what is being *reduces* to the question of what is substance.

For as 'is' (το εστιν) characterizes all things, not however, in the same sense, but one sort of thing primarily, and others in a secondary and dependent sense, so 'what a thing is' (το τι εστιν) unqualifiedly characterizes substance, but other things only in a qualified sense. (*Metaphysics* Z, 1030a 18ff.)

Aristotle draws a distinction between primary substance and secondary substance. Primary substances—this man, that horse—are the individuals to which various predicates are attached, or '*in*' which other individuals exist as particular qualities, relations, and so on. The secondary substance term, the fundamental *what* a thing is, belongs 'essentially' to it, while, other predicate terms may be attached to it only 'accidentally'. The individual substance as such can never be predicated of anything nor is it *in* anything. Now if 'to be' is always 'to be something or other', to be the bearer of true predicates, it follows that there cannot be an individual qua individual that can be said to exist independently of *what* it is or *what* it can be said to be. For Aristotle, therefore, it makes no sense —because there is no room in his system—to say that there is an individual which is a bare particular, devoid of properties, and especially of the essential properties that make it such-and-such a substance.[17]

3.9   Per Se *and* Per Accidens *Existents* [18]

The distinction Aristotle makes between *per se* existents (το καθ
αυτο ον) and *per accidens* existents (το κατα συμβεβηκος ον), while
fundamentally a distinction between types of existents (*ta onta*), can
perhaps best be understood when approached through the route of
predication, for in one sense a true predication articulates or determines an existent.

Suppose I point to some particular 'object' (where 'object' here is a
stand-in for some 'this', (τοδε, τοδι)) and say 'This is a man', or 'This is
red', or 'This is square', or in general utter a statement of the form
'This is ϕ', where 'ϕ' is a predicate term taken from one of the
categories, that is, it is either a substance-type predicate or a quan-
tity-type, quality-type (etc.) predicate. And suppose further that
what I say is true, that is, I have correctly or appropriately classified or
characterized the 'it' or 'this'. I can then use this true predication as a
warrant or basis for forming a designating phrase such as 'this-man',
'this-red', a phrase that might then be used as the *subject* of some fresh
predication, for example, 'This-man is musical'. Where the original
statement 'This is ϕ' establishes such a true 'predication', it is to be
thought of, more exactly, as giving the *identity* of the subject. Such a
'predication' can be thought of as 'collapsing' the 'predicate' into the
'subject' and thereby yielding the resultant phrase 'this-man', 'this-
red', and so on. Strictly speaking, the sentence 'This is a man' does not
have as its subject what is referred to by the word 'this' *alone*, for the
word 'this', alone, does *not* identify a subject. An individual subject is
always a 'this-ϕ'. I cannot say *what* 'this' refers to without already
using some classificatory, descriptive predicate belonging to one or
another category. Nevertheless, it may be useful for certain purposes—that is, to bring out certain similarities and differences—to
continue to speak *as if* the grammatical sentence 'This is a ϕ' ('This is
a man', 'This is red', and so on) are cases of predicative assertions
made of genuine *logical* subjects. Each 'this-ϕ' can now serve to refer to
or identify a *per se existent*, in the broad sense of this latter term. By 'the
broad sense' of *per se existent* I mean one which can be exemplified in
any of the categories, where the 'ϕ' of the 'this-ϕ' tells us *what* the 'this'

is, and again where the 'what' cuts across all the categories and is not to be restricted to the substance category alone.

In the narrower and more strict sense of '*per se*', however, only terms designative of *primary substances* will be *per se* existents; that is, the 'φ' will be a substance-type term, for example, 'man,' 'tree', and so on. The individual referred to will be a 'this-something' (τοδε τι); it will be a primary substance and will satisfy what Aristotle calls 'the what-it-is-to-be that' of a thing (το τι ην ειναι). In the case of *per se* existents that exemplify nonsubstance categories, for example, 'this-red', 'this-state-of-health', and so on, Aristotle would want to say, according to the terminology of the *Categories*, that they exist '*in*' a subject, that is, *in* a primary substance. Yet the fact that a *per se* existent is 'in' another *per se* existent, for example, 'this white' is 'in' 'this-man', does not make the former any less *per se* in this broad sense of the term, for purposes of contrast with a *per accidens* existent.

An important way of distinguishing what it is to be a *per se* existent, in the strict sense, namely, a primary substance, and that which is 'in' a subject is to note that a primary substance cannot undergo any *changes* in *what* it is without ceasing to exist altogether. In this sense *what* a primary substance is, is 'essential' to it. There can be no 'it', or individual *this-something* without its being a such-and-such. This-man cannot undergo a change with respect to being a man and still be *the same individual*, that is, without surrendering his *identity*. However, the *per se* existents that are 'in' a subject are, for the most part, states, conditions, quantitative features, relations, and so on which *can* change without affecting the identity of the subject, or primary substance. Indeed insofar as the individual substance *does* undergo change of one sort or another, it is change with respect to these 'accidents'. For example, this-man changes from having this-sitting posture to this-standing posture, from being 'this pale-faced' to being 'this ruddy-cheeked', and so on.

Now take the sentences (A) 'This man speaks Greek', 'This man is musical' or again the sentences (B) 'This surface is smooth', 'This surface is white'. The subjects of (A) identify a *per se* substance, the subjects of (B) identify a *per se* 'this-φ' in a nonsubstance category. What of the predicates in each set of classes? Let us assume the statements are true, that the predications hold, that they *do* belong to the identified subject. Aristotle would now say these statements establish *per accidens predications*, and the existents they determine are *per accidens existents.* By a *per accidens existent* is to be understood the entity referred to or identified by a phrase which now incorporates the predicate term along with the original subject term, in a compound expression. Aristotle appeals to this notion of *per accidens predication* as a way of making clear why we should speak of the entity referred to by this means as a *per accidens existent.* There is nothing, for example, in what it is to be a *man* that, as part of its definition, requires a man to know Greek or to be musical. (By contrast, if I were to say 'This man is an animal', the predicate 'animal' is part of the definition of 'man' and the phrase 'this-animal-man' would therefore continue to designate a *per se* existent.) Take the true statement of the form 'This ϕ is ψ', where 'ψ' is *not* part of the definition of 'ϕ'. Then by forming the compound phrase 'this ψ - ϕ' I should have a means for referring to or identifying a *per accidens existent*. In short, wherever I have a true *per accidens* predication—for example, 'This man is educated'—I can form a means for referring to a *per accidens existent*, namely, 'this educated man', or similarly 'this musical man', 'this white surface', 'this smooth surface', and so on. Each of these phrases can thus be used to refer to a *per accidens existent.* Let us further suppose that in the statements 'This man speaks Greek' and 'This man is musical' the phrase 'this man' refers to the same person in both cases. And let us suppose that both statements are true. I can then form a complex phrase 'this Greek-speaking, musical-man', and this phrase, too, would identify a *per accidens* existent. The presence of 'musical' along with 'man' is *per accidens*, but so, too, of course is the *co-presence* of 'musical' and 'Greek-speaking' with each other, and with 'man'. And the same type of analysis can be applied to the 'surface' example, so that 'this white, smooth surface' would therefore also be used to identify or refer to a *per accidens* existent.[19]

3.10   *Parmenides and Aristotle: A Brief Summary*

As we have seen, Parmenides's solution to the central problem of ontology is that of a rational mystic. The use of the word 'rational' here is meant to remind us of a twofold direction in which we have noted such concern on the part of Parmenides for rationality—first, in proposing the *'esti'* formula as a methodological postulate for *any* rational inquiry; second in not being content to retreat into silence on the level of apprehension of *to eon* (Being), but in undertaking to prove, by argument, its essential properties.

On the one hand, then, Parmenides would have us see how the presupposition of existence of that about which we would gain knowledge is an essential prerequisite for any rational inquiry. His '*esti*' formula is the prototype and matrix for a logician's analysis of the general structure of a proposition. Already in this earliest, primitive form of analysis of such structure, it points to the roles of reference and of predication in a proposition, and of how questions of the *existence* of the subject of reference and the *truth* of the predication asserted of the subject are to be viewed within this propositional context.

It is this logician's project of analyzing this cluster of concepts of reference, predication, and truth which Aristotle, in his own logical treatises, amplified and systematized in a form that was to remain the accepted orthodoxy for many centuries. Aristotle worked out the details of a theory of predication in the form of a theory of categories. One side of his theory of being is an account of the various senses in which 'to-be' is a matter of saying (predicating) what something is. But such a theory of predication is also intimately connected with a theory of what fundamentally exists. Aristotle's theory of existence (the other dimension of his general theory of being) is best seen as taking the form of a theory of substances, the primary constituents of the world of nature.

But there is another aspect of Parmenides's thought—that which has to do with *to eon*—which finds no parallel or echo in Aristotle's philosophy. Aristotle's approach to ontology reflects throughout the fact that he is basically a scientist, a logician, and a thinker preoccupied with the pluralities and diversities of what exists, not a mystic who has learned to abstract from that diversity and who dwells on the undifferentiated and utterly unique fact of the existence of the world as such.

Here we have, then, in the thought of Parmenides and Aristotle, both in what they share and in their divergences, two ancient models of what paths might be pursued in an inquiry into the nature of existence (being), and what distinctions, emphases, or projects such an inquiry might undertake to elaborate. As we turn from these ancient models to our own day, we shall note in the first place, a continued interest in ontological questions as filtered through a careful logical study of the semantic conditions for reference and of the nature of predication. We shall explore some current examples of such theories of existence, as approached through logic, and venture some proposals of our own.

Like Aristotle, however, modern logicians shy away from anything having to do with what Parmenides called *to eon*, with Being itself. Nevertheless, this side of ontology, I shall argue, forms a necessary complement to any study of the logic of the pluralities of existence. This aspect of ontology comes to the fore when we attend to what we should want to say—or leave unsaid—in dealing with the existence of the world as a whole. I shall myself, toward the end, briefly venture into this domain where logicians have feared to tread. While such conclusions as I shall arrive at are obtained through a route wholly different from that followed by Parmenides, in the end they converge upon and claim some kinship with what he had already long ago proclaimed.

Part II

Logic and Existence:
Some Current Theories

Chapter 4

Existence and Quantification

In addition to the development of a truth-functional, propositional (sentential) calculus, a major achievement of modern logic is
the construction of quantification theory in the form of a predicate
calculus. The analysis of the internal structure of propositions and,
in connection with this, the attention paid to the notion of predication, had been, of course, a primary concern of logic ever since the
days of Aristotle. However, in the hands of such major contributors
to the development of modern logic as Frege and Peirce, the notion
of what it is to be a *predicate* was much deepened and enlarged. It is
sufficient to recall here in particular the following advances. One is
the recognition given to the treatment of relational and many-place
predicates (functions of several arguments) in addition to those
normally studied in the classical Aristotelian-Scholastic tradition in
connection with the analysis of simple 'subject-predicate' types of
proposition—that is, those with monadic predicates. Another advance is the way in which for Frege a clear distinction is drawn
between the notion of predicate (or 'concept-word' in his terminology) and the singular terms ('proper names' in his terminology) that designate individual objects. Further, the way in
which predicates are attached to singular terms is also fruitfully
compared, by Frege, with the mathematical distinction between
function and *argument*.

There is, finally, another general direction in which modern
predicate calculi are set apart from traditional treatments of
predication. This has to do with the matter of quantification. In
traditional logic, especially in connection with the study of syllogis-

73

tic arguments and the distinctions among A, E, I, and O propositions, the syncategorematic expressions 'some' and 'all' were discriminated and studied in various employments. One of the ways, however, that distinguishes the pioneering studies of Frege, especially, in setting up the lineaments of a theory of predication, was the careful attention paid to quantifiers as a basis for achieving a clear formulation of the logic of sentences involving multiple generality. This was accomplished through the use of a special notational means for discriminating the quantifiers from the other components of a proposition, for example the variables of quantification and the predicate constants. And this in turn was accompanied by a close attention paid to the way in which sentences may be thought of as being constructed step-by-step, and in general as involving the distinction between sentences of atomic level and complex sentences, including those belonging to first and higher orders of generality.[1] This discrimination involved an important notational way of distinguishing the quantifiers from the way in which 'all' and 'some' were used, for example, in Boolean algebra to mark the exclusion or inclusion of classes. By linking the quantifiers with the role of binding variables, and also by distinguishing the operation of quantification from the predicative component of a quantified proposition, the way was thereby left open for what came to be a much-debated question of recent logic, namely the range and types of substitution instances or values to be given to the variables, the question as to what is to be understood by a 'value', and whether or not this range of values is to be restricted to individuals in a first-order logic.

The development of quantification theory from Frege to Quine is of great importance for any account of the varied attempts made by philosophers to explicate the notion of existence. Frege, Russell, Quine, and their many followers have offered the claim that it is only by appealing to the idea of quantification that we can give a satisfactory account and convey by precise means what existence is. Russell, for example, wrote: "When you take any propositional function and assert of it that it is possible, that it is sometimes true, that gives you the fundamental meaning of 'existence'. You may express it by saying that there is at least one value of x for which that propositional function is true." [2] And Quine, for example, has written: "Existence is what existential quantification expresses. There are things of kind F

if and only if $(\exists x) Fx$. This is as unhelpful as it is undebatable, since it is how one explains the symbolic notation of quantification to begin with. The fact is that it is unreasonable to ask for an explication of existence in simpler terms." [3]

Despite the fact that those in the Frege-Russell-Quine tradition have claimed to find in the language of quantification a way of explicating what existence is, it would be a mistake to infer that whoever, therefore, uses the predicate calculus is thereby committed to the philosophic view that it is only through the use of the particular (so-called 'existential') quantifier that we are able to express what existence is. For it is important to draw a distinction between the use of the quantifier symbolism and the reading or interpretation which that symbolism is given. Some have argued (and I find myself in broad agreement with their claims) that it is important to *keep separate* our notion of existence, and the way in which it is symbolized, from what is conveyed by the use of the quantifier as such. Belonging to this rival or nonorthodox camp of logicians are Leśniewski and his followers among the Polish school of logicians, and some of those more recently engaged in developing 'existence-free' logics and 'substitutional' or 'neutral' interpretations of the quantifiers.[4]

The interpretation of classical quantification theory as developed in the Frege-Russell-Quine tradition falls mainly in two subclasses. For one, as in Frege and Russell, quantification is essentially a matter of the instantiation of concepts; for the other, as in Quine, quantification is essentially a matter of the ontological commitment to certain objects or ranges of values for the bound variables. I proceed in the present chapter to examine both these strands of quantification theory and their bearing on the question of explicating the meaning of 'existence'.

4.1 *Quantification and Instantiation: Frege and Russell*

Frege's views on existence are to be culled from a number of his writings beginning with the *Begriffschrift*. Very often they take the form of brief remarks rather than extended discussions. Furthermore, his terminology sometimes undergoes change. I shall select for our present purposes one theme from among these materials, one that represents what we may think of as Frege's main point about the interpretation of the term 'existence'. This point comes out in a number of places, principally in his *Foundations of Arithmetic,* where he comments on certain important analogies between existence and number, particularly the number one. There are also brief comments on our subject in his essays "Function and Concept" and "On Concept and Object," among others. These views of Frege were taken up by Russell and recast in his own way, as we shall see shortly. It was through Russell's championing of this approach that it became a well-known and influential doctrine, accepted by many philosophers, among them Moore, Ryle, Ayer, and others. Russell's version of Frege's doctrine thus was disseminated even earlier than Frege's own writings themselves came to be more widely studied through the English translations of Austin, Geach, and Black.

The point that Frege makes about existence, and that I have characterized as his 'main point', is that existence is a second-level property of concepts. For Frege there is a fundamental difference between *objects* and *concepts.* An individual object is what is designated by a singular term, and a concept is what is conveyed by a predicate expression. In his later thought, especially, a concept for Frege is assimilated to what the mathematician calls a 'function'. In a more complete account of Frege's thought and its development than I shall undertake here, it would be necessary to distinguish several different ways in which he came to think of concepts and the predicates which designate them. Thus it is necessary to distinguish, as Dummett points out, between those simple predicates which form part of an atomic sentence, and that are *not*, strictly speaking, 'incomplete' or 'unsaturated', as contrasted for example, with complex predicates formed from complete sentences by omission of one or more singular terms, thus yielding predicates that *are*, in the proper sense, 'incomplete' or 'unsaturated'. Frege tended to simplify his account by regarding all predicates and their concepts as incomplete. Also, whereas Frege's later thought assimilates predicates to functional expressions, in line with a tendency to assimilate sentences to complex names, by contrast his earlier thought draws a distinction between predicates and functions, and of course between sentences and names.[5]

Again, it would be necessary to distinguish *atomic* sentences (formed from logically simple singular terms and simple predicates) from *complex* sentences, including in the latter category both those formed by the use of truth-functional connectives and general (quantified) sentences, the latter employing quantified variables in first- and higher orders of generality. (A first-order quantified general sentence is one in which the quantified variables range over individual objects, whereas in second- or, in general, higher-order generalizations the variables are not restricted to individual objects, and may range over properties, classes, and so on. In quantified sentences of first-order, the predicate(s) apply to individuals within the range of the bound variables as quantified by the universal or existential quantifiers.)

In a complete, simple, atomic sentence in which a name is used to designate an individual object or person, and something is predicated of that individual, we can distinguish the object designated by the name from the concept conveyed by the predicate expression and used to describe that individual. In the sentence 'Socrates is wise', 'Socrates' designates a person (object), and the expression 'is wise' serves as predicate (in Frege's terminology a 'concept-word') used to describe Socrates. Taken by itself, 'is wise' does not designate an object.

In the sentence we have just mentioned, the expression 'is wise' is a simple predicate in an atomic sentence, attached to a singular term ('Socrates') designating an individual. Another way in which we can construe the predicate '. . . is wise' is as an incomplete expression derived from a complete sentence by the omission of a singular term. Such a predicate expression, being incomplete, requires completion by some object-referring expression such as 'Socrates' to give us a complete sentence. An incomplete predicate expression of the sort we have just considered ('. . . is wise') will be said to be of the first-level. Its argument-place is to be filled by a singular term ('proper name') to yield a complete sentence.

A second-level concept ('second-order' in Frege's terminology in *The Foundations of Arithmetic*) however, would be one that applies to a first-level (first-order) concept, but not directly to an object. Otherwise put, a second-level predicate is one whose argument-place is to be filled by a first-level predicate. According to Frege, number concepts—for example, the number one—are to be thought of as second-level concepts. "If, for example," he writes, "we collect under a single concept all concepts under which there falls only one object, then oneness is a component characteristic of this new concept.

Under it would fall, for example, the concept 'moon of the Earth', though not the actual heavenly body called by this name. In this way we can make one concept fall under another higher or, so to say, second order concept." [6]

Frege now extends the same type of treatment to the concept of existence. It, too, is a higher-level property of a first-level concept. Indeed, we can predicate existence of concepts and only of concepts. To say that a concept exists is to say that a first-level concept has instances. The property of existence does not hold for the object(s) to which the first-level concept applies. It is, rather, that property of the first-level predicate (concept) which consists in the fact that the first-level predicate does apply. As such, therefore, existence is a second-level property of a first-level concept (as conveyed by a predicate). Where we have a true *atomic* sentence, by the rule of existential generalization we could say that this entails a general *quantified* sentence to the effect that there is at least one instance of the predicate in question. Thus if 'Socrates is wise' is true, then the general quantified sentence 'There is at least one individual who is wise' (or "The predicate 'wise' has at least one instance") is also true.

Frege gives an example of this approach to existence by considering a negative existential sentence. Take the sentence, 'There exists no rectangular triangle.' Frege says that this sentence "does state a property of the property 'rectangular . . . triangle'; it assigns it the number nought. In this respect existence is analogous to number. Affirmation of existence is in fact nothing but denial of the number nought." [7] This treatment of existence as a property of concepts is what is conveyed by the use of the *existential quantifier*. For example, the sentence 'There is at least one square root of 4' can be written in modern notation: '$(\exists x) x$ is a square root of 4'.[8] It can be read as saying that the concept *square root of 4* is not empty. Frege also comments that the sentence 'There is at least one square root of 4' is equivalent in meaning to 'The concept *square root of 4* is realized.' [9] This reading of the existential quantifier as 'there is' and as meaning 'the first-level concept (predicate) contained in the quantified statement is not empty, that is, does have at least one instance of application', is the substance of Frege's main view about existence. This sense of existence, conveyed by the expression *'es gibt'* in reading the quantifier, is the basis for Frege's coining at one point the term *'Esgiebtexistenz'* to mark this fact.[10]

An important consequence of the foregoing analysis of existence is drawn by Frege as regards the notion of individual existence. He claims that *insofar as we regard existence as a property of concepts*, it is wholly senseless to think of existence in this sense as belonging, or not belonging, to individual objects. In other words, singular existence statements are meaningless. "I do not want to say it is false to assert about an object what is asserted here about a concept," he writes. "I want to say it is impossible, senseless, to do so. The sentence 'there is Julius Caesar' is neither true nor false but senseless." [11] We shall find that Russell, who followed Frege in his general analysis of existence, follows him in this last point as well.

Let us sum up the foregoing points by commenting on the slogan " 'Exists' is not a predicate" as seen from the vantage point of Frege's philosophy.

To say that 'exists' is *not* a predicate, as ordinarily understood and accepted within the context of modern logic insofar as this is influenced by Frege's views, means the following: Let us assume that we are given a language that can be structured in accordance with the standard formalized distinctions of the predicate calculus. In this language, we make a broad distinction between atomic and complex sentences. *Atomic* sentences are sentences in which we can distinguish logically simple singular terms ('proper names', individual constants) and simple predicate constants attached to singular terms to yield such sentences. *Complex* sentences include sentences formed by the use of truth-functional connectives, as well as generalized sentences employing quantifiers and variables. General quantified sentences can be distinguished, among other ways, with respect to the *order* of their generality, that is, depending on the type of expressions that can be substituted for the variables bound by the quantifiers. Among such general sentences are those of *first-order*. These are sentences which contain individuals as their values, quantifiers that bind such variables, and predicates to be assigned to individuals. Quantifiers in this first-order language are of course to be distinguished from the predicates attached to individual variables or individual constants.

To say that 'exists' is *not* a predicate in a language (say a natural language such as English) that can be reconstructed in accordance with the foregoing specifications of the predicate calculus is to say that:

1. 'exists' is not a predicate constant in either an atomic sentence or a predicate in a general quantified sentence of first-order.

2. 'exists' is best reinterpreted as conveyed by the use of a quantifier in a first-order generalization, in which quantifiers are used to bind individual variables.

A further distinction—that between complete and incomplete expressions—as stressed by Frege, leads to another way of regarding the use of the expression 'exists'. *Complete* expressions are either singular terms or sentences, and are assigned to zero-level. *Incomplete* expressions form a hierarchy of first and higher levels, by omission of an expression of a given type from an expression of a lower level. Among such incomplete expressions we can distinguish *predicates*, not only with respect to whether they are one- or many-place, but also by reference to their level, that is, with respect to the type of expression that can be inserted into their argument place(s). For example, a predicate of first-level (formed by omission of a singular term(s) from an *atomic* sentence), will receive in its argument place(s) *singular term*(s) to yield a sentence that is either true or false. On the other hand, a predicate of second-level is an incomplete expression that receives first-level *predicates* in its argument place(s), rather than singular terms. And so on.

Now a quantifier as employed in a first-order generalization may also be considered as a *second-level predicate* since such a predicate, as an incomplete expression, receives *first-level predicates* in *its* argument places. A quantifier in a first-order proposition, qua *quantifier* (as distinct from predicates in the first-order proposition) takes *individuals* as values for the variables it quantifies. However, the quantifier, interpreted as *itself a predicate*, becomes a second-level predicate, taking *first-level predicates* in its argument-places. (Incidentally, the foregoing accounts for the reason I have distinguished in the present chapter the approaches of Frege and Quine, in their common adoption of a quantificational approach to 'existence'. Whereas Frege in his approach to existence stresses the treatment of the quantifier as a second-level *predicate*, Quine stresses the role of the quantifier as binding variables whose values are *individuals*.)

Thus, if one treats 'exists' as something that is conveyed by a quantifier in first-order logic, then since the quantifier itself may be considered as a second-level *predicate, this makes 'exists' also a second-level predicate*. To say a particular concept exists is tantamount to saying that the *concept is instantiated*; '. . . is instantiated (exists)' is thus to be understood as predicated of (first-level) concepts.

Hence, from the point of view of a modern, Frege-influenced logic, there is no *unqualified*, simple answer to the question "Is 'exist' a predicate?". The answer is 'No' or 'Yes' depending on whether we consider the use of *predicates* in atomic sentences and general sentences of first-order, where such predicates are applicable *only* to *individuals* (in which case our answer is 'No'), or recognize on the other hand the possibility of treating the quantifier of a first-order generalization as a *second-level predicate*, and therefore as applicable to first-level *predicates* (in which case our answer is 'Yes').

Russell claimed that "an unbelievable amount of false philosophy has arisen through not realizing what 'existence' means" [12] and offered his own constructive theory to help remedy the situation. That theory owed much, perhaps in its basic essentials, all, to Frege's account, although there is some difference in terminology as compared with Frege's. Russell touched on the theme of 'existence' in many of his writings, beginning with his essays "The Existential Import of Propositions" (1905), and the well-known "On Denoting" (1905), and continuing into *Principia Mathematica* and the *Introduction to Mathematical Philosophy*.

Already in his essay "The Existential Import of Propositions," in which he commented on some interesting proposals of the Scottish logician Hugh MacColl, Russell remarked on the fact that the term 'existence' is used in two different ways, depending on whether we consider its meaning in 'philosophy and daily life' or in that of 'symbolic logic'. These two meanings, he argues, are "as distinct as stocks in a flower-garden and stocks on the Stock Exchange, which yet are continually being confused or at least supposed somehow connected. . . . Until it is realised that they have absolutely nothing to do with each other it is quite impossible to have clear ideas on our present topic." These two distinct meanings are:

(a) The meaning of *existence* which occurs in philosophy and in daily life is the meaning which can be predicated of an individual: the meaning in which we inquire whether God exists, in which we affirm that Socrates existed, and deny that Hamlet existed. The entities dealt with in mathematics do not exist in this sense: the number 2, or the principle of the syllogism, or multiplication are objects which mathematics considers, but which certainly form no part of the world of existent things. This sense of existence lies wholly outside Symbolic Logic, which does not care a pin whether its entities exist in this sense or not.

(b) The sense in which existence is used in symbolic logic is a definable and purely technical sense, namely this: To say that A exists means that A is a class which has at least one member. Thus whatever is not a class (e.g. Socrates) does not exist in this sense; and among classes there is just one which does not exist, namely, the class having no members, which is called the null-class. In this sense, the class of numbers (e.g.) exists, because 1,2,3, etc. are members of it; but in sense (a) the class and its members alike do not exist: they do not stand out in a part of space and time, nor do they have that kind of super-sensible existence which is attributed to the Deity.[13]

Whereas in this passage Russell is prepared to take note of two distinct usages of the term 'existence', that of 'philosophy and daily life' on the one hand, and that of 'symbolic logic' on the other, by the time he came to write his "The Philosophy of Logical Atomism" in 1918 and other later works, he had himself clearly opted for the exclusive use of the logician. (Also, as we shall see, in these later writings he prefers to put the point about the meaning of 'existence' from the logician's point of view, in terms of 'propositional functions' rather than 'classes'.)

The whole burden of my own approach in this book is to argue that whereas the distinction noted by Russell in the passage quoted above is perfectly well taken, my own preference is exactly the reverse of Russell's. It is the usage of 'daily life and philosophy', in my opinion, which needs to be preserved and deepened, whereas the contribution of 'symbolic logic', I shall argue, has to do not with existence but at best with that of instantiation, a wholly different concept.

To return, however, to our summary of Russell's views: An especially full, lucid, and characteristic account of his position is to be found in his lectures on *The Philosophy of Logical Atomism* (1918).[14] In that discussion Russell makes basically two points. The first is that "existence is essentially a property of a propositional function. It means that that propositional function is true in at least one instance."[15] The second is that "existence-propositions do not say anything about the actual individual but only about the class or function." [16]

Whereas, as we have seen, Frege treats existence as a second-level property of first-level concepts, Russell prefers to couch essentially the same point by saying that existence has to do with a propositional function being sometimes true. In Russell's terminology: "A propositional function is simply any expression containing an undetermined constituent, or several undetermined constituents, and becoming a proposition as soon as the undetermined constituents are determined." [17] Consider, then, a propositional function with one variable x and a predicate ϕ. When such a propositional function is supplied with an expression which binds the variable in the way an existential quantifier does, we obtain a general proposition. And what this proposition says can now be read: "There exists an x such that x is ϕ [$(\exists x)\ \phi x$]." Russell also interprets this to mean ". . . [the] propositional function is *true in at least one instance.*" [18]

Another way that Russell also sometimes expressed the concept of 'sometimes true' is by making use of the term 'possible'. For example, he writes: "It will be out of this notion of *sometimes* which is the same as the notion of *possible*, that we get the notion of existence." [19] Again, he points out that "One may call a propositional function *necessary,* when it is always true; *possible,* when it is sometimes true; *impossible,* when it is never true." [20] But he conceded that this use of 'possible' may be "somewhat strange," [21] and it would be more helpful therefore in conveying Russell's characteristic claim to say that for him 'existence' is expressed most accurately by the use of the existential quantifier and that such use is to be taken as meaning 'sometimes true' as applied to a propositional function.

Whereas, then, for Frege existence is a *second-level* property of a concept, for Russell existence is a matter of *being sometimes true* and as holding for a *propositional function.* There is clearly, however, a kinship between these analyses, a kinship which may be captured by appealing to the idea of *instantiation.* Both Frege's and Russell's account of 'existence' are differently formulated versions of the same basic idea that existence is a matter of instantiation—the 'applying', 'holding', 'having instances', 'being sometimes true', when said of a 'concept' or 'propositional function'.

Given Russell's fundamental agreement with Frege on what 'existence' means, it follows for Russell, as it did for Frege, that it is a complete philosophical mistake to speak of individuals existing, or to admit singular existence statements, that is, statements logically predicating existence of an individual. Russell claims: ". . . the individuals that there are in the world do not exist, or rather it is nonsense to say that they exist and nonsense to say that they do not exist." [22] Russell suggests that a basic fallacy underlies this way of talking, namely, the fallacy of "transferring to the individual that satisfies a propositional function a predicate which only applies to a propositional function." [23] Thus, "If you say that 'Men exist, and Socrates is a man, therefore Socrates exists', that is exactly the same sort of fallacy as it would be if you said 'Men are numerous, Socrates is a man, therefore Socrates is numerous', because existence is a predicate of a propositional function, or derivatively of a class. . . . If I say 'The things that there are in the world exist', that is a perfectly correct statement, because I am there saying something about a certain class of things; I say it in the same sense in which I say 'Men exist'. But I must not go on to 'This is a thing in the world, and therefore this exists'." [24]

We may mention, finally, that when Russell came to formulate the Theory of Definite Descriptions (a theory that had as one of its principal purposes the removal of the paradoxes associated with making ostensible reference to nonexistent entities), he showed how one may treat existence claims (whether affirmative or negative) in connection with such individual entities by means of the ideas and techniques we have just been examining. Thus, for him definite descriptive phrases that ostensibly serve as the logical subjects of propositions have to be re-expressed in such a way that the descriptive content becomes part of the predicative component of the proposition. Furthermore, any apparent logical predication of existence with respect to an individual is to be re-expressed in the language of quantification, which then links existence with the instantiation of properties. In dealing with sentences that ostensibly predicate existence of an individual, where this individual is referred to by a *proper name*, Russell's procedure would be to first replace that proper name by an appropriate set of *descriptive terms* and then use the devices of quantification to express the fact that there is one and only one individual or instance that has those characteristics, that satisfies that description. Thus, if we were given a statement such as '*a* exists' where '*a*' is an ordinary proper name, the first step would be to reduce '*a*' to a set of descriptive expressions, and then by use of a quantificational operator express the fact there is (there exists) one and only one instance of the descriptive characteristics in question. To say 'the ϕ

exists' (where 'the ϕ' is a definite description) is tantamount to saying 'the x satisfying ϕx exists'. This is symbolized in *Principia* as "E! $(\imath x)$ ϕx". The symbol 'E!' is given the following definition:

$$\text{"E! } (\imath x)\,(\phi x). \; = \; : (\exists c)\text{:}(x)\phi x. \; \equiv \; x = c\text{"} \qquad \text{(Df.) [14.02]}$$

that is, "there is an object such that ϕx is true and x is c but not otherwise." It would be incorrect to treat 'E!' as a genuine predicate assignable to an individual, since as shown by the foregoing defini-tion, it reduces to the use of the existential quantifier, and a quantifier is not a (first-level) predicate.

Take the sentence 'The author of *Waverley* exists.' In accordance with what we have just said, it is necessary, on Russell's view, to re-express this in such a way that the phrase 'the author of *Waverley*' is no longer the logical subject, nor the term 'exist' any longer the logical predicate. 'The author of Waverley exists' is to be rewritten in philosophically more acceptable language as "the propositional function 'x writes *Waverley*' is true for at least one and at most one x." Let this individual be designated by 'c', that is, x is c. Then to say 'The author of *Waverley* exists' is to say "that there is an entity c such that 'x wrote *Waverley*' is true when x is c, and is false when x is not c. 'The author of Waverley' as a constituent has quite disappeared there, so that when I say 'The author of *Waverley* exists' I am not saying anything about the author of *Waverley*." [25]

These views of Russell have exerted an enormous influence in the history of twentieth-century philosophy. For example, Ryle used these ideas to stage an attack on, and to argue for, the elimination of what he called 'quasi-ontological predicates'. In his well-known essay "Systematically Misleading Expressions," Ryle argued that when such predicates as 'exists', 'is a being', 'is real', or 'does not exist', 'is unreal', 'is fictional', and the like are used in sentences in which names such as 'Mr. Baldwin' or 'Mr. Pickwick' are their appropriate sub-jects, they yield examples of systematically misleading expressions. The remedy for the kinds of mistakes, fallacies, and futile ontologiz-ings that we get involved in when we use such predicates to make supposedly genuine ontological claims, is to be found, according to Ryle, in using the techniques of Russell's theory of descriptions, or, what comes down to the same thing—since it is based on it—the rewriting program and interpretation of quantificational logic as

Russell understood it. Ryle puts the matter as follows: "There is a class of statements of which the grammatical predicate *appears* to signify not the having of a specific character but the having (or not having) of a specified *status*. But in all such statements the appearance is a purely grammatical one, and what the statements really record can be stated in statements embodying no such quasi-ontological predicates. And, again, in all such quasi-ontological statements the grammatical subject-word or phrase *appears* to denote or refer to something as that of which the quasi-ontological predicate is being predicated; but in fact the apparent subject-term is a concealed predicative expression, and what is really recorded in such statements can be restated in statements no part of which even appears to refer to any such subject." [26]

In evaluating the foregoing claims, I shall concentrate on what the various accounts have in common, the thesis, namely, that the only philosophically sound analysis of the concept of existence is that which takes existence to be a matter of instantiation. What the several versions agree upon is that that to which we ascribe existence or of which we predicate existence is something general, namely, a concept or first-level predicate (*'Begriffswort'*) in Frege's terminology, or a propositional function, in Russell's terminology. I shall not stop, therefore, for our present purposes, to critically explore the relative advantages, if any, in describing existence with Frege as a higher-level *property* of general concepts, or with Russell as a matter of a (general) propositional function *being sometimes true*. For it is more important, for our purpose, to concentrate on what these accounts have in common than upon their differences. And if we succeed in showing some inherent weaknesses in giving an analysis of 'existence' which relates it exclusively to that which has to do with the instantiation of general terms, then we need not go on to estimate the relative advantages of describing instantiation as a higher-level property of concepts or as a matter of a propositional function 'being sometimes true.' I shall accordingly in what follows focus on this central, underlying point: Is existence a matter of the instantiation of general concepts? (The phrase 'general concepts' is perhaps an allowable redundancy, for *all* concepts are by their nature general, i.e., capable of reapplicability, just as a function allows for application in connection with different arguments.) The thesis I shall argue for is that it is philosophically unsound to treat 'existence' in this way.

We may agree, at the outset, that the term 'exists' is in fact sometimes used in the sense of 'has instances', 'is sometimes true', 'applies', and so on. But let us remember that our task here, which is philosophical, is not one merely of recording the facts of linguistic usage. Our task is to arrive, if we can, at a philosophic theory as to how it would be best, for philosophic purposes, to use the term 'exists'. And this is no longer a matter of acknowledging an empirical fact of usage. It is rather a matter of taking note of this or that *proposal* as to how, in the interest of developing a sound conceptual scheme, we ought to use the term 'exist' as part of such a scheme. Nor am I denying the obvious fact either that we are being offered the invitation to accept the *proposal*, embodied in the philosophic theory we have been examining, to construe 'exist' as meaning 'instantiation'. What I wish to argue is that the philosophic theory which claims that existence is, at bottom, a matter of instantiation, and that the 'existential quantifier' is to be read as conveying this meaning of 'exists' (i.e., as 'instantiation') are proposals we are not obliged to accept, and in fact that we should resist. In short, what I wish to argue is that it would be best to reserve the term 'exist' to represent something quite *different* from instantiation. Nor, in saying all this, am I to be understood as in any way denying that the notion of instantiation is an important philosophic concept, and that we are to make all necessary efforts to become as clear as we can about how we should understand *it*. All I am interested in claiming is that the notion of *instantiation* is so different from what the term 'exist' ('existent', 'existence', etc.) should be reserved to mean, that terminologically we do well to keep these two conceptual matters entirely separate and not use the same term to convey or represent both.

(What some people mean by saying that individuals exist, Frege would prefer to describe as the *wirklichkeit* of those individuals. Geach, who has called attention to this side of Frege's thought, translates *'wirklichkeit'* as 'actuality'.[27] We can say that an individual has *wirklichkeit*, that is, is [or was] *actual*. If we were also to use the term 'exist' as having this meaning, Frege would maintain, it would be necessary to distinguish this meaning of 'existence' as *'wirklichkeit'* and as applicable to individuals, from 'existence' as *'es gibt ein'* ['is instantiated'] and as applicable to concepts. The term *'wirklichkeit'* cannot apply to concepts, and the term 'existence' in the sense of 'instantiation' cannot be applied to individuals. Frege himself reserves the term 'existence' to mean '*es gibt ein*' and as having to do with the instantiation of concepts. In the present discussion, I am confining my attention to *this* use of the term 'existence' as 'instantiation'. My criticism of Frege's analysis is therefore in part terminological, since I question whether one should reserve the use of the term 'existence' when what is meant is 'instantiation of concepts'. On the other hand, Frege's [unfortunately only brief] comments on '*wirklichkeit*' do seem to me quite relevant for a discussion of existence. Russell's account of existence, in exploiting Frege's analysis of existence as instantiation, fails to acknowledge at all what Frege at least took note of in his appeal to the notion of '*wirklichkeit*'.)

One way of summarizing the point I am making is to say that while the term 'exist' undoubtedly is used in ordinary discourse, and for some philosophers, too, in their technical writings, both to make an instantiation claim about some concept and also to make an ontological claim about the existence of some entity in the world or about the existence of the world itself, it is advisable not only to distinguish these latter ontologic claims from instantiation claims, but to reserve the term 'exist' for use exclusively in connection with making ontological claims of the latter sort. In saying this I am, of course, also criticizing and dissociating myself from those philosophers who do not recognize a tenable distinction between making an instantiation claim and an ontological claim, since for them whatever legitimate meaning attaches to what I have called 'an ontologic claim about existence', reduces to, is tantamount to, and is identical in meaning with, making an instantiation claim concerning some concept. For philosophers, such as Ryle, who belong to this school of thought, the only legitimate meaning of 'exist' is that which is conveyed in making an instantiation claim. This position seems to me to be utterly misguided. For not only should I wish to argue for the importance, first of all, of keeping quite distinct (1) making instantiation claims about concepts, from (2) making ontologic claims about the existence of individuals in the world as of the world itself; but I should go further, in urging that whereas the concept of instantiation is a perfectly useful and important concept, it need not have anything to do with existence, and that we should restrict the family of terms centering around 'exist' to what is involved in making ontologic claims about individuals to be found in the world and about the world as a whole itself. Nor, of course, am I arguing that we should in any way try to reduce the notion of instantiation to that of making ontologic claims, that is, to existence claims, since I believe these are equally *bona fide* enterprises, and that there is no need therefore to eliminate either one in favor of the other on the grounds that one is somehow 'more fundamental'. I am simply urging that we avoid the confusion that comes from using the same expression, 'exist', to cover these quite different types of philosophic concepts.

Let us agree, then, as a way of upholding the above differentiation, to use the term 'exist' ('existent', 'existence') in connection with properly ontological remarks, claims, assignments, and to use the expression 'there is (are)' to mark instantiation claims. Then 'there is' is not to be used where 'exist' ('existence' 'existent') is to be used, or vice versa. Further, the expression 'there is' ('there are') is to be understood as having a univocal meaning of its own, despite a multifarious variety of examples of its use. It was, for example, a mistake on Ryle's part to argue that to say 'minds exist' and 'bodies exist' is to use the term 'exist' in two different senses. He writes: "A man would be thought to be making a poor joke who said that three things are now rising, namely the tide, hopes, and the average age of death. It would be just as good or bad a joke to say that there exist prime numbers and Wednesdays and public opinions and navies; or that there exist both minds and bodies." [28]

Now where Ryle uses the term 'exist' I should use the term 'there is (are)', for this is how he understands the term 'exist(s)'. In the examples Ryle uses, he is dealing with what I have called 'instantiation claims'. Thus to say, for example, 'Minds exist' is to say 'There are minds' and this means: 'The concept *mind* has instances'; and similarly 'Bodies exist', is to be rewritten as 'There are bodies' and means: 'The concept *body* has instances'. Now the important point is that the expression 'there is (are)' has *the same meaning* in both statements, whether one is talking about minds or about bodies. Indeed the use of 'there is' to mark an instantiation claim cuts across all sorts of different subject matters, and can be used in connection with predicates ('*F*'s) as widely varied as you please, while itself remaining univocally constant. It simply means that the predicate '*F*', whatever that might be, holds or applies for at least some cases or instances. And these cases or instances *need not, although they might, for certain of these*, be further characterized as themselves 'existing' or as being 'existents'. Thus one might make the instantiation claim that *there are* instances of 'dragon' or 'prime number' as readily as that there are instances of 'is wise' or 'building'. In pointing to Socrates or the Empire State Building, respectively, as instances for the predicates (concepts) 'is wise' and 'building', we can say of the examples given, of the individuals referred to, that each exists or is an existent. But I can also give as examples of the applicability of the predicates 'dragon' and 'prime number', the sentences 'Fafner is a dragon' and '3 is a prime number'. However we should not say that the expressions 'Fafner' and '3' refer to anything *existent*. The expression 'there is (are)' used to carry an instantiation claim is thus topic-neutral. In this respect the use of 'there is' can be compared with other logical constants or syncategorematic expressions, for example: 'most', 'or', 'and'. As logical constants these have a univocal meaning and do not change their meanings when used in connection with variously different descriptive, nonlogical expressions. For example, the word 'and' does not change its meaning as we go from 'He is tired *and* he is hungry' to 'The rational numbers are real *and* the irrational numbers are also real'. Similarly the expression 'there is (are)' to make an instantiation claim preserves a constancy of meaning regardless of the predicate expressions to which it is attached. The use of 'there is (are)' in 'There are no computers that work faster than the human brain' and 'There is no largest prime number' exhibits the same meaning of 'there is'.

It does not follow that if we can say some concept is *instantiated* (what we can express by saying 'there is an *F* ') that the *instance* must be an *object* or that it *exists*. In *some* cases of instantiation this may indeed be the case, but surely not in all. For example, if I say 'Cows exist' is to be re-expressed to read 'There are cows' (in order to prepare us to distinguish *existence* from *instantiation*), and if in turn the sentence 'There are cows' is to be understood as saying 'The concept *cow* has instances', then we may ask with respect to these instances whether or not *they exist*. And in this case, if I select some appropriate example— say this cow Bossie in the meadow before me—I should indeed say this individual (object) cow does *exist*. On the other hand, suppose I have the sentence 'Virtue exists', and I translate this to mean 'Virtue has instances' (i.e., 'The *concept* virtue is in fact instantiated') and by way of example of this truth offer the sentence 'Wisdom is a virtue', then with respect to *this* instance, that is, what is conveyed by the term 'wisdom', I surely need not say it designates an individual or object of some sort. Indeed far from this being the case, we should say 'wisdom', which is our instance here, is at bottom a concept, that is, it should be treated as a nominalization of the predicate, functor, or concept 'is wise'. And of this concept, I should say with Frege, that it is not an object or an individual. Moreover, it would be absurd to say it exists in the way this cow Bossie does. The same kind of analysis, it may be expected, could be given for other putative objects—for example, mathematical ones—so that, for example, 3 as an instance of 'number' need not be thought of as an object, not even an 'abstract' one.

In short, with respect to instances of a concept, we need not say that the mere fact that we can give such instances obliges us to say that these instances are in every case objects or individuals, much less that they exist. We need not be ontically committed to the existence of individual objects simply by asserting or accepting the true statement that there are instances of some predicate *F*, or by assuming therefore that the instances are always objects or individuals.

One important way of bringing out the difference between the meaning of 'there is' as used in making an instantiation claim and the use of 'exists' or ('existent') as in ontologic remarks is to say with Frege that the former is a second-level property of a concept, as conveyed by a first-level predicate. On the other hand, 'exists' (or 'existent') holds for, or applies to, individual objects or persons in the world, not for predicates. The term 'existent', I suggest (and as I shall more fully examine later), is best taken as a semantic index that attaches to the referring device (proper name or definite descriptive phrase) used to identify an individual constituent of the world. It is the individual in the world that is the existent. The term 'existent' is a semantic index that together with appropriate referring (denoting) devices serves to pick out an individual in the world. And it is this individual, as an extralinguistic ontologic constituent of the world—for example, Socrates (not 'Socrates'), the table on which I write, the planet Mars, and so on—that is the *existent*. The individual constituent of the world is thus in no way to be conceived as a concept or a predicate. It would therefore be utterly senseless to apply the concept of instantiation to *it*. We cannot, for example, say 'There is Socrates' and mean by this what we mean when we say 'There are wise men'. For it makes no sense to say that an individual can be instantiated; and instantiation is what we mean, or ought to mean, when we say 'there is F', where 'F' is a predicate term or concept.

Conversely, we cannot apply the expression 'existent' or 'exist' to predicate terms (concepts), for a predicate does not in its own right refer to, or name, an individual in the world. Predicates are not referring devices in the way in which singular terms ('proper names') are, and do nut, qua predicates, designate individuals. Nor is a predicate itself an individual. At best a predicate *applies to* instances. For some concepts the instances are individuals that are constituents of the world. And it is of *these* individuals that we can say that *they* exist, but not of the concepts that apply to them. Nor can we say of any concept qua concept, *whatever* it be, that insofar as it has instances, that it *exists*. Existence is something that has to do with individuals, not with concepts. And this is the exact reverse of what Russell and his followers claim.

The subject of individual existence as treated in accordance with the instantiation theory is unsatisfactory. Its treatment of what we are to understand by 'individual existence' suffers from both artificiality and confusion. In attempting to subsume the notion of individual existence under the rubric of what it means in general to speak of there being an instance of some kind, type, or description, violence is done to the wholly distinct idea of individual existence. In straining to accommodate the notion of individual existence in the procrustean bed of instantiation, one fails to bring out in an illuminating way the distinctive idea of individual existence. At best what is accomplished by the methods indicated is an application of the notion of instantiation. To say an individual exists, on this approach, is only to say that one and only one instance of a type, kind, or description is to be found. Yet to say this sort of thing is still only to advance the idea of instantiation. Instantiation, however, is something which holds only for concepts; however, concepts are not individuals. And while it makes sense to say concepts are instantiated (terms expressing them can be applied and reapplied to different cases and on different occasions), this cannot be said of individuals. Individuals cannot in any way be said to be instantiated. Yet it does make sense to say an individual exists, and since it does, we must carefully distinguish the sense in which an individual exists from the general idea of the instantiation of concepts, even where such instantiation is confined to a single instance. Indeed the charge of artificiality reduces therefore to the more serious charge of confusion. To say that, in the manner indicated, one has reduced the notion of individual existence to that of unique instantiation is in effect to run together two ideas that are philosophically of a completely different order.

Futhermore, in concentrating, as it does, on the notion of instantiation, the treatment of existence within classical quantification theory, as interpreted by Russell and his followers, fails to draw the necessary distinctions with respect to individuals in a way that would clarify our primitive intuitions. It suffices to be an individual, for modern logic, that it be a *bona fide* example of some descriptive characterization. However, to say the table in my study exists, or Napoleon existed, cannot be assimilated to the way in which we can say there is a prime number between 6 and 11 or there is a unique individual called 'Santa Claus'. What we need is specification of what individual existence comes to that will differentiate those individuals that do exist, because, as we ordinarily say, they belong to the world, and those instances of a concept which can in no way be said to belong to the world. The interpretation of quantification as essentially a matter of making an instantiation claim fails to provide this distinction, yet this desideratum is one that must be met if we are to have an adequate ontology and a logic that can serve to express it.

4.2   *Quantification and Ontological Commitments: Quine's Views*

Our discussion of quantification, up to this point, in connection with the Frege-Russell approach and its reading of the quantifiers, has stressed the way in which existence is to be understood essentially as a matter of *instantiation*. However, Quine, although he shares in the Frege-Russell tradition of looking to quantification to help us clarify and express the meaning of 'existence', stresses the matter of *ontological commitment* rather instantiation. What this comes to, in his reading of the quantifiers, is the claim that we are saying something through their means about *entities*. And, depending upon what entities are taken as the possible values of our quantified or bound variables, we commit ourselves to this or that *ontology*: we declare through their means what we believe there is. A matter of central

importance for the understanding of Quine's view is the interpretation or reading of the quantifiers. Quine adopts what has come to be
known as the 'referential' (or 'objectual' or 'ontological') interpretation. According to this view, the use of quantifiers to bind variables involves making a general statement about certain *entities* which
are the values of the variables in question.

Quine insists, correctly enough, to begin with, on making a distinction between *naming* (or referring) and *meaning* in connection
with the various terms used in our discourse. "Meaning, let us
remember," he writes, "is not to be identified with naming. Frege's
example of 'Evening Star' and 'Morning Star', and Russell's of
'Scott' and 'the author of *Waverley*', illustrate that terms can name
the same thing but differ in meaning. The distinction between
meaning and naming is no less important at the level of abstract
terms. The terms '9' and 'the number of the planets' name one and
the same abstract entity but presumably must be regarded as unlike
in meaning; for astonomical observation was needed, and not mere
reflection on meanings, to determine the sameness of the entity in
question." [29]

Although Quine, beginning with his earliest writings, makes a
sharp distinction between naming and meaning, and although in a
sense he has never abandoned this basic distinction, it should also be
noted that according to his later writings the vehicles par excellence
for naming are *variables*.[30] Variables as bound by the quantifiers are
the vehicles for accomplishing reference to the extralinguistic entities, objects, or values with which discourse deals and whose existence
is assumed in making such reference. What are ordinarily called
singular names (for example 'Socrates', 'Pegasus', and so on) are,
according to Quine, to be paraphrased into descriptions in the
manner Russell showed. This is to be done not only for the purpose
Russell had, which was that of resolving certain paradoxes, but for
purposes of achieving a regimentation of discourse through translation into the canonic language of quantificational logic. The language of logic that accomplishes this regimentation requires only
general predicates, bound variables, and other logical devices to
secure the kind of reference accomplished in ordinary language
through the use of proper names and other singular terms. Accordingly, singular names are in principle dispensable: "Names are a red
herring." [31] What remains are variables as bound for accomplishing

reference, the values selected by binding, and the predicate or predicates asserted to hold true of the object or objects thus selected. Thus, given '*a*' as a proper name in an ostensibly referential position in a sentence of the form '. . . *a* . . .', we can rewrite such a sentence in the form '($\exists x$) ($x = a$ and . . . *x* . . .)'. ' $= a$' can now be treated as a *predicate* term. " 'Socrates' becomes a general term that is true of just one object, but general in being treated henceforward as grammatically admissible in predicative position and not in positions suitable for variables. It comes to play the role of the '*F*' of '*Fa*' and ceases to play that of the '*a*'." [32] And this maneuver, Quine argues, is especially helpful in dealing with a sentence such as 'Socrates exists' or 'Pegasus exists.' " 'Pegasus exists' becomes '($\exists x$) (x is Pegasus)' and straightforwardly false; 'Socrates exists' becomes '($\exists x$) (x is Socrates)', with 'Socrates' as general term, and probably true (with timeless 'is', of course). 'Socrates' is now a general term, though true of, as it happens, just one object; 'Pegasus' is now a general term which, like 'centaur', is true of no objects." [33]

Further, Quine rejects the view that syncategorematic terms designate anything extralinguistically. This would apply not only to such formal or logical connectives as the truth-functional 'and', 'or', 'if . . . then', 'not', but to *predicate* terms in ordinary discourse as well. Of predicate terms we can say at best that they *apply to, hold true* of extralinguistic *objects*. A variable that is meaningfully bound by a quantifier in first-order discourse must be an *individual variable*. It makes no logical or ontological sense, however, to bind predicate variables since they do not designate anything whatsoever, qua predicates. Nor do they have values or entities which are designated by their substituends. Yet Quine allows that in using individual variables we may have, in principle, any sort of individual objects as the values of such individual variables. These may be ordinary individual objects in space and time, or such abstract entities as universals, properties, propositions, or mathematical objects. What our ontology is—what our ontological commitments are—will be indicated by what in our theories we subscribe to, as existing, as being "what there is". As recast in the canonic language of quantificational logic, this will be revealed by what *kinds* of individual objects we are prepared to quantify over. For in quantifying over them we implicitly affirm that these exist; we commit ourselves to the belief that there are such entities, extralinguistically, and as constituting what exists objectively and as objectually real. This is all done by means of the language of quantifiers because of the way the quantifiers are to be read, according to Quine. For him the universal quantifier '(x)' is to be read 'for each entity x' and the particular quantifier '$(\exists x)$' is to be read 'there exists (or there is) an entity x such that . . .'[34] As a nominalist in a broad sense, Quine believes that the only real entities are *individuals*. But his nominalism is generous and tolerant enough to include within its scope all types of individual objects, ranging from ordinary objects in space and time to universals and mathematical objects. In any case, the reading of the quantifiers would be the same, and as having the same meaning, whatever the kinds of individual objects which we allow in our ontology. "When we say, for example,

$$(\exists x)\,(x \text{ is prime}.\ x > 1,000,000),$$

we are saying that *there is* something which is prime and exceeds a million; and any such entity is a number, hence a universal." In general, then, *"an entity is assumed by a theory if and only if it must be counted among the values of the variables in order that the statements affirmed in the theory be true."*[35] And this criterion of ontological commitment, in using the quantificational form of discourse as its clue, maintains "no distinction is being drawn between the 'there are' of 'there are universals', 'there are unicorns', 'there are hippopotami' and the 'there are' of '$(\exists x)$', 'there are entities x such that'."[36]

Whether a nominalist ontology can be austerely restricted to allow *only* individual objects in space and time ('nominalism' in a more specialized sense) is a question on which Quine seems to have shifted his views from an early espousal and inclination in the direction of this more austere type, to the more liberal construal of nominalism indicated above. And he has come to admit, in his more recent writings, that he has "no high hopes of getting an acceptable system of the world without admitting some universals, namely classes, among the values of the variables."[37]

The important point to remember in all this, then, is that the quantifier itself, in binding individual variables, is read as saying something about what exists, about what there is independently of our discourse. In making a generalization involving a universal quantifier, for example '$(x)\,(\phi x)$', we are saying something about *all* of the constituent individual objects or values which fall within the range of the variable x thus quantified. In the case of the generalization involving the particular quantifier, for example in '$(\exists x)\,(\phi x)$', we are saying something about *some* of the individuals falling within the range of the variable x. Where the domain of values is finite, the universal quantifier can be paraphrased or defined in terms of a finite series of conjunctions in which each conjunct represents a particular value of the variable to which the predicate applies. In the case of the particular ('existential') quantifier, the expansion for the finite domain would be given in terms of a finite series of alternations. These equivalences cannot be offered in the case of an infinite domain of individual values for our quantified variables. Alternative strategies are available here for conveying the meaning of such universal or particular quantifications. In any case, the important point for our present purpose is that in either case, whether for finite or infinite domains, on Quine's view, a domain of individual objects or entities is being posited, assumed, or committed to in our quantifications.

One important consequence of this view of the quantifiers must now be noted. It comes out in the way Quine treats a statement such as 'Pegasus is a flying horse.' According to him we must regard this statement as *false*. For we cannot regard 'Pegasus' as naming an individual object that exists. There is no object to which we can assign the name 'Pegasus'. In rewriting the original sentence, therefore, in accordance with the language of quantification, and as an illustration of the technique proposed in Russell's theory of definite descriptions, we would say:

> 'There is an x such that x is a flying horse and x is
> (identical with) the winged horse of Bellerophon.'

But this sentence is false, since there is no such individual. The existence condition is false, and therefore the description (predicate) 'is a flying horse' does not hold for any individual object belonging to the domain of objects over which the variable x, as quantified, ranges.[38] This treatment of the sentence 'Pegasus is a flying horse' is Quine's solution, too, to what otherwise would be a counterexample to an accepted law of quantificational logic, that which goes by the name of 'existential generalization'. For the law of existential generalization is a rule of inference which sanctions going from a true statement, as premiss, in which a constant expression is used with which is concatenated some predicate expression, to a conclusion in which an assertion is made employing the existential quantifier, but without making explicit the existence of the value denoted by the constant expression which was asserted in the premiss, and yet where now in connection with the variable so bound the original predicate expression is also attached: $F(a) \rightarrow (\exists x)\ F(x)$. *If* we were to regard 'Pegasus' as a name that has an individual designatum, we should be obliged to say that since Pegasus does not exist, from this we should, by the rule of existential generalization, be led to infer that '$(\exists x)$ (x does not exist)' which would be a contradiction.[39]

Quine's theory of ontological commitment and his approach to questions of existence are directly affected by his interpretation of the role of the quantifiers. Indeed these are so intimately related that for him they are not separable. He writes: "The existential quantifier '$(\exists x)$' is the distilled essence of existential talk. All imputations of existence can be put as existential quantifications." [40] Any critical judgment of Quine's views ought, therefore, to begin by considering the matter of how to interpret the quantifiers.

In the first place, while we may agree it is important to adopt in a general way Quine's broad distinction between naming and meaning, there is no reason to accept Quine's program of seeking to eliminate names altogether and to replace them by bound variables as the instruments of reference. For it is questionable whether in any actual usable language, particularly for use in *making reference* to individual existents, we can dispense altogether with some referential devices for accomplishing identifying reference to individuals. When Quine suggests, for example, that 'Socrates' as a *general term* is *true of one object*, we have a right to ask *of which* object that putative predicate 'Socrates' is true. And unless we had some linguistic means of picking out that individual object, and naming it, we could not establish the sentence which corresponds to that clause which is 'true of one object' in Quine's account. We cannot, in other words, dispense entirely with singular referential devices in any usable language that deals with individual existent objects. Ultimately, the usability of a formula making use of bound variables and predicate expressions, if it is going to be applied in the case of singular reference, will have to seize upon some device such as a demonstrative pronoun (along with the accompanying descriptive terms) to *pick out* the individual meant. A variable, even if restricted to a single value, cannot do this without falling back on some referential device that *is* successful in picking out such a particular individual.

Quine writes: "The whole category of singular terms can, in the interest of economy, be swept away in favor of general terms, viz., the general terms which correspond to those singular terms. For let '*a*' represent any singular term, '*F*' any corresponding general term, and '. . . *a* . . .' any sentence we may have cared to affirm containing '*a*'. Then we may instead dispense with '*a*' and affirm '($\exists x$) (*Fx* and . . . *x* . . .)'. *Clearly this will be true if and only if '. . . a . . .' was true.*" [41]

Now whatever the apparent moves in behalf of 'economy' in eliminating the use of the singular term '*a*' by converting to the sentence '($\exists x$) (*Fx* and . . . *x* . . .)', if the *truth* of the latter depends for its truth on the statement containing '*a*' ('. . . *a* . . .') (as Quine himself points out in the sentence I have italicized) then, just as clearly, the use of '*a*' has *not* been completely eliminated from our language insofar as we are obliged to, and in fact *do* use language to make reference to a particular individual and say something about it. If the use of regimented discourse can get along without incorporating the use of singular constants, this is only because such regimented language depends for its relevance, applicability, and truth upon the use of language that *does* involve singular referential terms to begin with. Therefore in any successful usable language for dealing with existence on an individual level, a basic grammatical category should be reserved for *individual names*. We do well to include such individual names, to begin with, in our language and to keep them distinct from the general predicative expressions applied to the objects they designate. They are not and cannot be replaced in every case by predicate terms combined with quantified variables.

A second point on which we shall diverge from Quine has to do directly with the reading of the quantifiers. For Quine the quantifiers are *objectual* quantifiers: they say something about the values, the objects, the entities over which the quantified variable ranges. For him, to use a variable as quantified is to make reference to the extralinguistic values of that variable.[42] But in a language which allows individual names that are referential as well as referentially empty (as in the names of fictitious "individuals") the quantifiers are to be read differently. In such a language we should allow that there are two types of individual *names* we may employ: those that make extralinguistic reference to existents, to constituents of the world, and those that are the names of fictitious "individuals" and so do not have any reference to what exists, to any constituents of the world. Hence, it is not the case that in such a language the use of a quantified individual variable commits us by that very fact to positing that there are, extralinguistically, values, or objects, or entities. For only if we use referential individual names are we so committed, or are we making such ontological, existential reference. But not so if the individual name we should use, in replacement of the individual variable, were an empty individual name. Therefore since in such a language we do not wish to say that the use of an individual name as such necessarily involves us in reference, we are not able to say that the use of a bound variable commits us to an objectual reference.

We must make an important distinction, then, between a *substituend* (which is a linguistic expression) and a value (in Quine's sense), that is, an extralinguistic object or entity. Individual variables can receive substituends as replacements, and among these some substituends will be referential names, and so have extralinguistic objects to which they refer. Other substituends will be individual empty names that have no extralinguistic reference and do not designate any entity whatsoever in the world.

We must therefore dissociate the matter of making an existence commitment from the use of the quantifier. It is not the case for us, as it is for Quine, that "quantification is an ontic idiom *par excellence*." It is therefore misleading to call the symbol '($\exists x$)' the *existential* quantifier, or to read it as saying 'there *exists*', or even '*there* is . . .' insofar as the latter phrase is read with an existential or ontological force. Let us therefore use the neutral reading 'For *some* . . .' for '($\exists x$)', just as we should use the reading 'For *all* . . .' for '(x)' in '(x) ϕx,'; we shall then label the first the *particular* quantifier, the second the *universal* quantifier. To use the particular quantifier in a language which allows for nonreferential as well as referential names need not per se involve us in making any ontological commitments. It merely asserts, in a sentence of the form '($\exists x$)(ϕx)', that for *some* substituends of the variable x, we should find that we obtain true sentences, that is to say, the predicate holds when attached to the individual name functioning as argument or logical subject in that sentence. For example, if our predicate were 'fearless' and our language allowed for the use of names of fictitious individuals, we could substitute the name

'Siegfried' (of Wagner's *Ring*) as an example of the 'x' in 'For some x, x is fearless' to obtain a *true* sentence.

Given Quine's view of how we should read the quantifiers, it follows that we cannot express by means of the quantifier that there are certain *values* of the bound variable which do *not* exist. For to be a value of a variable *is* to exist. One way of expressing this is to say that 'everything exists', that is, all the values of any bound variable exist: '$(x)\ (x = x)$', from which a singular existence statement 'y exists' can be derived and which can be expressed, '$(\exists x)(x = y)$'.[43] In order, therefore, to say that 'something does not exist', for example, 'Pegasus does not exist' in quantificational language so understood, it is necessary to transform what at first glance seems like a value for a variable (Pegasus) into a set of *predicate* expressions, and then to say with the aid of the quantifier that *there is no* value of the variable to which that predicate applies.

Once we abandon, however, the reading of the quantifiers which takes them to commit us to the existence of values, and regard them instead as governing certain ranges of linguistic expressions, as substituends, then we need not agree that 'everything exists'; and we need not transform sentences which deny existence to what is represented by an individual name into sentences in which we have transformed names into predicates.*

---

* The criticisms of the referential view of quantification I have voiced are in partial agreement with those, like Hintikka, who would rid quantificational logic of 'existence-presuppositions'. However, there are other respects in which some of these critics of Quine do not go far enough in their overhauling of the 'referential' view. Hintikka, for example, agrees with Quine that the range of *bound* individual variables is that of existent individuals. Where he disagrees with Quine is with respect to the substitution instances of *free* individual variables—which, he allows, could include as substitution instances nonexistent individuals. (J. Hintikka, *Models for Modalities*, pp. 33, 38, 41-42, 121.)

Why, however, make the point only with respect to *free* individual variables? Why not, also, *bound* variables? Hintikka is still operating with the reading of the quantifiers as saying something about *existence*, i.e., 'for all existent values' or 'for some existent values' of the bound variable. Once we drop the existential or existence-committing reading of the bound variables, we need not think of modifying only the matter of allowing as substitution instances nonexistent individuals for the free variables alone, but can extend the same possibility to the bound variables as well. Hence all we need in reading the quantified formulae are the universal 'for all (values of) x' and the particular 'for some (values of) x', and can drop the stipulation that the bound values of the variable must be existent ones.

4.3   *A Critical Summary*

Let us stop to take a brief backward glance at the development of quantification theory from Frege to Quine, with respect to the claims made in behalf of that theory as having a bearing on questions of existence.

Frege and Russell stressed the use of 'some' as essentially connected with the making of an instantiation claim about some concept (thereby exhausting what they took to be the basic meaning of 'existence'). On the other hand, Quine thinks of the use of 'some' as essentially connected with the making of ontological (existential) claims about individual entities.

In connection with Quine's view, I have argued that the use of the particular quantifier need not be read as making any *existential* claim. Whether the mathematician talks about *some* irrational numbers, the comparative mythologist about *some* flying horses, the psychologist about the mechanical aptitudes of *some* persons, the linguist or logician about the symbols in *some* language, the use of the term 'some' does not as such involve any ontological commitment to the *existence* of what is being talked about. Questions about ontological commitment are a separate matter, to be settled independently through appropriate philosophical analysis.

Again, the use of 'some' can, of course, be linked with the making of an instantiation claim as Frege and Russell stressed. However, making an instantiation claim about some concept is not to be thought of as *thereby* tantamount to the making of an existential or

---

If the use of bound variables is to be read as saying 'For all existent values of x' and 'For some existent values of x', then we face the question how, on this reading of the quantifiers, we are to use the language of the quantifiers, in the form of the use of bound variables, to say something either about all or some values of the variables which are not restricted to existent values. To say with Hintikka that we can take care of statements about nonexistent individuals through the use of substitution values for free variables, would seem to be insufficient. It should be possible, and would be desirable, to be able to use the quantifiers for binding variables where the values are not restricted to existent values, and where the use of bound variables does not range only over existent ones.

ontological claim. If a mathematician says 'Some numbers are irrational' and this is understood to mean the mathematical concept of irrationality has instances, this need not involve making ontological claims about the *existence* of such numbers. To determine whether, or in what sense, numbers *exist* is something that needs to be settled independently of, and in addition to, the claim that there are *instances*, among numbers, of such and such a mathematical property.

It follows from all this, specifically, that there is not some special philosophic solution to the general ontologic problem of existence to be found in the mastery of the logician's rules about the use of the particular quantifier in the predicate calculus.

There is, finally, the matter of what we are to make of the treatment of the concept of individual existence within the framework of the predicate calculus. We have noted, especially in connection with the use of quantificational formulas as brought to bear in the matter of conveying the notion of individual existence, a curious failure to do justice to this fundamental idea. With Russell, especially, this gets assimilated to the notion of instantiation. For Quine—while in his own special sense of 'existence' only individuals exist—this sense has been so broadened and neutralized as to lose all genuine ontologic value, since such individual existence need no longer be thought of as restricted to what has space-time locus in the world. Further, the whole orientation of the standard predicate calculus tends to subordinate, and in a sense, reduce, the expression of the form of a singular sentence to that of a general sentence, characteristically employing, for this purpose, quantified variables suitably restricted to a single value for the variable. This priority assigned to the general sentence and in particular to *general* existential sentences tends, therefore, to discourage any special attention to the notion of individual existence in its own right, and to the fact that it is, from an ontological point of view, the fundamental notion.

These biases and orientations are not, however, common to all contemporary logicians. Many moved beyond and outside the dominant orthodoxy of the tradition established with the publication of *Principia Mathematica*. The varied developments that mark the post-*Principia* generation include the work of those logicians who have returned, to some extent, to the guidance of the older Aristotelian tradition and to the lessons to be learned by paying attention to the resources and clues of *ordinary* language. In the work of Geach and Strawson, for example, one finds such a greater readiness to deal with the notion of individual existence from within the framework of ordinary language and in terms of a renewed emphasis upon the traditional distinctions between subjects and predicates. In the following two chapters I shall examine the views of these two philosophical logicians who accept (or seem to accept) it as proper to say that individuals exist.

Chapter 5

'Exists' as a Tensed Predicate

The terms 'existence' and 'time', taken jointly as well as singly, collect a wide range of philosophic themes. These themes obviously interconnect at various points. However, we need not assume that there is any single correct way of surveying or crisscrossing the conceptual terrain made up of these interconnections, nor even that in the literature there is some well-trodden path for doing so.

One obvious point of contact is already manifest on the level of ordinary language and in the way we talk of individuals as still existing or no longer existing. Ordinary grammatical rules allow us, for example, to describe an individual by the use of the verb 'to exist' in its tensed, participial, or gerundive form as a grammatical predicate. We say, for example, "The Parthenon, though mutilated, still exists". But whatever the sanction provided by grammar, the question of how—for purposes of critical philosophic understanding—we are to construe the concept of individual existence and the temporal distinctions that fit in with this concept is not settled simply by an appeal to linguistic habits or rules. On the contrary, the philosophic task (some would prefer to say the task of logic) is still to be carried out. That task consists in formulating an acceptable theory, a set of *proposals,* critically arrived at, as to how we *should* express ourselves if we are going to be clear about the connections between individual existence and time.

There are already available a number of alternative suggestions as to how this interest may be satisfied. Some do not hesitate to endorse the use of 'exist' as a predicate, and as tensed, for purposes of describing an individual. Others, following an important clue in the development of modern logic in its rebellion against treating 'exists' as a predicate, would fall back on the devices of quantification theory to convey all that needs meaningfully to be said in connection with existence. Others still (for example, A. N. Prior), without abandoning the quantificational approach, have sought to modify the orthodox versions of that approach by the introduction of tense-operators to accommodate what we should want to say on the side of time. Interlaced with these discussions there is, too, the continuing debate, inspired in large part by McTaggart's distinctions, as to whether questions of temporal location are best conveyed, in his terminology, by A-series talk in terms of 'past', 'present', and 'future', or in B-series talk of 'earlier than', 'later than', and 'simultaneous with'.

In the present chapter I shall consider the thesis that 'exists' can be treated as a descriptive predicate applicable to individuals, and where the predicate so used can be tensed, or, in general, given a temporal specification.

My purpose in examining *this* thesis is to kill two birds with one stone. First, and quite apart from the temporal question—that is, whether we can treat 'exists' as a *tensed* predicate—there is the prior and, in a sense, logically independent question, whether 'exists' is to be regarded *at all* as a descriptive predicate applicable to individuals. And to examine this question, let it be said at once, will be my *primary* interest and concern. I shall shortly consider a clear, important, and recently formulated attempt to rehabilitate the classic view that 'exists' can, in fact, in certain cases, function as a predicate in this role. Insofar as this approach directs a well-merited attack on the quantificational view as supposedly all-sufficing for the analysis of existence, it is to be applauded. At the same time, I shall argue that it does not completely succeed in making its own case for 'exists' as a descriptive predicate applicable to individuals. And I shall myself later propose that we should reject *both* the 'quantificational' and the 'descriptive predicate' views in favor of what I shall refer to as the use of *semantic indices*. Thus instead of subscribing to the claim that if 'exists' is not to be analyzed in accordance with the use of quantifiers, we are left only with the *sole* remaining possibility, namely, that 'exists' is a descriptive predicate, we shall see that these do not, in fact, exhaust the alternatives. There is also the 'indexical' view which I shall touch on briefly in this chapter and examine more fully in Chapter 7.

There is a second general purpose to the following discussion. For in the course of examining the view that 'exists' can be treated, in certain of its uses, as a descriptive predicate applicable to individuals, we shall find at one stage of the argument that a natural way, it would seem, of supporting that view is the fact that in ordinary language we not only use 'exists' as a predicate but also use it in various *tensed* ways. And such surface grammatical clues, it might be argued, are to be taken as revealing the deeper philosophical truth—indeed the truth of ordinary elementary experience—that everything passes, that nothing abides. And this, surely, ought to encourage us to say that we can *predicate a temporal existence of every individual.* I shall undertake to examine the worth of this position too. It would seem to bolster the claim that 'exists' *is* a genuine descriptive predicate. And yet I shall, in the end, be driven to reject this view as well. For if we shall want to say, ultimately, that 'exists' is not a genuine descriptive predicate applicable to individuals, and if this can be upheld, then *a fortiori* it cannot be a *tensed* predicate either. If 'exists' goes as a predicate it also goes as a *tensed* predicate.

Yet what shall we do with the undeniable and unexceptional rudimentary experience about the temporally bound character of what we think of as individual existents? Here let me say, by way of anticipation, that one feature of my discussion will be a certain dialectical treatment that seeks to deal in a mediating way with the tension that arises from trying to do justice to the conflicting claims that, on the one hand, individual existence is essentially time-bound, and yet, on the other hand, that the concept of existence has nothing to do with time.

5.1   *'Exists' as a Genuine Predicate of Individuals: Aquinas and Geach*

Although it is not a widely shared view among philosophers at the present time, there are those who staunchly defend the view that 'exists' *can* be used as a genuine predicate applicable to individuals. Geach is one such philosopher, and he suggests that in Frege also one finds acknowledgment of this view, as we noted previously. It is true that Frege's name is more frequently invoked in connection with a different conception of existence—one that holds or applies to *Begriffe* (concepts). Frege's notion of *'wirklichkeit'* as predicated of individuals is to be sharply distinguished from the sense of 'existence' conveyed by the expression *'es gibt ein'* ('there is'), where the latter is used in connection with concepts. The confusion of these two concepts of existence, Frege claims, would be the grossest possible fallacy. Geach would follow Frege in this distinction. Geach also claims to find virtually the same basic position in Thomas Aquinas.

According to Geach, Aquinas's analysis of 'existence' is also grounded in the necessity of drawing a fundamental distinction between the use of 'exists' in the sense of 'there is' as this applies to some concept, general term, description, or form *'F'*, and existence in the sense in which this can be predicated of an individual qua individual. In the first case, we are saying there is at least one thing which satisfies the description *'F'*, that *'F' qua* form or kind has instances. In the second case, as in the sentence 'Socrates no longer is (or exists)', we are saying something of an individual. According to Geach, this distinction is reflected in Aquinas's use of the concept of *esse* (or the verb *est*). For the notion of *esse* corresponds to the 'individual existence' sense of 'existence' as contrasted with the 'there is' sense. Accordingly, in examining the connection between the notions of existence and time in the Thomistic framework as this holds for individuals, we may confine ourselves to the *esse* sense of existence.[1] Geach translates *esse* as 'actually existing'. He points out that "an individual may be said to 'be', meaning that it is at present actually existing." [2] Further, he suggests, it is this 'present-actuality' sense of *'est'* that "corresponds to the uses of the verb 'to exist' in which we say that an individual thing comes to exist, continues to exist, ceases to exist, or again to the uses of 'being' in which we say that a thing is brought into being or kept in being by another thing." [3]

Geach takes the sentence 'Joseph is not and Simeon is not' as uttered by Jacob, and says of it: "It would be quite absurd to say that Jacob in uttering these words was not talking about Joseph and Simeon but about the use of their names. Of course, he was talking about his sons; he was expressing a fear that something had happened to them, that they were dead. We have here a sense of 'is' or 'exists' that seems to me to be certainly a genuine predicate of individuals." [4]

I shall not stop to inquire to what extent Geach's account of Aquinas correctly states what Aquinas held. It will be sufficient for my purposes to examine Geach's formulation of the theory that 'exists' is a *bona fide* predicate applicable to individuals whether or not this does square with the view Aquinas did in fact hold. I shall call this formulation the 'Geach-Aquinas view'.

We must now ask whether this thesis is a sound one. Shall we agree that 'exists' can be used as a tensed predicate applicable to individuals? We cannot answer this question with a simple 'yes' or 'no'. For we should need to separate out the several different components in this question and examine in greater detail the senses in which they are to be understood. We shall find that while there are some features of the thesis with which we might readily agree, there are others we shall be inclined to reject. In the course of disentangling these various strands of the thesis and offering a differential critical assessment of it, I shall take advantage of certain distinctions to be found in Aquinas as well as of some terminological proposals that Geach himself introduces.

In giving his exposition and interpretation of Aquinas's views on individual *esse*, Geach makes two principal points that bear directly on our present theme, and in my account I shall consider these separately.

The two points in Geach's account that I shall be concerned with are: (1) the connection between saying an individual exists and saying the individual can be characterized as a such-and-such, or as engaged in such-and-such (where the 'such-and-such' is to be filled in by some term or terms *other than* 'exist'); (2) the doctrine of *individualized form* in Aquinas, its relation to the notion of *esse*, and what it means to speak of an *individualized esse* as an *'act of existing'* (*actus essendi*). (The first of these sides of Geach's thesis will be examined in the present section, the second will be examined in Section 5.3, below.)

One aspect of the Geach-Aquinas thesis is the claim that insofar as existence is predicable of an individual, it is so in virtue of some specific form that may be predicated of that individual. Aquinas expresses this as: "quodlibet esse est secundum formam aliquam" (Ia. q. 5 art. 5 ad 3 um), and Geach interprets this to mean, "there is no such thing as a thing's *just* going on existing; when we speak of this, we must always really be referring to some form or nature, X, such that for that thing to go on existing is for it to go on being X. (For a man to go on existing is for him to go on being a man—one and the same man; for a statue to go on existing is for it to go on being the same shape; etc.) *Esse*, therefore, is always related to some form or other." [5] In connection with the same point, Geach elsewhere writes: "For it is in this sense of 'exist' that we say a thing goes on existing; and for a thing to continue to exist is for it to be the same X over a period of time, where 'X' represents some *Begriffswort*; and this in turn means the persistence in an individual of the form expressed by the predicable expression 'X'. Thus, a man continues to exist in that the baby, the youth, and the grown man are *the same man*; and this means the persistence in some individual of the form, *Begriff*, that answers to the *Begriffswort* 'man' ".[6] In accordance with this same point Geach also points out "that as regards living beings 'to be' has the same reference as 'to live', *vivere viventibus est esse* (Ia q. 18 art. 2)." [7]

How shall we understand all this? There are two possibilities here. (I shall discuss these possible interpretations in linguistic terms, but this is only a convenience—for exactly the same points as we shall make could also be made, indeed would need to be made, in ontologic terms.)

One possible interpretation is this:

(a) Given a sentence in which 'exists' ('existed') is used as a predicate in connection with the name (or other referring device) for some individual, we should be able to *replace* every instance of the word 'exist' ('existed') by some *other* term, some particular *Begriffswort* which (i) describes the individual in question and (ii) such that, in connection with the *Begriffswort* so used, we can use appropriate *tense* devices. In this case 'exist' may be thought of as a *place-holder* for other expressions, and where one or another term (e.g., 'lives', 'is a man', 'is a building', etc.) can be used for the sake of clearer understanding in place of 'exist'. Further, in connection with the 'time' aspect, while we do use the verb 'to exist' in present, past, and future tenses as well as in participial and gerundive forms, we should need to replace those tensed or participial forms of 'exist' by *other verbs*. This can be done basically in two ways: (a) we can replace 'exist' directly by some other verb, for example 'exists' by 'lives', or (b) by replacing 'exist' (existed') by some particular adjectival or sortal expression accompanied by the use of the verb 'to be' as copula. The tensing of the copula would then convey the relevant time distinctions, for example, *'is now* alive', *'was* alive', and so on. Nor need we confine ourselves to the use of the tensing of the copula or of the verb that replaces 'exists' as the only or the most fundamental way of conveying time distinctions. Nothing in our analysis precludes the possibility of introducing and using the time-ordering of events by the use of calendar (time-co-ordinate) systems, clock-measuring devices, and so on. All of these time-ordering and time-measuring descriptions will be included along with, and in conjunction with, the use of other descriptive expressions to specify the particular character (the *F*'s) of the events being temporally described, and where *all* such descriptive expressions (the *F's* plus the time-marking devices) replace the use of the term 'exist'.

(b) Another line of interpretation is this. Given a sentence in which 'exists' ('existed') is used as a predicate in connection with the name or other referring device for some individual, it is never sufficient to have 'exist' ('existed') *alone* as the predicate. One must always add to the term 'exist' some other appropriate, determinate *Begriffswort*. Thus instead of saying 'Socrates existed' one should say 'Socrates existed-as-a-living-man'; instead of saying 'I exist' one should say 'I exist-as-a-living-man', and so on, since, according to Geach, an individual exists as some definite form or nature.

The difference in the interpretations (a) and (b) is reflected in the way we should interpret the remarks of Geach quoted above. At one point he says: "*Esse* is always related to some form or other." And if we ask what such *relation* consists in, then we get one kind of answer (what corresponds to our interpretation (a) above), when we take another sentence also quoted earlier as our guide, namely, "As regards living beings 'to be' has the same reference as 'to live'." I take 'has the same reference as' to mean 'can be replaced by'. In this case 'is related' means 'is related as a synonym for', 'is replaceable, as a putative description, by the more precise description . . .'. On the other hand, to say 'something cannot just go on *existing*' might mean 'to exist is always to exist-as-*X*' or '. . . to exist-as-*Y*', and so on. Similarly, one should not say '*S is now*', or '*S was*' without supplying to the tensed copula which now, on this interpretation, does proxy for 'exists' ('existed'), some additional expression, for example, 'living man'. We should then get interpretation (b). Here we could interpret the statement "*esse* is always *related to* some form or other" as meaning that the relation is always between the term 'exist', which we use along with some *other* term, to that other term, so that instead of disappearing or being replaced, it continues to serve as part of a complete predicative expression.

In short, the difference between interpretation (a) and interpretation (b) is that on (a) 'exists' is always a *place-holder* for some more determinate verb, for example 'lives', whereas on (b) 'exists' is an *incomplete* predicate, and we obtain a definite sentence only when some determinate, descriptive predicate is *added* to it, for example as in 'exists-as-a-living-man'.

Were we to stop at this point, however, it would seem we should be obliged to say that Geach's original goal of rehabilitating the use of 'exists' as a *bona fide* predicate applicable to individuals, and able to stand on its own feet, has not been successfully reached. For it turns out that 'exists' is a feeble verb, after all, lacking its own power to serve as a determinate predicate expression. On one interpretation, it is so feeble it disappears altogether, and needs to be *replaced*, while on the other interpretation, though it does survive, it does so only in tandem with another verb or expression, and where it is the latter that gives the entire hyphenated expression its descriptive content. If this were all there is to the Geach-Aquinas thesis, one would have to record its failure. However laudable Geach's concern to show the limitations of the Russellian or quantificational view as all-sufficing, we should have to say about his own resuscitative efforts on the verb 'exists' as an expression that can serve as a descriptive predicate applicable to individuals, that they did not succeed.

But this is not the end of the matter.

5.2   *Existence and Time*

What if we have been too hasty in our assessment of Geach's position as stated thus far? If, to be sure, 'exists' is merely a place-holder (as in interpretation (a)) for some other verb or genuine descriptive expression, we should have to insist it is eliminable, and that's the end of the matter. But have we been entirely fair in our criticism of interpretation (b)? Even though, on that interpretation, 'exists' functions along with some other expression, one might wish to say it may nevertheless play an indispensable role for ontology, at least, in being included along with such other expressions. In short, it may be argued, the inclusion of 'exists' ('existed') *adds something* to our understanding that we should not otherwise have without its presence. And what it adds, one might be inclined to say, is precisely the way in which, *when itself tensed,* it calls attention to the time-bound character of all things. The very fact that we constantly use such expressions as 'did exist', 'does exist', 'continues to exist', 'ceases to exist', and so on points to our need to call attention in some fundamental way *other than* by the use of ordinary tensed expressions (i.e., expressions other than 'exists'), to the sheer fact that *existence itself is essentially a temporal matter.* And should we not, therefore, acknowledge *this* important contribution of the verb 'exist' *as tensed,* to the total predicative component of a proposition about some individual? Let us stop to consider this possible move. I shall argue that, far from being salvageable, Geach's argument, thus far, is indefensible, and that the attempt to retain the essential role of 'exists' as a tensed verb for ontological purposes is unsuccessful. I propose to argue, in other words, that 'exist' when taken as a tensed verb does *not* conform in any clear way to the normal requirements for a tensed verb.

In general if a verb is used as a predicate applicable to some individual we should normally expect that its use in a particular sentence serves to describe in some way the subject to which it is being applied: the verb possesses some *descriptive content.* Further, since we are dealing with a verb which is capable of being tensed, we should normally expect, too, that the tensed use of the verb will indicate something of the *time when* that which the verb describes takes place. Let us look into these matters now, and we shall do so first in the context of relatively simple cases of the use of tensed verbs, before turning our attention to the case of 'exists'.

There are different ways we might undertake to classify verbs with an eye to bringing out their different time-schemata, that is, how they manifest or imply certain patterns of time-determinations.[8] One important basis for classifying verbs in this regard is suggested by the difference between verbs that allow for the use of continuous tenses and those that do not. We can say, for example, 'The wheel is rotating on its axle' or 'I am playing my viola', but we cannot say 'The bullet is hitting the target' or 'I am knowing French'. Verbs (whether tensed in the present, past, or future) that possess continuous tenses can be taken generally to describe some *process* or other that *takes time,* that endures over a *stretch* of time (however long or short), and that allows, too, generally, for discrimination within the particular process involved, of successive stages, phases, or steps, however imprecisely specified or varied or irregular these stages, phases, or steps may be.

On the other hand, in the case of verbs that do not allow for continuous tenses, we cannot say that some process is going on over a period of time, or that what is being described involves some discriminable successive stages in this process. Within this latter class of tensed verbs, the noncontinuous ones, we should find it useful to make a subdivision between two groups of such verbs. Consider, for example, the sentences 'I know my own telephone number', and 'He won the 3-meter race'. 'To know' and 'to win' are both noncontinuous verbs. We cannot ask, correctly, 'How long does it take you to know your own telephone number?' Nor can we ask, correctly, 'How long did it take him to win the race?' Yet the difference is brought out by the fact that we can ask with respect to a verb like 'know', 'For how long have you known your telephone number?', although we cannot ask, correctly, 'For how long did he win the race?' Thus whereas it is possible, without describing a *process*, to say that someone knows something for a certain period or stretch of time, we cannot say that someone wins something over a period of time. The reason for this is that in the former case—knowing—we are dealing with a state or disposition, which, qua *state* or *disposition*, may be correctly ascribed to an object or person as being true of it over a stretch of time. However, in the case of a verb such as 'win' or 'hit' we are not dealing with a state or disposition but with the *terminus* or *achievement* of some process, such that whereas the process takes time (endures over a period of time), the terminus or achievement, like *any* instantaneous point within the process (including for example, its start), takes place *at* a given moment of time. We can say, 'I have known my telephone number for the last five years' but not, 'He won the race for five minutes'.

Now what of 'exist'? We do undoubtedly use 'exist' in tensed ways, from a purely grammatical point of view. But does this mean that 'exist' represents a *process* of some sort? This suggestion seems supported by the fact that we do, after all, use the verb in *continuous* tenses. For example, we say 'This building has existed ever since the turn of the present century', or again, 'The now existing tension in Northern Ireland is greater than it was ten years ago', and so on. But if these verbal clues are to be taken as suggesting that we regard existing as a process—What are its stages, phases, steps, or sequences *qua existing*? (The term 'existing', let us remind ourselves is not here taken as a stand-in for some other verb, but as having its own distinctive meaning.) There do not appear to be any. To exist, at any time, means—if it means anything at all—the *same* thing: there are not any stages, degrees, increases, decreases, developments, successions in existing *as such*.

To this latter point it might be objected that we are overlooking a way in which we can take existing as a process involving various discriminable stages. And the objection might be put thus. Consider 'viola playing' as a process in which distinct stages or phases are discriminated, for example placing the fingers on the strings, drawing the bow, and so on. Now since we do not say that placing the fingers on the strings *as such* is *viola playing*, and so on for the other phases or constituent activities, yet we do speak of them as phases, stages, and so on, wherein is the difference from the situation in the case of 'exist'? Why should we not allow for existing what we allow for viola playing, and say that the stages, phases, and constituents of existing are all the varied activities, processes, and so on, that we find going on in the world or its components, and that together, but not taken singly, they make up the process of existing?

To this objection, however, we can reply as follows. Whereas we *do not* say that placing the fingers on the strings, alone, is viola playing, and we *do* say that the phase of placing the fingers on the strings is to be *distinguished from* the phase of drawing the bow, in the case of existing we cannot say the same sort of thing. For any putative stage or phase of existing can also be described by saying that *it exists*, and moreover insofar as that constituent phase or stage does exist, it is *not* discriminable *qua existing* from any other stage or phase of existing.

In contrast to the foregoing type of objection to our refusal to regard existing as some type of process, another type of objection, coming from an altogether different direction, might be made to the same refusal. It might be said, for example, that we can consider existing to be the limiting case of processes that are in varying degrees relatively *unstructured*. Thus one might offer the case of walking as relatively unstructured in one sense, namely as involving the *same* kind of performance throughout—taking one step at a time, *throughout* the time that one is walking—as contrasted say with the more intricately structured process of moving one's legs in a ballet (where roughly the same units of bodily movements are *not* present during any temporal slice of the time it takes to perform the ballet). Why, in other words, should we not regard existing as the limiting case of an unstructured process in this sense, such that there will be throughout the process of existing always the same thing going on?

To this one would need to reply, however, that the notion of a *completely* unstructured process—which a *limiting case* of unstructured process would be—seems to lack all meaning. For in what sense can we speak of a process here at all? How is such a 'process' to be identified and distinguished from other processes? Even walking, as a relatively unstructured process, has a structure in which distinct minimal units of such a process, that is, *steps*, can be discriminated. However, it does not seem possible to identify anything which we can call, in a comparable way, *units* of existing that together make up, or are constituents of a 'process' of existing. Hence to insist on calling existing a process, even a limiting one of relatively unstructured processes, does not seem to be at all warranted or helpful.

Are we to say, then, that 'exist' is not a verb marking a process but only an *achievement, terminal point*, or other *instantaneous point* of some process? This, too, seems unacceptable. For of *what* process is existing the terminus, achievement, or other instantaneous realization? If someone were to answer: "Of divine creation", the answer brings with it its own well-known problems. Moreover, divine creation is not a process in the sense in which I am using the latter term in the present discussion, namely, as something exemplified in any natural or empirically observable sequence. Moreover, we do use the verb 'to exist' in continuous tenses, and this is not true of 'achievement', 'process terminal', or 'instantaneous realization' verbs.

Is 'exist' then perhaps a verb that describes a *state* or *disposition*? But there are at least two fatal objections to this. First, whereas a state or disposition is latently present in some subject over a stretch of time and becomes manifest at particular times, we should hardly want to say that existence is a latent state or disposition. Existing, if it is anything, would seem to be a continuing and explicit matter. (I am leaving aside for the moment such phrases as 'coming to exist' or 'ceasing to exist'.) Further, whereas we should normally wish to say that a state or disposition is to be found in, or is at some point acquired by, some already existing subject, we can obviously not say the same sort of thing about existing. If existing were itself a state or disposition, *in* what or *of* what is it such? The suggestion is incoherent.

But what other alternatives are there for construing 'exist' as a tensed verb? There do not seem to be any. As even this cursory survey would seem to suggest, there are serious obstacles in the way of treating 'exist' as a verb which easily conforms to the time-schemata of ordinary verbs of process, state, or instantaneous realization or achievement. As a verb, therefore, it would seem to balk our efforts at finding any obvious links with time, at least as far as the tensing of ordinary verbs would show those links.

There is, however, one more set of cases we must examine before we reach any general conclusion. This set includes such expressions as 'starting to exist' and 'ceasing to exist'. For example, Geach, as we saw, claims there is a predicate use of 'exist' in which one says that an individual came to exist, still exists, no longer exists, and so on. If our criticisms of treating 'exist' as a predicate are to be upheld, we shall need to consider such phrases as 'started to exist' and 'ceased to exist' when used predicatively of an individual.

Surely again with respect to these expressions, there is no question that they occur in everyday use as predicates in everyday discourse. The only question we are raising is whether this is to be taken as adequate ground for purposes of a philosophic reconstruction of ordinary language and to regard such use as indicative of the presence of a predicate descriptively applicable to an individual and that can be tensed. Nor, of course, are we in any way questioning the universally shared and uncontested elementary experience that all things come to be and pass away. For it would clearly be the height of absurdity to challenge the use of 'exist' in such ordinary ways as when we say 'so-and-so began to exist' or 'so-and-so no longer exists'. Our question, rather, is whether we can take the surface grammar as indicative of what we should take to be the conceptual truth about 'existence'.

Consider the simple everyday uses of 'start', 'cease', and the like, in sentences with verbs other than 'exist'. We say 'The water started to boil a moment ago', 'It stopped snowing early this morning', 'The performance ended at 11 o'clock', and so on. Expressions such as 'starting', 'ending', 'ceasing', and so on are appropriately used in connection with processes of one sort or another. We need not, for our purposes, here undertake any examination of the question whether an ontology constructed out of individual things is or is not more fundamental than one constructed out of events. In either case, as long as we continue to use the terminology of 'things', as distinguished from 'processes', we recognize that it is not possible to speak of things, as such, as starting or ending but only of *processes*. Where we do use the terms 'start', 'stop', and so on, in connection with things, we always do so explicitly or tacitly in connection with processes of one sort or another. We say, for example, 'The pot full of water started boiling a moment ago', or 'Heifetz's concert (that is, his *playing*) ended at 11 o'clock', and so on.

Now what are we to say of the use of such expressions as 'started to exist', 'ceased to exist', and so on? Clearly the pattern of these expressions is modeled on the kinds of examples in which, as in 'boiling', 'running', 'playing', we are dealing with processes of one sort or another. And since there is no question of what it means to say 'so-and-so started to run' or 'so-and-so stopped running', we assume that we can also speak of 'so-and-so starting to exist' or 'so-and-so ceasing to exist'. But our previous discussion has sought to bring out the difficulties in regarding existence as some kind of process, disposition, state, or instantaneous moment during some process. And the same points we made earlier in connection with 'existing' will serve us again in dealing with 'started to exist', or 'ceased to exist'. Once more we acknowledge that it makes perfectly good sense to speak of 'being born', 'dying', 'being made into a chair', 'ceasing to have the shape and usability of a chair', 'starting to boil', and so on. All of these expressions deal with specific processes, activities, or states of things. But existing is not among them. Where we do use the term 'existing' as a synonym or placeholder for one of these specific processes, states, and so on, of course we can say that in *this* role it makes sense to speak of starting or ceasing to exist. This is the case, for example, where in the case of human beings, one may say 'I came into existence (or I began existing) in 1913'. But here 'to come into existence' ('to begin to exist') is another way of saying 'I was born in 1913', or 'My life began in 1913'. And similarly if we should say 'My desk started to exist in 1950', what this means is that it emerged from a particular carpentry shop as this desk in 1950, and began to serve in that capacity from that time on. And so on for all similar cases. The use of the term 'exist' as a surrogate for some specific, time-bound, time-assignable process, with its beginning, duration, ending, is perfectly innocuous, since we can replace the term 'exist' by this or that *descriptive* verb.

I conclude from all this, that of the two interpretations we offered above of what it might mean to say that 'exists' as a tensed verb can be predicated of an individual, it is at best the first rather than the second interpretation that could be defended. And this would mean, as we have said, that 'exist' in this case is a protean place-holder verb that needs to be replaced in every instance of its use by some particular *Begriffswort*, some particular descriptive verb or predicate before one can say that we have a *bona fide* predication with respect to an individual, or before we can consider the tensing or other time-specifying assignment with respect to that predicate.

Now if *this* is one way in which we are to understand what it means to say 'exists' can be predicated of the individual, and that such a predicate can be used in various present or past tensed forms as applied to that individual—I think we may readily assent to the thesis *so understood*. There need be no objection certainly to replacing the sentences 'Socrates existed' by 'Socrates lived', 'I exist' by 'I am now alive', or to say that 'Joseph is not' is to be understood as, and therefore, to be replaced by, 'Joseph is dead'.

If *this* is what is meant by saying that 'exists' is predicable of individuals then too the matter of understanding the relation of 'time' to 'existence' can be reduced, at least as a first step, linguistically considered, to the matter of the use of tenses or other time-markers (e.g., dates, clock readings, etc.) in connection with the verbs (or other predicative expressions in general) that *replace* 'exists'.

5.3 *Existence as Individualized Form*

But this conclusion, it will rightly be argued, does not really capture the point of the Geach-Aquinas thesis. In effect what the foregoing analysis and its result leads to, it will be said, is the elimination of the concept of existing as a distinctive, central, and irreducible concept. And this result does violence to the basic interest of the philosophy we are examining.

Let us turn then to the other side of this theory—what in Geach's terminology is discussed under the rubric of the doctrine of 'in-

dividualized forms'—to see whether we might find a more acceptable line of thought for treating 'exists' as a *tensed predicate* that can be
predicated of an individual.

This other aspect of the Thomistic notion of *esse*, as interpreted by
Geach, concerns the sense in which for Aquinas we can say there is
an *individual esse* or individual *actus essendi*. To understand this notion, it is necessary to examine what Geach calls the notion of
'individual form'. The phrase 'individual form' is introduced by
Geach in order to distinguish it from *form* 'tout court' or 'simpliciter'.
The term 'individual form' is Geach's, but he insists that the distinction is present in Aquinas himself and that if we did not make
the distinction, Aquinas's account of 'form' would be incoherent. By
'*form*' (simpliciter) we are to understand any general concept or
descriptive term that can be predicated of individuals. Such a
general term is not to be taken with the Platonists as designating an
entity in its own right. Its role, rather, is like that of a function in
mathematics (as Frege was later to make clear). We may adapt
Frege's metaphor and say that a form or concept is 'unsaturated' or
'incomplete' and requires, for its use in predication, completion by a
subject term to which it is attached. The expression '. . . is wise', for
example, would be such a form or predicate, and we can put in place
of the blank represented by dots a proper name, for example
'Socrates', 'Plato', and so on, to get a complete sentence. Thus '. . . is
wise' does not designate or refer to some entity Wisdom; it is to be
used or applied, rather, in describing this or that individual, so that
we can thereby say something, whether true or false, of that individual. Now whereas form in general or simpliciter is, qua general,
applicable to more than one individual, and is qua form, too, 'incomplete', *individualized form*, by contrast, is individual, as such, and
'complete'. "A form is as it were a function that takes an individualized form as its value for a given individual as argument." [9]
The difference is illustrated by the expressions '. . . is wise' and 'the
wisdom of Socrates'. The latter phrase consists of an abstract noun
corresponding to the predicate '. . . is wise', followed by the genitive
of the subject.[10] Aquinas's term '*quo*' ('that by which') is indicative of
the presence of an individual form. Thus '*quo* Socrates sapiens est'
('that by which Socrates is wise') corresponds to the individualized
form 'sapientia Socrates' ('the wisdom of Socrates'). Whereas an
expression for a predicate, concept, or form (simpliciter) cannot

properly occupy a subject position in a sentence, since it does not refer to anything, the phrase that conveys an individualized form (for example, 'the wisdom of Socrates') *can* be used in subject position, since it refers to something genuinely individual.

Now this notion of what it is to be an *individualized form* is invoked by Geach in expounding Aquinas's views with respect to the notion of an individualized *esse* or *actus essendi* (act of existing). The individual *esse* is to be distinguished from such individualized forms as the wisdom of Socrates, the whiteness of Socrates, and so on. For while there is no continuing to exist that is not a continuing to be a so-and-so—some particular *F* (man, red, wise, etc.)—nevertheless it is necessary to distinguish, according to Aquinas, the *existing* of x (the *esse* of x) from 'that whereby' x is an *F* (the individualized form *F*).

The individual *esse* of each individual, far from being something he (it) may share with other individuals, is his (its) alone. Thus the individualized *esse* of each individual is, in this respect, unlike some form *F* which appears now as a general form (simpliciter) and now as an individualized form. For in the case of an *F*, 'wisdom', we can say that insofar as two individuals are both wise (that each is wise) it is because they are *alike* in respect of their *F*-ness, and this despite the fact that the wisdom of one is *different*, qua *individualized form*, from the wisdom of the other. This is *not* so, however, in the case of *esse*. For "when x *is* and y also *is* the *esse* of x and the *esse* of y are in general different as such. (Ia, q. 3 art. 5: *Tertio . . .*)" [11]

"In the fairy-tale," as Geach remarks, "all the human members of the family and the family cat shared a single life, that is, a single *esse* (*vivere viventibus est esse*); and when the betrothed of the youngest daughter took a pot-shot at the cat, its death was the death of the whole family. In actual families, animality is common to all the members of the family, including the cat, but *esse* is not, and so killing the cat has no such consequence. So, although for a man or cat to go on existing is precisely the continued existence of his animality, that is, the persistence of a certain individualized form in continuously renewed matter: nevertheless we must recognize a real distinction between his animality and his *esse*." [12] Accordingly, Geach maintains, "there is an unbridgeable distinction between *esse* and any form *F*-ness whatsoever." [13]

Now in one sense I think we may agree with the claim that there is an "unbridgeable distinction between *esse* and any form *F*-ness whatsoever." But I think too that we need to be careful in how we formulate that distinction. Geach, following Aquinas, is ready to treat '*esse*' as an individual form as derived from the *verb* taken as designating an *act of existing*, whereas, it seems to me, we do better by couching the matter in terms of the use of the quasi-substantive expression '*existent*'. The latter expression is in no way to be thought of as derived from a tensed verb or a tensed predicate, or as a predicate to which any time specifications are assigned. I use the expression 'quasi-substantive' to suggest that whereas a genuine substantive (in general a sortal) term is at bottom a *descriptive* term (for example, 'table', 'horse'), the term 'existent', not being descriptive but rather ontological, cannot form a (genuine) substantive in this sense; the term 'existent' is thus a *quasi*-substantive from a logical point of view. However, from a purely *grammatical* point of view it is as genuine a substantive as any other.

I should be perfectly willing to employ the notion of an *individual esse*, if this meant simply an *individual existent* where the phrase 'individual existent' (*esse*) is tenseless (since all individual names are, as such, tenseless).

The difference in approach may be brought out and illustrated by the way in which we can treat the cognate expression 'actuality'. Geach writes: "A provisional explanation of actuality may be given thus: *x* is actual if and only if *x* either acts, or undergoes change, or both." [14] The noun 'actuality' and the adjective 'actual' are thus explained for Geach in terms of the supposedly more fundamental verbs 'to act' and 'to undergo change'. But this, I submit, prepares the way for treating actuality or *esse* ultimately as if it itself were some *special type* of activity or change, some *F*, in short. Our previous analysis has shown the dangers in this way of talking. While I should not deny that as far as individuals are concerned, their existence is always the existence of an individual of this or that kind, as involving a whole complex of *F*'s, individual existence is not to be included among the *F*'s. The individual *esse* of an individual is not to be listed among the *F*'s (the verbs, adjectives, sortal nouns) which are used to *describe* the individual. The converting of *esse* into a verb (and tensing it) lends itself, however, to this type of assimilation and confusion. It would be better to keep the term 'actuality' as a substantive rather than reduce it by derivation to the verb 'to act' (or 'to undergo change'). As for *esse*, again it would be best not to assimilate this to the idea of an *actus essendi*, an *act* of existing, but instead to use the noun-substantive expression 'existent' as itself fundamental and not derivable from the verb 'existing'.

Since the predicates we use to describe an individual may also occur in fictional discourse, we should not be able to tell merely from the use of tensed verbs, dates, clock-readings, and the like, that what is being described as happening or having happened to an individual did take place to an individual existent. When attached as an 'ontological marker' or 'semantic index' to individual names or definite descriptive phrases, the term 'existent' serves as a reminder that we are dealing with a genuine part of the world, as contrasted with what is only fictional or imaginary.

A principal function, then, which the term 'existent' performs will be to indicate that the individual name or definite description is attached to a *bona fide* constituent, fragment, or part of the world as a whole, that it is not fictional.[15] To say something is an actuality or an existent is to say it is a real, individual part, or fragment of the world as a totality of existents. (The world itself, however, is *not an individual existent.*) The term 'existent' is thus another term, another way of referring to an individual. It does so, however, in abstraction from and without paying attention to the special characteristics, the *F*'s that otherwise characterize it. It is not the task of the term 'existent' to classify or describe the particular kind of thing or occurrence to which the individual belongs or to which it may be assigned, for example to say it is a 'cat' or 'a lightning flash'. This is to be left to the predicational (conceptual) role of general terms. Nor is it the role of the term 'existent' to make any allusion to, or convey anything about, the various time-determinations in which an individual is involved. This again is to be left to the various specialized devices, such as dates, clock-readings, and the tensed use of verbs that are employed in describing the states, activities, changes, processes in which the individual is involved, as for example, when we say, 'Peter ate his breakfast and then went to school', or 'The Second World War ended in 1945'. Whatever time features or time-determinations are to be assigned to an individual existent are in no way to be inferred from the fact that it is an existent; these are rather to be established and conveyed separately by virtue of the specific descriptive terms that can be used predicationally to fix it in some particular time order.

To summarize briefly, then: My discussion has stressed the way in which we may legitimately regard 'exist' as a tensed verb for purposes of a logical grammar, but only insofar as it is merely a place-holder for a tensed verb that is genuinely descriptive, and where it is the latter verb that allows of temporal determination, and hence is genuinely predicative. When not taken as a place-holder for another verb, I have argued that it is best not to think of 'exists' as a tensed verb or predicate at all; rather we should use the substantive expression 'existent' in connection with an individual. Its use is at once that of a semantic index, as attached to the name (or other referring device for an individual) to signify that the individual being referred to is real, that it is a fragment of the world and as another way of referring to that individual. However, in this capacity the term 'existent' does not serve as a descriptive characterization of that individual, nor carry with it any tensed or other temporal determinations.

5.4   *Appendix*

I should like to illustrate the advantages of making the types of distinctions with respect to the use of the term 'exists' in connection with an individual that I have been examining in this chapter, by considering at this point an argument due to G. E. Moore.

Moore writes: " 'I don't exist now' and 'this doesn't exist now' are self-contradictory. But 'I might not have existed now (at t_1)' or 'This might not' are not, because what they mean is merely that there would have been no contradiction in my saying of myself in the past 'I shan't exist at t_1' and will be no contradiction in my saying of myself in the future 'I didn't exist at t_1'." And Moore adds: "No one could, of course, have said of 'this' in the past 'this won't exist at t_1' unless this did exist at the past moment in question; nor could anyone say of 'this' in the future 'this didn't exist at t_1' unless 'this' exists at the future moment in question." [16]

Let us sort out the following sentences in Moore's own statement of the argument.

(1)   'I don't exist now' (when uttered myself at any time)
(2)   'This doesn't exist now' (when uttered by anyone at any time)
(3)   'I might not have existed now (at t_1)' (when uttered by myself now, at t_1)

(4) 'This might not have existed now (at t_1)' (when uttered by someone
     now, at t_1)
(5) 'I shan't exist at t_1' (when uttered by myself at a moment t_{1-n} in the
     past, i.e., earlier than t_1)
(6) 'I didn't exist at t_1' (when uttered by myself at a moment t_{1+n} in the
     future, i.e., later than t_1)
(7) 'This won't exist at t_1' (uttered by someone at a moment earlier than t_1)
(8) 'This didn't exist at t_1' (uttered by someone at a moment later than t_1)

Sentences (1) and (2) when uttered at anytime by myself or anyone
else, are self-contradictory. Sentences (3) and (4) are not self-contradictory because, according to Moore, what they mean is conveyed by (can be replaced by, as equivalent in meaning) sentences
(5) and (6) for (3), and by (7) and (8) for (4), and these are not
self-contradictory, since they could be true or false. Moore's analysis
is perfectly correct; there is no question that sentences (1) and (2) are
self-contradictory and sentences (3) and (4) are not self-contradictory. But Moore seems quite ready to use 'exist' as a tensed verb (e.g.,
'I shan't exist at t_1', 'I didn't exist at t_1', 'I don't exist now') or as a verb
permitting modal qualifications; for example, 'I might not have
existed now (at t_1)', and so on. If my own earlier analysis has any
merit, it would appear that we should need to distinguish among
these various sentences *different* ways in which the word 'exists' functions. And the reason why the overall analysis as given by Moore (that
(1) and (2) are self-contradictory, whereas (3) and (4) are not) is
sound, can be shown to be supported by the kinds of distinctions with
respect to the uses of 'exist' that I have been arguing for. I shall
distinguish these as sense (a) and sense (b). In sense (a), 'exist' is used
as a place-holder for some other verb that functions in a predicative
way; in sense (b) 'exists' conveys a semantic condition for the successful referential use of the subject expression of some sentence,
whether that subject expression designates a person or an inanimate
object.

   Consider, first, sentence (1): 'I don't exist now.' (a) The reason why
it is self-contradictory to utter this sentence is twofold: first, 'exist'
here is a place-holder for (or can be taken as meaning, in this context)
'am alive', and it is pragmatically self-refuting for a person who is
alive, as evidenced, among other things, by his actually uttering a
sentence, to say 'I am not alive.' His very behavior belies what he is

saying. (b) Second, the use of the first-person pronoun 'I' requires that the pronoun have a referent and insofar as that referent can be identified (by anyone, including the speaker) as a *real constituent of the world*, that referent can be called, ontologically speaking, an *existent*. Here, unlike the first interpretation of the use of the verb 'exist' (a), 'exists' is not a place-holder for another verb at all, but rather a term that, when the sentence is rephrased as a whole, introduces the ontological term 'existent'. As such, the term 'existent' is not derivative from a verb, nor something that allows auxiliary temporal terms to be attached to itself. This ontological term is relevant, however, to an analysis of the semantic conditions that need to be fulfilled in successful reference. In order for the term 'I' to be correctly used, for example, there must be a referent which is *an existent,* that is, a real constituent of the world.

When we turn to sentence (2), it is clear that the reason why it is self-contradictory, is precisely of the same sort as the reason given under the second line of analysis given for sentence (1) (i.e., under (b), above). Here when we say 'This doesn't exist now' we are saying something self-contradictory because the demonstrative pronoun 'this' requires as a condition for its successful semantic use, a referent which is an existent. In order for the term 'this-(F)' to succeed referentially, there must be *an existent- (F)* which is being designated or identified. The use of the word 'exists', then, is *not* here a place-holder for some specific verb or other *predicate* term that we might otherwise wish to predicate of the subject this-(F); for example, 'This-(book) is *red*', 'This (man) is *running*'. Rather, the reason why 'This doesn't exist now' is self-contradictory is that, insofar as one is correctly using the demonstrative word 'this' now, or at any time, there has to be an existent target for the *subject* term itself.

In (1) 'exists' can function as a place-holder for another verb as predicate, and as tensed, for example, for the term 'am alive' whereas in both in (1) and (2) 'exists' as an ontologic term also functions as a semantic condition for the use of the subject term of the sentence.

Once we make the distinctions I propose, and as applied to the analysis of sentences (1) and (2), we can extend the same type of analysis to sentences (3) and (4), or indeed to sentences (5) and (6) and to (7) and (8) (Moore's replacements for sentences (3) and (4), respectively). For once again in sentences (5) and (6), the use of the word 'exist' can be understood in the sense of being a place-holder or rough equivalent for 'live'. 'I shan't exist at t_1' means 'I shan't *be alive* at t_1', and 'I didn't exist at t_1' means 'I wasn't alive at t_1'; and these, of course, are not self-contradictory. We might also take the use of the word 'exist' in the other way—as replaceable by the ontological term 'existent', and as relevant to a semantic analysis of the referential role of 'I'. Thus to say 'I shan't exist at t_1' can be analyzed as meaning: "The *existent* which is the referent of the term 'I', where the term 'I' is used by myself at t_{1-n} (now) can be identified by myself or others *now*". However, I shall not be able to use the term 'I' at time t_1 because I shall no longer be *alive*. With respect to sentences (7) and (8) (as Moore's analysis for sentence (4)), the word 'exist', as used predicatively, might again be taken as a place-holder for some verb or other predicate expression that is appropriate for the particular *kind* of subject the demonstrative pronoun 'this' here helps to identify. Thus, if the term 'this' were supplemented by a particular sortal or characterizing term ('F'), and were to become say, 'this man', then the entire sentence should read, 'This man won't be alive at t_1'. On the other hand, it might be suggested that the principal use of 'exist' in (7) and (8) has to do with the semantic reference of 'this (F)'. In this case what, for example, (7) ('This won't exist at t_1') means, is: the expression 'this (F)' *now* (at t_{1-n}) has a reference to an existent; however, it will not be possible for anyone to use the expression 'this-F' at the moment t_1, if the expression 'this-F' is intended to stand for the same object, one having an identity in time from t_{1-n} to t_1, for at time t_1 the expression 'this-F' in this sense will *not* have as a referent *the same existent*.

Chapter 6

Existence as a Presupposition

6.1 *The Meaning of 'Presupposition'*

Suppose you and I are sitting at a table, and as I point to a particular bowl on the table I say: "That bowl is silver-plated." Again, let us suppose that in the course of giving a lecture on ancient philosophy I utter the statement, "Socrates often used irony in his remarks." Or, finally, consider the statement we might find in a book on astronomy: "The planet closest to the Sun has an extremely high surface temperature." These would all be examples of singular subject-predicate statements. In each of them the expression serving as the subject refers to some object or person that can be temporally located in the past or present. The expression serving as the subject in the first of the examples above involves the use of a demonstrative pronoun ('that') together with a descriptive expression ('bowl'); the second consists of a proper name ('Socrates'); and the third is a definite description ('the planet closest to the Sun'). They are all examples (though they do not exhaust all the possible types) of referring devices. In normal circumstances the use of one or another of these referring devices accomplishes what we may call, following Strawson, an *identifying reference*: the demonstrative pronoun, proper name, or definite description helps the auditor or reader to pick out a particular object or person.[1] It is this particular object or person about which the predicate of the given statement goes on to say something purportedly informative.

Strawson has argued that in speech-act situations of the kind described, that is, speech acts in which identifying reference is made by a speaker to an audience by means of a subject term of a subject-predicate statement, there normally would not be an explicit assertion made by the speaker about the existence of the subject being identifyingly referred to. Its existence is presumed to be known or taken for granted, along with other items of knowledge about it in a general background of knowledge. This background of presumed knowledge, for different cases and in different situations, will have varying degrees of richness. Strawson characterizes the presumption of the item of knowledge about the *existence* of the subject a *presupposition*.

A statement *A* is said to *presuppose* another statement *B* if and only if *A* is neither true nor false unless *B* is true; (equivalently, the truth of *B* is a necessary condition for the truth or falsity of *A*).[2] Thus the truth of the statement "That bowl exists" (*B*) is a *necessary condition* for the statement "That bowl is silver-plated" (*A*) to be either true or false. The statement "That bowl is silver-plated" presupposes the statement "That bowl exists."

The relation of presupposition needs to be distinguished from the relation of entailment. Where *A* entails *B*, the conjunction of *A* and the denial of *B* results in a straightforward contradiction; since the truth of *B* is a necessary condition for the truth of *A*, it would be self-contradictory to affirm *A* and at the same time deny *B*. In contrast, where *A* presupposes *B*, the truth of *B* is a necessary condition for the truth *or* falsity of *A*. Here it would be a "different kind of absurdity," not simply one of contradiction, to conjoin the affirmation of *A* and the denial of *B*.[3]

Despite the above clarification about the basic difference between presupposition and entailment, there are a number of unclarities and ambiguities connected with Strawson's use of the concept of presupposition. Strawson has formulated the presupposition relation in somewhat different ways on several different occasions, and these formulations seem to oscillate between two accounts of what presupposition is.[4] According to the first account, as one critic has pointed out, "when a meaningful sentence is uttered by a speaker of the language on a certain occasion, then a necessary condition for the statement thus made to have a truth value is that the (main) referring expression in the sentence has, on that occasion, a reference"; and according to the second account, "when a meaningful sentence is uttered by a speaker of the language on a certain occasion, then a necessary condition of the speaker's thereby making a statement is that the (main) referring expression in the sentence has, on that occasion, a reference." [5] Whereas the second account denies that there is any statement at all when there is a reference failure, the first account maintains there is one but only denies that it has a truth-value. I shall, however, not stop to explore this ambiguity in Strawson's account, since my concern at the moment is not primarily with the notion of truth-value gaps, but with exploring what we are to make of the status of the presupposed statement having to do with the existence of the referent of the subject term. And here I find that there are other unclarities and ambiguities in Strawson's account to which we must call attention.

For when we examine the various passages in which Strawson appeals to the concept of a presupposition relation, there is a certain ambiguity in the statement of what that relation is. (1) In one sense, the presupposition relation marks, as we have just seen, a logical relation between statements, where the statements so related are fundamentally two, namely, the presupposing statement (A) and the presupposed statement (B). This presupposition relation is to be contrasted with the entailment relation. The difference between presupposition as a logical relation and entailment is one of logical properties: their tables of truth-values (or truth-value gaps) differ. It is thus not a matter principally of what is or is not asserted, for in *both* relations it is necessary to make explicit the respective antecedents and consequents for the respective relations, in order that their corresponding truth-values (or truth-value gaps) may be assigned. (2) In another sense, however, Strawson thinks of a presupposed statement in a presupposition relation as one *tacitly accepted as true,* as contrasted with one *explicitly asserted.*[6] Strawson stresses that the presupposition of existence is *not* asserted when he wishes to contrast this sense of presupposition (that is, as something tacitly accepted as true) with what is explicitly asserted. The second of the discriminated senses of presupposition—that which has to do with the matter of *assertion*—comes to the fore when he deals with the use of sentences in speech-act situations, and from the point of view of speech-act analysis. The first sense of presupposition (that which has to do with distinguishing it as a *logical relation* from other types of logical relations) comes to the fore when he wishes to express the distinctive formal logical properties of the presupposition relation.

Thus far I have treated the second meaning of presupposition as having to do basically with a contrast between what is explicitly stated as over against what is not asserted at all, that is, with what is left implicit or tacit. This matter of 'assertion', however, is complicated by a further unclarity or ambiguity in Strawson's account. At one point Strawson remarks (in connection with utterances in which definite identifying reference is made to actual historical individuals): "I shall take it as understood that the existence of the individuals referred to in such utterances is *presupposed rather than implicitly asserted* in the making of such utterances." [7] We must now ask: What does it mean to *contrast* presupposed utterances with those implicitly asserted? Indeed what does the phrase 'implicit assertion' *mean*? According to the way the term is used in this passage, we should need to contrast a presupposed utterance not only with an explicit assertion, but with an *implicit assertion* (whatever that means) as well. Are we to say that presupposed utterances are always implicit (unexpressed), or are they also capable of being made *explicit*? Obviously it would be necessary for Strawson to allow the latter, since the specification of the logical relation of presupposition, for any given case of statements so related, would require that these should be made explicit in order that we would be able to evaluate the truth-values of the presupposing statement, given the truth-value of the presupposed statement. But if that which is being presupposed is not even implicitly asserted, what is its logical form when made explicit? Is it a statement? And wouldn't it have to be a statement in order for it to have a truth-value so that the presupposing statement can be assigned *its* truth-value? One of the preliminary difficulties, then, in Strawson's account of presupposition, as it applies to the matter of existence involved in acts of identifying reference, is that he does not provide any clear way of reconciling the two following apparently conflicting claims: (1) In order for there to be a presupposition relation, there need to be at least *two* statements, each of which can be judged with respect to its truth-value. In particular, the presupposed statement '*S* exists' needs to be *true* in order for the presupposing statement to be either true or false. (2) The presupposed 'existence-factor' is not either implicitly or explicitly *asserted*. (But a special difficulty of (2) is this: If we could not formulate the existence of the subject to which identifying reference is being made, as a *statement* which *can be* asserted, and its truth-value assessed, how can the relation of presupposition hold for *A* and *B*?)

The only way I can see of clearing up this unclarity is to say that when Strawson denies that the presupposed statement is an implicit assertion he is using the term 'assertion' to mean 'making a predication'. But this is not the only way in which he uses the term 'assertion'. *We* should then need to distinguish two different senses of 'assertion' in order to take note of this ambiguity in his employment of this term: In one sense of 'assertion' what is asserted, whether explicitly or implicitly, is always an assignment of a predicate to a subject. In another, 'assertion' means whatever is explicitly uttered as a statement. In this sense of assertion, what is presupposed is not asserted because it is not explicit. Let us designate these two different senses of assertion as assertion$_1$ (a statement which qua statement requires a predicate) and assertion$_2$ (an explicit utterance of a statement of any assignable logical form). What Strawson might be taken as saying then, is this: whether what is presupposed is or is not asserted$_2$, in any case it is not asserted$_1$.

6.2   *What Is the Logical Form of 'S exists'?*

If this be accepted, then the question I wish to consider next is this: What can we say about the logical form of the existence-factor statement when it is converted from being a tacit (unasserted$_2$) presupposition to an explicit assertion$_2$? What can we say, in other words, about the logical form of the utterance '*S* exists'? How shall this be construed?

Let us begin by recalling the fundamental role which predication plays in the understanding of the logic of statements. Strawson would seem to wish to argue for the logical and philosophical soundness in general of regarding the subject-predicate statement as the basic type of statement, and as adequate to dealing with "most of the propositions we are day by day concerned with." [8] Predication, he tells us, "is the ascribing of something to an individual, or to some, none or all of a class, where the existence of the individual or of the members of the class is presupposed." [9] Accordingly, in a subject-predicate type of statement we can distinguish two main, explicitly present, items: "If we are to be able to say how things are in the world, we must have at our disposal the means of doing two complementary things, of performing two complementary functions: we must be able to specify *general types* of situation, thing, event, etc. and we must be able to attach those general specifications to *particular cases*, to indicate their particular incidence in the world." [10]

Whatever the fundamental role of the subject-predicate statement, it is, at any rate, an open question as to how, for this type of statement, the presupposed existence factor or presupposed existence statement is to be logically classified and its form made clear. That it is not itself an explicit item but only a presupposed item in the initially given subject-predicate statement, attached, as it were, to the referential use of the original subject term, has been brought out. But our question has to do with the logical form of the presupposed statement '*S* exists' when this is made explicit. What is Strawson's answer to this question? Once again, I must report that I do not find a single, clear, positive answer to this question. He has, to be sure, faced this question from time to time, and I shall briefly survey what he has to say by way of giving an answer to our question.

One of the claims that Strawson repeatedly makes is that the sentence we are concerned with is *not* to be construed as being of a subject-predicate type, in any other than a purely grammatical sense. He writes: "when an expression which looks as if it might be used to make an identifying reference to a particular (or, for that matter, to a plurality of particulars) is followed in a sentence by the word 'exists' (or 'exist'), we cannot coherently take the first expression as functioning in a particular-referring way, i.e. as making an identifying reference to a particular (or to certain particulars). To attempt to do so would make the sentence unconstruable." [11] The reason why it would be unconstruable as an ordinary subject-predicate statement is that we should be faced with an absurd consequence. We must now stop to explore what this absurd consequence is, according to Strawson, since he does not say what this is in the passage from which we have quoted. But he does make the point elsewhere. For example, taking as his illustrations the sentences 'The man-in-the-moon does not exist' and 'The man-in-the-moon does exist', he argues that "we cannot coherently construe the substantival expression as a referring expression; for to do so is to construe it as carrying, as a presupposition, precisely that content which the proposition as a whole asserts or denies. We are therefore required, in this case, to find a different way of construing the proposition." [12] In discussing the case of the traditional four basic types of categorical propositions, in his earlier book *An Introduction to Logical Theory*, he points out that "if we tried to assimilate a statement of the pattern '*x*'s exist' to any of the four forms, or to regard it as a subject-predicate statement at all, we should be faced with the absurd result that the question of whether it was true or false could arise only if it were true; or that, if it were false, the question of whether it was true or false did not arise. This gives a new edge to the familiar philosophical observation that 'exists' is not a predicate. When we declare or deny that 'there are' things of such-and-such a description, or that things of such-and-such a description 'exist', the use of the quoted phrases is not to be assimilated either to the predicative or to the referring use of expressions." [13]

Before going on to consider what positive proposals Strawson makes to deal with this situation, let us stop to examine the argument as he has given it thus far. And let us consider what he has to say in particular with respect to the existential presupposition for a *singular* subject-predicate statement. The presupposed statement for '*S* is *P*' where *P* is some predicate other than 'exists' is '*S* exists'. Now if '*S* exists' as the statement to be analyzed were taken as a putative subject-predicate type statement, then, *on the assumption that every singular subject-predicate type statement presupposes another statement making an existential claim*, the presupposed statement for the statement '*S* exists' would also be '*S* exists'. And Strawson's argument is that for the presupposing original statement '*S* exists' to be true or false, the *presupposed* statement '*S* exists' would need to be true, and this is absurd. Or again, if the presupposed statement '*S* exists' is false, the original *presupposing* statement could not be either true or false, since the question would not arise. And this, too, is absurd. Now, in order for this argument to be valid, we should need, in the first place, to accept the assumption that *every* original singular subject-predicate statement presupposes another statement expressing the existence claim, and that this would apply to the statement here taken as original, the putative subject-predicate statement '*S* exists'. But why should we make this assumption? What if we were to reformulate the assumption to read that every original singular subject-predicate statement *except* '*S* exists' presupposes *another* statement expressing the existence claim? This ruling would be tantamount to saying that the presupposition rule (the rule that any ordinary singular subject-predicate statement presupposes another, an existence statement) does *not* hold for the existence statement itself. Another way of putting this ruling is to say that not every use of a referring expression carries

with it a *presupposition* of the existence of the individual referred to by
the subject term; specifically, where the referring term occurs in a
sentence along with the grammatical predicate 'exists', it does not
carry with it any such further presupposition. We should then not be
faced with the consequence mentioned. To make this ruling, of
course, would require justification, and in particular would involve
the decision of how we are to treat the term 'exists' in the statement '*S*
exists'. Thus we might at least leave the door open to investigate the
possibility that this can be done in a plausible or convincing way.

We gain some support in considering this possible emendation by
examining another argument for rejecting the classification of the
statement '*S* exists' as an ordinary subject-predicate statement.
Wherever we have the logical pattern of presupposition, we can
always distinguish the original presupposing statement and the
presupposed statement since the statements will always be *different*.
And the grammatical predicate of the presupposed statement in the
case we are concerned with will always be 'exists'. However, it is by no
means clear in what way the application of this pattern to the original
statement '*S* exists' as a putative subject-predicate statement, and to
its presupposed statement (which is also '*S* exists'), gives us two *distinct*
statements. In what way can we *first* evaluate the truth-value of
the presupposed statement *before* we evaluate the presupposing
statement; or evaluate the presupposed statement as a *condition* for the
determination of the truth-value of the original statement? Since
there is but *one and the same* statement in both cases which appears both
as presupposing and presupposed statements, the operation of *separate* truth-value evaluation breaks down and is inapplicable. This
again argues for the possible advantage of not considering the
statement '*S* exists' as falling within the *ordinary* pattern of subject-
predicate statements.

6.3   *Strawson's Proposals*

Rather than explore alternative routes of dealing with '*S* exists' as a
subject-predicate statement, though of a possibly distinctive kind,
Strawson, in his *Introduction to Logical Theory* and *Individuals* suggests
that we should abandon the attempt to treat the use of the sentence '*S*
exists' as a subject-predicate type of statement. He proposes instead

in these writings that we regard the statement as an existential statement, in the sense of modern logic, or rather as part of such an existential statement. "Fortunately," he says, "there are idioms available which allow us to escape from the misleading suggestions of the form described [that '*S* exists' is of the subject-predicate form]; and these are the idioms which are reconstructed in logic by means of the device of existential quantification. The expression which looks as if it might be used in a particular-referring way is replaced by a predicate-expression corresponding to it in sense, and the word 'exists' appears merely as part of the apparatus of quantification. Thus we allow that particulars can be said to exist without committing ourselves to the incoherent attempt to construe existence as a predicate of particulars." [14]

I find the foregoing passage quite puzzling. On the one hand, Strawson apparently invites us—by his use of the phrase 'existence-presupposition' earlier in the passage from which the foregoing was taken—to continue to think in terms of his own presupposition theory as the best way, in general, of dealing with subject-predicate statements, in preference to the analysis provided by quantification theory. Yet when he comes to face the question of how to formulate the so-called 'existence-presupposition', he calls upon the resources of the quantification theory, which makes everything explicit, and does not appeal to the notion of presupposition at all; *it* treats the existence factor, not as a matter of an existence presupposition, but, as he correctly reports, as conveyed by "a part of the apparatus of quantification." In 'canonical form' the existence condition is explicitly 'asserted', in the sense of being conveyed by the use of the existential operator as applied to a quantified variable. This explicit appearance of the existence factor appears in the standard form of an existential statement of quantificational logic along with two other components in the case of a singular statement, namely, the uniqueness condition and the predicative component. The schema for such a statement reads

$$(1) \qquad (2) \qquad\qquad (3)$$
"(There is)(one and only one x) that (has (or is) P),"

where (1) is the existence factor, (2) the uniqueness factor, and (3) the predicative factor.

Which, then, is Strawson's view of how to treat the existence factor? Can he provide his own analysis of the existence presupposition as a *complete* statement separate from the presupposing statement and as presumably required by his presupposition theory? Or must he call in the apparatus of quantification theory when he has to deal with the existence factor, thereby admitting the weakness and unavailability for this purpose of his own approach? He cannot coherently say that when it comes to stating what the logical form of the existence factor is, we should fall back on the quantificational form, for that is to grant the claim of the logical reconstructionists and is tantamount to abandoning his own point of view. If, in making explicit the existence factor, we need to appeal to the quantificational form, why not do so from the very beginning? And is not this to admit that, whatever be the merits of the presuppositional analysis in pointing out something about the explicit and tacit sayings in a *speech-act* approach, when it comes to giving the explicit *logical form* of what we are committed to in our utterances, the presuppositional analysis fails us, and we need to turn to the logician's reconstruction? I find no clear answer to these questions in Strawson's account.

Strawson himself, I suspect, was aware of this problem, and undertook to deal with it in a fresh way in his paper entitled "Is Existence Never a Predicate?" [15] His answer to the question posed by this title is a qualified *negative*. He there proposes to show how 'exists' *can* be used predicatively, that is as a logical and not simply as a grammatical predicate. In order to do so, Strawson first develops a point originally made by G. E. Moore in the latter's well-known paper, "Is Existence a Predicate?" Moore had pointed out in connection with the use of a sentence whose logical subject is 'tame tiger' and whose logical predicate is 'growl' that we can use *any* of the following quantifying adjectives: 'all', 'most', 'many', 'some', 'a few', 'no', 'at least one' to precede the subject term. However, where our subject is 'tame tigers' and the (grammatical) predicate is '*exists*', we can use any of the foregoing quantifying adjectives *except* '*all*' and '*most*'. Strawson proposes to use this distinction as the basis for determining what are logical subjects and predicates as distinguished from being merely grammatical subjects and predicates. The test is the following: "Given a grammatical subject and predicate, then it is a necessary condition of their counting as a *logical* subject and predicate respectively that if the grammatical subject admits of starting off with *any* of the quantifying adjectives, then it should admit of starting off with them all (with, where necessary, i.e., where 'at least one' is involved, a change from singular to plural or vice versa)." [16]

Strawson now uses this criterion to argue that there are some cases in which 'exist' *can* be used as a logical predicate. He gives the example of a child who is given a classical dictionary to look at, and is told by the person handing him the volume, "A good proportion of the characters listed are mythical, of course; but most of them existed" (or conversely).[17] Since the sentence 'Most of them existed' makes perfectly good sense in this situation, and since according to the criterion previously stated, wherever a quantifying adjective like '*most*' or *any* of the others can be meaningfully used, we are prepared to say that the subject of a sentence in which this occurs is a logical subject, therefore 'exists', according to the criterion, must be accorded the status of being a logical predicate in this sentence. If so, however, we still have an explanation to seek, for, wherever we have a logical subject used referentially, there is a presupposition of existence connected with the use of that subject. How, then, in the present case, are we to satisfy this requirement? What is that whose existence is presupposed in using the subject term, such that we can be said to use the term 'exists' as a logical predicate for the subject 'characters in this book'?

This is the question to which Strawson next addresses himself. And in order to answer it he first introduces the notion of a *presupposed class*. A *presupposed class* is a class the existence of the members of which is presupposed. According to Strawson, in this situation there is a presupposed class of characters (those listed in the dictionary). The *existence* of this class of characters is presupposed since it consists of the class of characters being *talked about*, *discussed*, or *described*. However, as a class it is 'ontologically heterogeneous', for it includes as *subclasses* characters which genuinely existed in history, along with those which are legendary, fictional, and so on. With this approach, therefore, we can show 'exist' to be used as a logical predicate—that is, where it makes reference to a certain subclass of *objects or persons talked about*. In a similar way, Strawson argues, we can show how the term 'exists' can be made to function predicatively relative to subjects that are conveyed by singular terms. Take the case of the two sentences 'King Alfred did exist', 'King Arthur did not exist'. "We have only to see the names as serving to identify, within the *heterogeneous* class of kingly characters we talk about—a class which comprises both actual and legendary kings—a particular member of that class in each case; and then see the predicate as serving to assign that particular member to the appropriate subclass. Thus 'exists' appears as a predicate, and not as a predicate of a concept; but as a predicate of some, and not of other members of the heterogeneous class. What, on this model, we shall have to regard as presupposed by the use of the name in each case is not the existence in history of an actual king with certain actual characteristics, or the existence in legend of a legendary king with certain legendary characteristics, but rather the existence-in-history-or-legend of an actual-or-legendary king with certain actual-or-legendary characteristics." [18]

What shall we say of this account? Let us note, to begin with, that the term 'exists' (or 'existence') is used both in connection with certain classes and in connection with certain individuals.

1. As for its use in connection with classes, Strawson uses it in connection both with regard to what he calls a presupposed class of things talked about as well as in connection with *one* of the subclasses of the presupposed class. The presupposed class is an ontologically heterogeneous class, insofar as its subclasses—those included among the things talked about—are of diverse ontological types; they include existence, or the subclass of existing things. This ontologically heterogeneous class is a presupposed class because its existence is not explicitly asserted. Yet its existence as the ontologically heterogeneous class of things talked about is taken for granted in a given context, as in the example given. Now it is worth noting in passing, in connection with this class whose existence is presupposed, that unlike the account which Strawson gives of a subject term that is actually employed in a singular subject-predicate statement (for example, 'Socrates is wise')—the existence of whose referent is presupposed—the presupposed class in the present use of this term does not function as a *subject term* in a subject-predicate sentence. As a presupposed class its existence is established, not by the use of a term as such, but by the *context of discussion*.

Now we might agree that this need not count against the advisability of our thinking of this class as a presupposed class; still we also need to be clear that the notion of presupposition has now been widened to include not only the presupposed existence of an entity being referred to by a term explicitly introduced as a subject term in a statement, but as having to do with a class of matters *not* specifically linked with the use of a subject term in a statement. Allowing for this extension of the notion of presupposed existence, let us now examine somewhat more closely what it means to say *this presupposed class exists* insofar as it is the 'class of things talked about'. The phrase 'things talked about' is ambiguous. In one sense 'things talked about' is the class of talkings, of things said, of utterances, statements, discussions, and so on. These are all affairs of human beings doing certain things. The episodes and the discussion exist because human beings themselves exist, and their talkings, musings, and interchanges, among others, are so many overt or silent *speech acts*. Now if the presupposed class exists in *this sense* (as it undoubtedly does), then are we to say that the subclasses of which it is composed are also so many different species of particular kinds of *speech acts?* Is the subclass of 'existence' or 'fiction' the class of existent things *talked* about, or of fictional things *talked* about? This does not seem likely. We turn then at this point to the other meaning or emphasis to be given to the expression 'things talked about'. For the use of the phrase 'things talked about' can, because of the use of the term 'about', be given another interpretation: it is not the speech acts, the episodes of talking, but rather the referents, the objects or targets of these acts of reference and description to which we should attend.

Of these two meanings of the phrase 'things talked about', I would interpret Strawson to be saying that the presupposed class exists because it is a *class of talkings* and the talkings exist, that is, the *first* of the above discriminated meanings. However, the ontological diversity comes in, not from the fact of talkings, since we could talk history as well as fiction, but in the *different ontological* statuses of what is talked *about*. Accordingly, the subclass of existence, if it is going to be *ontologically* discriminated from the class of fiction, must be a class of *entities* not a class of *talkings*. In this case we should have to say that the sense in which we say 'exists' attaches to the ontologically (not descriptively) homogeneous *subclass* of things that exist, does *not* attach to the ontologically homogeneous subclass of fictional entities. And if this is so, it is misleading to speak of the *presupposed class as made up* of ontologically heterogeneous subclasses. Indeed, in the sense in which the presupposed class exists, as a class of *talkings*, that class belongs as a subclass to the class of existing things, rather than the other way around. (There are very many other kinds of things that exist and that belong to the class of existing things besides talkings.) Also, if the presupposed class is a class of talkings and the so-called subclasses are classes of entities, then we cannot properly speak of the various *ontological* classes of *entities* as being *subclasses* of the class of *talkings*. However, if Strawson were to say that by the presupposed class he does not mean simply the class of *talkings* but the class composed of the ontologically diverse subclasses of entities of the things talked *about*, then, of course, it makes no sense to say, to begin with, that that class itself exists, since at best it only includes as a subclass the things that exist; it includes, however, other types of entities as well, and surely, therefore, the entire class cannot have the same ontological status as belongs only to one of its subclasses. Of course, to put the question this way only reminds us of the great danger in speaking of the various ontological 'subclasses' as composing or collectively constituting some all-inclusive class, and in assuming, furthermore, that it too can be assigned some ontological status. We might very well be inclined to reject altogether, therefore, at this point any talk of an 'inclusive class' that is allegedly composed of so many 'subclasses'. (To follow through this criticism, which I shall not do at this point, would lead to one possible interpretation of the dictum 'being is not a genus', a dictum I believe to be sound.) Because of the foregoing difficulties and unclarities in Strawson's position, it seems to me he has not fully succeeded in giving an analysis of how 'exists' can be used predicatively in connection with a *plural* subject.

2. Let us now turn to the other prong of Strawson's analysis and see whether he is any more successful in showing how we might use 'exists' predicatively in connection with a *singular* subject. He argues that we can use the term predicatively as in the statement 'King Alfred existed' because we can fall back on a parallel strategy to that employed in connection with using the term 'exists' in connection with a plural subject (as in 'Most of the characters in this book existed'). Once more, to say '*x* exists' (where '*x*' is a singular referring expression) is to use the term 'exists' predicatively, for it takes advantage of a presupposition of *the context of discussion*, rather than of a presupposition in connection with the use of the term '*x*' itself. But what is this presupposition, and how does it function to give the desired result?

I do not find in the passage quoted earlier, in which Strawson sets out his reply, that he has given us a single reply; indeed I find two. I should like, before moving on to my main critical objection to his approach in general, to stop to call attention briefly to these. The first of these answers appears in the following sentences from the beginning of the passage: "King Alfred did exist, King Arthur did not. We have only to see the names as serving to identify, within the heterogeneous *class* of kingly characters we talk about—a class which comprises both actual and legendary kings—a particular member of that class in each case; and then see the predicate as serving to assign that particular member to the appropriate *subclass*." [19] Here, as in the case of dealing with predicating 'exist' of a plural subject, the technique is to use this term in the same sense in which it appears as marking off a *subclass* (the class of things that are actual *kings*). (Strictly the subclass 'actual or existent kings' is itself a sub-subclass, since it is included within the wider subclass of *all* things that are actual or exist.) To say 'King Alfred exists' is to take the term 'exists' (or 'is actual') from the sub- or sub-subclass 'actual kings'. And this subclass is part of the wider presupposed class of kingly characters talked about, which includes actual as well as legendary kings. The only point I should wish to make in connection with this version of the solution is that it has all of the weaknesses already mentioned when we discussed this type of strategy as used to deal with 'exists' for plural subjects. I shall not repeat these criticisms here.

Let us move on, however, to what seems to be a different answer altogether, one that Strawson offers in the concluding sentence of the passage quoted earlier. He there says: "What, on this model, we shall have to regard as presupposed by the use of the name in each case is not the existence in history of an actual king with certain actual characteristics, or the existence in legend of a legendary king with certain legendary characteristics, but rather the existence-in-history-or-legend of *an* actual-or-legendary king with certain actual-or-legendary characteristics." [20] Now the difference between this version of the solution and that quoted earlier is that Strawson here—in appealing to a presupposed background from which to extract the use of the term 'exists'—appeals to a background formulated in *singular* terms. It is no longer, as in the earlier account of presupposition, a matter of representing a *subclass* of actual or legendary kings. He uses the expression '*an* actual-or-legendary king with actual-or-legendary characteristics'. Now this expression, I take it, is intended to identify some special type of *individual* as the presupposed background. I must confess, however, that I find it difficult to understand this. What kind of individual is it that is 'actual-or-legendary' with 'actual-or-legendary characteristics? Such an 'individual' would seem to be a monstrous ontological hybrid whose only claim to identity as an individual is that which derives in this instance from the spurious use of hyphens. If we were to give the entire passage its most generous interpretation, we should not be obliged to take seriously this (perhaps inadvertent) use of the expression *'an* actual-or-legendary king'; rather, we should regard it as simply another way of conveying the basic device mentioned earlier, that, namely, which appeals to the use of *subclasses* as part of a wider presupposed class. If so, our main concern must be with evaluating the soundness or helpfulness of *this* ('subclass') interpretation.

And here it seems to me there is an underlying difficulty with this entire strategy that I have not as yet touched upon, a difficulty, moreover, that is of a far more serious nature than any of the others already mentioned. It is this. Strawson's strategy in attempting to show how 'exists' can be used predicatively in connection with an individual, is to fall back on the use of the term 'exists' as it occurs in marking off a certain *subclass*, the subclass of actual or existent things, which in turn is part of 'presupposed (ontologically heterogeneous) class'. But have we really helped ourselves very much by falling back on this subclass? Indeed, have we not simply postponed and shifted our original question (that is, how to deal with '*x* exists') by saying this is to be done by turning to the *subclass* to which it is related and from which it derives the warrant for the use of the term 'exists'? For how is the subclass itself established or demarcated? If this is to be done extensionally, do we not have to fall back on the *singular statements* out of which the subclass is to be built up—the indeterminately large array of singular statements '*a* exists', '*b* exists', '*c* exists', and so on? And what have we gained thereby? For are we not back with our *original* problem, that is, how we are to understand, for example, '*a* exists'? On the other hand, if we should attempt to avoid this charge of circularity by rejecting the procedure of specifying what the subclass of things actual or existent is in extensional terms, and would wish to say simply that the term 'exists' as it appears in connection with the subclass is to be understood *intensionally*, we then face the question as to what *this* means: Is 'exists' to be thought of as definable, or as a primitive, undefined term? Whichever answer is given, it would seem the *same* answer as is given for the use of the term 'exists' in connection with the *subclass*, can be given for the use of the term 'exists' in connection with an *individual*, as in the statement '*a* exists', and so on. We should not, in other words, have gained any deeper understanding of how 'exists' is to be used predicatively by detouring to the use of this term as applied to an entire *subclass*.

6.4   *Concluding Remarks*

While the foregoing discussion has tended to be largely critical of Strawson's analysis of existence in terms of the notion of presupposition, there is no need to reject completely the value of this notion for such purposes. On the contrary, some fruitful suggestions emerge from Strawson's discussion, and they will be basic to our own positive account in the final section of this book. Two lines of thought, specifically, are worth pursuing.

One would consist in showing in detail what it means to say—given the distinction between what is *fictional* and what is *real*—that one *presupposes*, on a given occasion, that one or another of these *uses of language* is being exhibited. Thus in normal circumstances a storyteller and his audience will presuppose that the storyteller is making use of language for *fictional* purposes. On the other hand, those reading, say, a report of a laboratory experiment in a scientific journal will presuppose that language is being used for the purpose of describing observations of what *actually* happened. The contrast between the fictional and the real is undoubtedly therefore a distinction we find it important to make. However, what this presupposed distinction amounts to (how it is to be analyzed) is not clarified by appealing to the notion of presupposition itself; it needs to be supplied independently. In particular, how that distinction bears on the project of explicating the form of the sentence '*S* exists' still confronts us. In the following chapter I shall make some suggestions as to how this analysis is to be accomplished.

Meanwhile there is another clue for the analysis of '*S* exists' brought to light by the notion of presupposition (and some of the things Strawson says about it, *en passant*) that is also worth following up. To accept it as true that something exists—for example, this table, Socrates, King Alfred—is at the same time to presuppose that it belongs to some wider class or whole and *that it exists in virtue of that membership or belonging*. Insofar as some particular thing exists, it does not do so in any self-sufficient and completely isolated way. Rather its existence is bound up with some more inclusive whole of which it is an element or part. Once more we shall not find the materials for analyzing this idea by restricting ourselves to the notion of presupposition. But that we presuppose such a background, class, or whole to which some particular object or event belongs, and in virtue of which we say it exists, *this* is an idea of fundamental importance. It will be explored in Chapter 8. We shall consider there the notion of what it is to be an individual existent, and its crucial relation to the existence of the world as a whole.

Part III

Toward an Ontology of Existence

Chapter 7

Individual Existents and Semantic Indices

As our discussion up to this point has repeatedly stressed, a satisfactory account of existence (or its complement—an analysis of the
meaning of 'existence') would need to do justice to two interrelated
aspects of this theme: (1) the way in which we are to think of what it
is to be an individual existent, and our propositional representation
of it, and (2) the nature of the totality of existents, that is, the world.

We have already seen how, at the dawn of ontology in the West,
Parmenides and Aristotle, each in his own way, approached this
broad topic. For Parmenides the two sides of this question were still
very much at the center of his attention. His treatment of what it is
to be an individual existent, as something knowable, was approached through his acceptance and use of the 'esti' formula (the
prototype of the logician's examination of the structure of a
proposition) with respect to which the roles of reference, predication, and truth can be studied in their interrelations. For
Parmenides, too, the nature of existence (Being) can be approached
on a level where the distinctions among individual existents recedes
into the background and is replaced by a concentrated attention
upon the sheer fact of the Being of the world itself, which he calls '*to
eon*'. It is this side of existence that for him was of principal interest,
and to a degree that virtually obliterated all other concerns by the
intensity of its presence.

By the time we reach Aristotle's ontology, the one-dimensional
interests of the logician and the natural scientist have replaced the

149

two-dimensional character of Parmenides's philosophy. The discernment of *to eon*, in the way this preoccupied Parmenides, has virtually disappeared and is replaced by an interest in the foreground of multiplicity and change, and in the logical character and empirical truth of our discourse about this foreground.

The approach to existence by contemporary logicians, when seen in broad perspective, is a continuation and deepening of the sort of thing we find in Aristotle. Once again we find a preoccupation, among other things, with how to systematize and construe our use of language so that we could be clear about what it is we mean when we say something exists. The logicians we have examined do not always agree with one another as to what that 'something' is, nor how to conceive of 'existence' in connection with that 'something'. But they have been at least in broad agreement that it is through the analysis of our use of language that we can best approach what it means to say that something exists. And, like Aristotle in their concentration upon this problem, they have largely ignored that dimension of existence which is the topic of Parmenides's account of *to eon*. (Nor, of course, would the apparatus of logical symbolism or semantic analysis in any case be competent to deal with this side of existence at all; for existence on this level transcends all such instruments of intelligibility or conceptual knowability.)

Our examination of this heritage, both of ancient models as well as the samplings from some of the mainstreams of current investigation, has yielded a variety of fruits, including both points of deep appreciation and agreement as well as points of disagreement. It is time now to try, in some fresh way, to take stock and to attempt to sketch the outlines of an acceptable philosophy of existence.

Such a philosophy, first of all, would need to be an *ontology* of existence rather than primarily or exclusively a *logic* of 'existence'. Yet, of course, it would be necessary to satisfy the legitimate and important requirements of logic. And as a way of focusing on this aspect of the problem, we should wish to find a way of satisfactorily analyzing, for logical purposes, the structure of a singular existence statement ('*S* exists'). This I attempt in the present chapter.

At the same time, no satisfactory treatment of the *logic* of singular existence statements can ignore or get very far without considering what it is to be an individual existent, that is to say, what its *ontologic* character is. *This* question, however, is part of the wider question of the relation of individual existents to the world as a whole. And this in turn raises the further question of what we mean by 'the world'. I deal with this latter cluster of themes in the final chapter.

In trying to find a philosophically satisfactory analysis of the singular existence statement ('*S* exists'), we have examined thus far three main types of theories: (1) the classical quantification theory, (2) the tensed-predicate theory, and (3) the presupposition theory. We have found that while each of these theories contains a number of plausible and valuable proposals, in the end each taken as a whole proved unacceptable. Is it possible to give an analysis that would fare any better?

The thesis I shall argue for is that what is conveyed by the sentence 'Socrates exists' is best represented by what I shall call a 'semantic index'. The index is to be attached to a singular term, for example 'Socrates', as this is employed in a sentence whose predicate is *other than* 'exists', for example in the sentence 'Socrates is wise'.

By a *semantic index* I mean a symbol that indicates the referential status of the term to which it is attached. The expression 'referential status' can itself be understood in two ways, and I must stop, therefore, to say something about how I am using it in the foregoing characterization of *semantic index*. In one of its meanings, the referential status of an expression has as its prototype the name-bearer relation, that is, the relation that holds between a singular term (such as a proper name) and the object it denotes (its referent). In another, broader, sense of the expression 'referential status', the referential status of an expression is the semantic role it performs, of one sort or another, in contributing to the truth-conditions (the truth or falsity) of the sentence as a whole in which that expression occurs. In this latter sense, the referential status or semantic role of an expression need not be restricted to singular terms or, therefore, to the prototypical name-bearer relation of such singular terms, and may be used with respect to *any* expression in a sentence.[1] In what follows, I employ the expression 'referential status' in the first of the above meanings; that is, referential status will have to do *only* with singular terms, not with the semantic role, in the broader sense, of *any* type of expression.

A semantic index, then, is to be attached to the singular terms of sentences containing such terms. Singular terms, with their appropriate semantic indices, are concatenated with simple predicates (in atomic sentences) or occupy the argument places of sentences with one-place or many-place first level predicates. Accordingly, a semantic index cannot be attached to the predicate of a sentence, for semantic indices have to do with matters of reference (of designation and denotation) in the sense we have specified, whereas predicates, not being themselves singular terms, will be said not to have any referential status at all, that is, no actual or possible *referents*.

The notion of a semantic index will be invoked, in particular, in order that we may be able to properly analyze a sentence such as 'Socrates exists'. To make clear the meaning and warrant for taking 'Socrates exists' as something to be represented by a semantic index, will of course require analysis, and this we now proceed to give.

7.1 *Linguistic Resources; Natural and Artificial Languages*

Let us begin by taking note in a preliminary way of the linguistic resources we have at our disposal for carrying out our investigation and for formulating such results as we shall be able to achieve.[2] The principal resource, of course, is that of the natural languages; for example, English, French, German, and so on. Language, in the form of one or another of the natural languages, is the basic or primordial form on which we invariably fall back and is thus never totally replaced even when more refined and technical, symbolic means become available for one or another specialized purposes. But however indispensable and richly sustaining the distinctions of vocabulary and grammatical structure embodied in such ordinary natural languages may be, it is also the case that the kind of linguistic supplementation that is offered by the careful and deliberate construction of various special symbolisms serve special needs and meet special criteria that are not adequately met by the resources of natural languages. These special symbolisms or deliberate constructions are of various types, including the calculi of the logician and mathematician. Nor, in taking note of these, need we be guided by the assumption that among those that are either already available or yet to be constructed there is some *ideal* language. The search for some ideal language, an absolutely perfect symbolism that would once and for all lay bare the structure of reality and at least in principle be adequate for all cognitive purposes, has, as we know, frequently fired the imagination and inspired the hopes of many philosophers. We need not subscribe to the possibility or actual availability of such an ideal language in order for us nevertheless to acknowledge the contributions which a plurality of standardized and artificially constructed symbolic systems can make to the reform, improvement of, and refinement upon, ordinary language. For each such constructed system can then be judged relatively to the needs that prompted its construction and its success in meeting those needs.

It is in this spirit that we can approach the construction of a specially constructed artificial language or logical symbolism, as an additional resource to those of ordinary language, and as giving us the tools and refined standards by which to clarify, appraise, and even transform the kinds of formulations we might otherwise make in our discourse. And this policy, I submit, can profitably guide us in our own inquiry in ontology. Accordingly we need not abandon our use of ordinary language and seek to everywhere replace it by the use of a preferred symbolic language, even if this were possible. We should rather continue to use ordinary language (in our case, English), but under the proviso that where an explicit philosophic question is raised about what our use of such language commits us to, specifically as far as our ontological views are concerned, we shall call upon our considered selection of some preferred, artificial, reformed, and symbolic language to recast in precise terms what it is we wish to say. Since our total project is to gain some understanding of the concept of existence in connection both with individuals and the world, a first major step in this direction would obviously have to consist in undertaking an explication of the concept of individual existence. For this purpose, therefore, we shall need to consider first what special language of an improved or reformed sort we might choose to serve as our model symbolic vehicle.

Among various specially constructed artificial languages, when considered from a logical point of view, that is, with respect to their basic grammatical (syntactic and semantic) categories, we may distinguish many different types. Let us assume that in order to have any language we shall be interested in, it will be possible to isolate the following basic elements: (1) First of all, there are those unities of discourse we call *propositions* (statements, sentences), and that are capable of being appraised in terms of 'truth' and 'falsity'. The combination of expressions 'Socrates is wise' is a proposition, since we can ask with respect to it "Is it true or false?" (2) Second, we shall recognize a set of expressions we call *nouns* or *names*, in the widest sense. Under this rubric we can include singular proper names (e.g., 'Socrates', 'Pegasus'), general nouns (e.g., 'man', 'triangle', 'mermaid'), adjectives (e.g., 'red', 'sour'), pronouns (e.g., 'he', 'they', 'this'), and definite descriptions (e.g., 'the tallest building in the world', 'the smallest prime number'). A crucial way of distinguishing various artificial languages will be in terms of what are taken as the basic constituent expressions under this heading of 'nouns' or 'names'. Some might wish to select only singular terms (e.g., proper names, definite descriptions, etc.), and where furthermore such singular terms are restricted to those that refer to entities in the world. Others, again, might select only singular terms but allow these to be divided among those that have reference to individual existent entities in the world, as well as those that do not have any such reference and can, for example, represent nonexistent fictional "individuals". Still others, while also restricting themselves entirely to a language which recognizes only singular terms, might add to this list of possible singular terms the names for abstract entities; for example, for universals such as Wisdom or for mathematical objects such as the number 3. Still other languages might broaden the name or noun base by allowing in addition to singular terms, general names (e.g., 'man', 'triangle') as well. And there are still other possibilities as well.[3] (3) Finally, we shall say that in any artificially constructed language there will be a set of *functors*, that is, expressions that are able to form more complex expressions. These will include, for example, proposition-forming functors (e.g., predicates, truth-functional connectives) and name-forming functors (e.g., the definite description operator, i.e., 'the' attached to a descriptive predicate).

There are many different families of artificial languages that may be constructed, depending on what specific types of choices are elected within each of these broad categories. For our purposes we need not undertake to explore the range of possibilities here in any systematic or thorough way, although the matter is of great interest to logic and a theory of language. Among this range of possibilities, there is no singly correct or ideal language. As previously remarked, the construction and use of a language is a relative and pragmatic matter. Its adequacy is to be judged in terms of the kinds of subject matter and problems we wish to deal with and the kinds of results we hope to achieve. At any rate, since in our present investigation we are concerned with clarifying the philosophic problem of existence, it will be sufficient to declare what type of artificial language we propose to choose as our model and guide, even though we continue to use for the most part the vocabulary and syntax of ordinary English. For this purpose I propose to adopt as our model an artificial language that has the following characteristics:

Within the wide class of 'nouns' or 'names', we shall confine our attention and limit our discussion to those expressions that are 'names' for individuals, and are to be classified therefore as *singular terms*. By a 'singular term' we shall understand any linguistic expression that serves to pick out an individual from a domain of other individuals. Proper names (e.g., 'Socrates') will be one species of such singular terms. We shall also include under the heading of 'singular terms' definite descriptions, for example, 'the natural satellite of the Earth', as well as demonstrative expressions used in conjunction with some descriptive expression and that succeed in identifying the individual meant, for example 'this table'. Singular terms, further, will be subdivided for our purpose into two groups: those that refer to individual constituents of the world, and those that have no such reference, and are in this sense 'empty'. Among the first group are such singular terms as 'Socrates', 'The Empire State Building', 'this table', 'that lightning flash'; among the latter, 'Pegasus', 'Cerberus', 'Mr. Pickwick', 'The Ring of the Niebelungen'.

I shall leave aside such putative singular terms as 'Wisdom', '3', and so on, that are taken by some philosophers as names for abstract entities. There is no compelling necessity to posit such entities. What are supposedly singular terms for such special entities can be re-expressed so that they can be shown to belong, more properly, to the category of proposition-forming functors in our language, rather than to the category of singular terms. Briefly the situation is this. What for an atomic or a first-order proposition is a predicate can be re-expressed as an argument for a second-level predicate and therefore as forming a higher-order proposition when attached to a new proposition-forming predicate. Thus, given a proposition such as 'Wisdom is a virtue', the term 'Wisdom', which is a nominalization derived from an atomic or first-level predicate expression in a proposition such as 'Socrates is wise' or 'There is at least one individual who is wise', is now put in the argument-place of a second-level predicate, in this case '. . . is a virtue' to yield the given sentence. However, while many philosophers treat the use of the name 'Wisdom', for example, as a singular term for an abstract entity, and so as a name that can be used in an atomic sentence or as an argument in a first-order proposition, it is best (because in satisfaction of Occam's razor) to regard the term 'Wisdom' as merely a nominalization either of a simple predicate in an atomic sentence or of a first-level functor ('. . . is wise') in a first-order general (complex) sentence. It is therefore a *pseudo*-singular term. This obviates the need to posit a special domain of abstract entities or universals as the referents of these pseudo-singular terms. The independent being of such entities is an illusion created by our grammar, an illusion that can be dissipated by operating with a language restricted to the use of singular terms of the sort we have indicated.

However, the treatment of fictional "individuals" needs to be separated from the treatment given to those abstract entities called 'universals'; and so we shall leave room under the heading of 'singular terms' for fictitious "individuals" in addition to those for real or existent individuals. Stipulations about the use of singular terms for fictitious "individuals" do not, however, carry with them any ontological commitments. We need not introduce into our ontology, therefore, any separate and independent domain of fictional *entities* to correspond to, and serve as the *referents* of, the names for fictional "individuals".

7.2 *Fictional "Individuals"*

Let us stop to consider briefly this last point. A work of fiction is a human creation. Socrates is a person; Mr. Pickwick is a character. An author can create characters, he cannot qua author create persons. The author of a work of pure fiction is not concerned with describing some actual state of affairs. He invents a state of affairs and what that state of affairs is, is what he says it is. Here then is the chief difference between a sentence such as 'Socrates is wise' and 'Mr. Pickwick wore knee breeches'. The first statement gives a description of a person who is a part of the world of individual existents. Socrates as an existent is not produced by an exercise in language. In the case of factual statements about existent individuals there must already exist the individual about which something is being said. A factual statement is beholden to the given existence of the subject and restricted in the kinds of predicates it can truthfully ascribe to that subject. Neither type of restraint holds in fiction. The author is not given a subject already existent. He invents his subject, and what he assigns to that subject, for which he assigned an individual name, is completely a matter of choice on his part. In order to read and understand Dickens's novel we do not need to presuppose the existence of Mr. Pickwick, since the name 'Mr. Pickwick' does not refer to an existent individual at all. The name 'Mr. Pickwick' was introduced by Dickens in the course of writing a long series of sentences whose totality is *The Pickwick Papers*. Apart from that book there is no Mr. Pickwick. In the case of the sentence 'Socrates is wise' we need both to understand the terms used and to know whether the statement, as a factual statement, is true or false. To know whether the statement as a whole is true or false requires a determination of what the actual state of extralinguistic affairs is, to know whether the predicate terms apply to the entity designated by the subject term. In the case of the sentence 'Mr. Pickwick wore knee breeches' all we need to do is understand the predicate terms and their concatenation with the name 'Mr. Pickwick'—an expression that is devoid of any *existential* reference.

In order to understand the referential status of a name such as 'Mr. Pickwick' without being obliged to assign an existent, ontological referent to that name, and in order, further, to come to some decision as to what to make of the question of the truth or falsity of sentences about fictional "individuals", it will be helpful to take advantage at this point of the well-known distinction between *sense* and *reference* first introduced by Frege. Although Frege applied this distinction to various types of words and expressions in a sentence as well as to a sentence as a whole, we shall consider this distinction for our present purposes only as it applies to singular terms, and use as our illustration the distinction between two types of proper names, one for an existent person, the other for a fictional character.

In the case of the use of an ordinary name of a person, the

distinction between the sense of that name and its reference amounts to this. The *sense* of a proper name consists in the particular way we have in identifying the person in question, the referent of the name. Thus we normally have various items that make up such sense, although these need not completely coincide at any given time with the sense of the name attributed to that name by other users of that name. The sense which the name 'Socrates' has would normally include such descriptions as 'the teacher of Plato', 'the husband of Xantippe', 'the philosopher who drank the hemlock', and so on. Some one or a combination of such senses will serve to identify the person who is the referent of this name.

Moreover, different expressions that have different senses may yet have the same reference. The sense of an expression determines the reference that an expression has, not the other way around. Indeed the situation where two names have different senses although they have the same reference can be, in some cases, genuinely informative. This was the point made by Frege's example of the use of the expressions 'The Evening Star' and 'The Morning Star'—two expressions that have different senses, yet in having the same reference, are items in an identity statement that is far from trivial. By the sense, then, of a name we mean the way for identifying an object, the criterion we have for picking out the object. For a name to have a *reference* in the ordinary, everyday case an object or person can be identified that (who) is the bearer of the name. And in such cases the object or person, as the referent of the name, is an independently existing entity in the world. A child is born and given a name in a baptismal ceremony or by filling out a birth certificate. And even where we are no longer able to directly confront the referent of a proper name, say because the individual person is long since dead, there may be sufficient support through a linkage of evidence to provide a warrant for making reference to that person in the past.

Yet in natural language one may use names or other singular terms not only to make reference to what is an acknowledged constituent of the world. The use of creative imagination or, in linguistic terms, the construction of fresh and novel combinations of terms taken from the already available resources of language make possible the introduction of expressions (singular terms, in particular) whose senses do not already have some evident and acknowledged association with some independently existing object, event, or person.

We may for present purposes, distinguish here roughly two types of cases. In one a name or singular term, to which a precise sense is given, is introduced with the intention of designating some actual individual in the world—with the expectation that it will in fact be found to have a referent in the same way in which already normally accepted names have their referents in individual constituents in the world. Assuming that the description or sense given to the term is a coherent one, the referent among existent objects may be found with which the name can then be correlated, and where the sense given to the name can then be used as a means for identifying the object. For example, parents, in advance of the birth of a child, may pick out a name for it. When Adams (and Leverrier) on the basis of precise calculations with respect to mass, position, and so on, gave definite descriptions to the putative trans-Uranian planet (subsequently named 'Neptune'), a referent was found for their descriptions after a sense for that singular term had already been specified. On the other hand, when Leverrier also predicted another hitherto undetected planet adjacent to Mercury (to which the Imperial Astronomer assigned the name 'Vulcan'), no such actual referent was in fact eventually found. The name continued to have sense but lacked a reference. In both of these latter, astronomical, examples there was an intention on the part of the scientific investigator to refer to an actual object. However, in one case the intention succeeded, because confirmed; the other was to be set down as a case of failed reference, though possessed of sense. Where the sentence containing a singular term has a referent in the world, and the properties predicated of it apply, the sentence is true. Where the singular term has no referent at all in the world, the sentence is neither true nor false, although the singular terms and predicates and therefore the entire sentence continue to have sense.

Such cases of successful or failed reference need to be distinguished, however, from those uses of creative imagination (or the use of the resources of language in novel constructions) where there is no intention to refer to actual objects (or persons, events) in the world. The invention of "individuals" through the giving of names to such "individuals" and the sense(s) these names have by virtue of what is said about these "individuals" is not for the purpose of identifying

actual individuals in the world or for the purpose of making factually true assertions about actual individuals in the world. Such,
broadly, is the situation in *fiction* (or better still, *pure fiction*). (Our
interest here, for the moment, is in pure fiction and not in those uses
of fictional discourse which, in their own indirect, symbolic way may
be thought to say something 'true' of the actual world; nor again
shall we consider those mixed and complicated uses of discourse in
which along with reference to actual and genuine constituents of the
world, are combined the uses of terms that have only fictional status:
for example, Tolstoy's use of the names 'Natasha' and 'Napoleon' in
War and Peace.)

In purely fictional discourse the assignment of a proper name to a
character is given *sense* by virtue of the various things the author says
about the "individual" so named. More accurately, the name is
given the sense it has as a result of being concatenated in the
sentences in which it appears along with various predicates and
descriptions. And yet, since the primary intention of this type of
discourse is not to give a factual description of the actual constituents of the world but only to 'entertain', or in general to exhibit
and exercise the imagination and thereby also perhaps indirectly
cast light on the actual world, we do not look for or require referents
that are genuine constituents of the world for the singular terms
introduced.

However, it may be said, there is a sense in which Dickens in
writing his novel does *refer* to Mr. Pickwick when he uses the name
'Mr. Pickwick', and there is a sense too in which we can say the name
'Mr. Pickwick' *in* the novel has a reference. (Both of these ways of
thinking of the reference of 'Mr. Pickwick' *in* the novel need to be
distinguished from the way in which a literary critic, say, or a reader
of Dickens's novel can *refer to* and talk *about* what Dickens says in the
novel.)

But if 'Mr. Pickwick' does have a reference and it is not a constituent of the world, what then is its *referent*? We could reply in either
of two ways: We could insist that a fictional name has *no* reference,
since in making a distinction and contrast between sense and
reference for ordinary names in nonfictional discourse we need always to keep the two distinct even when the terms 'sense' and
'reference' are considered in connection with fictional discourse.
And since there is no clear referent for a name in fiction, *it has none*.

On the other hand, we can modify our use of the term 'reference' to accommodate what we may wish to say about fictional discourse. In this case, we could say, the *referent* of 'Mr. Pickwick' is the *sense* which is given to the use of that expression in Dickens's novel. For fictional names, in short, the reference *reduces* to the sense. Here the term 'reference' (for singular terms) will be so modified as to allow us to say that for them their sense coincides with their reference. In support of this second view of the matter, we could say that sense, in general, is wholly a matter of the *understanding* of the terms in a language. It will be acknowledged, we shall assume, that the predicates and descriptive terms used in fictional discourse are the same as they are in factual discourse. The senses of the terms will be the same. On the other hand, it will be the matter of the reference of the singular terms that will differ. Whereas in factual discourse we can separate their sense from their reference, in the case of fictional discourse we *cannot*.

Provided we make clear in what way we are using the term 'reference'—that is, in its strict or modified meaning, we can choose either of these alternatives.

Now what about the matter of truth and falsity? Once again we are confronted by a matter of decision, of how we choose to use the terms 'true' and 'false', just as earlier we were confronted with a decision about the strict or modified use of the term 'reference'. In this case, too, we may wish to insist that unless a basic or atomic sentence contains a singular term that not only has a sense but a referent in the form of a constituent of the world, the predicates applied to that "individual" will be neither true nor false of "it". And on this stipulation, since the singular terms in purely fictional discourse are not intended or required to have any such reference, we should be obliged to say, on this ruling, that the sentences of purely fictional discourse are neither true nor false. And this is a position one may surely adopt and that indeed finds favor with many philosophers, including Frege himself.

On the other hand, bearing in mind a classic and parallel distinction between 'formal' and 'empirical' truth, we may wish to extend in an analogous way the notion of truth to fictional discourse. The truth of fictional discourse will of course be admittedly different from the formal truth of mathematics, since the criterion for truth in fictional discourse is not—as it is in those cases where one speaks of formal truth—a matter of a statement being true when it is a validly derivable consequence from other statements within a deductively organized system. In the case of fiction, the truth of what is said is established simply by being written or uttered by the author. Whatever he says about his characters, provided it does not violate any rules of the language or of logical consistency, thereby becomes *true of* the characters he invents. The only false statements an author can make would be those that violate the rules of logic, for example attributing two contradictory predicates to the same "individual" in the same work of fiction.

In order to understand the name of a character introduced in a novel, we need, as we read the novel, only some subset of the various things the author says about that character in order to understand the sense of the name. For as we progress in our reading of the novel, the name occurs in always new sentences whose predicates are, in those sentences, added to the sense which the name already has on the basis of the things previously said about the subject of these new sentences. Not only are the sentences which explicate the sense of the character's name already true by virtue of what the author had previously said, but as we add new sentences in which the name appears, we enrich the sense of the name for further uses of that name in still other sentences. And so on.

Shall we use the term 'individual' in connection with what the name of a character introduced in fiction represents even though what it represents is not an individual existent? Shall we speak of fictional *individuals*? The question is in part a terminological one, calling for agreement or convention. The important thing is to distinguish between the species of individual names or singular terms. If we insist on using the term 'individual' to represent only what are individual existents, extralinguistic objects in the world, then we shall not be able to speak of Mr. Pickwick or Pegasus as 'individuals'.

Nevertheless there is, after all, some analogy and parallel between the use of the names 'Pegasus' or 'Mr. Pickwick' and 'Socrates' on the one hand, as contrasted with the use of general names (sortal nouns or characterizing adjectives) as descriptive functors in our language, whether these are attached to the use of fictional names or names for existent individuals. The one set (for example, 'Mr. Pickwick', 'Pegasus', and 'Socrates') are individual names; '. . . is a person', '. . . is a man', '. . . is a flying-horse', '. . . is wise', '. . . wears knee breeches', and so on, are general terms, attachable to different individual names to yield in their own special ways true or false propositions. To take cognizance of these parallels, we are pushed in the direction of assimilating 'Pegasus' to 'Socrates' and not to '. . . is a flying-horse', '. . . is a man'. We are inclined therefore to regard 'Pegasus' as an individual name 'standing for' an individual, whereas '. . . is a flying-horse' is a general functor or predicate expression.

Should we not, therefore, also allow fictional *individuals*? The tension between these two lines of argument, on the one side discouraging us from treating Pegasus as an individual, on the other side encouraging us to treat Pegasus as an individual, calls for some resolution. I propose to mediate between these conflicting pressures by using double scare-quotes around the word 'individual' ("individual"), whenever we wish to describe the use of an empty individual name, but not when we refer to an individual existent. Thus, Pegasus is a fictional "individual", Socrates is an individual. The use of double scare-quotes for the word 'individual' reminds us of the *extended* use of the word 'individual' to accommodate this special sense of 'individual' when used to describe what fictional singular terms or names stand for.

7.3   *Semantic Indices*

At this point I should like to introduce, as a supplement to the grammatical categories we have thus far considered—names, propositions, functors—a new device to be used in conjunction with singular terms, namely, a *semantic index*, as previously defined. The need for a semantic index in connection with the language we have chosen arises from the fact that the semantic category of singular terms includes two groups, those that refer to extralinguistic entities in the world, and those that have no referential uses of this kind. It is in order to discriminate these two types of singular terms that we need semantic indices. For a semantic index, when attached to a given singular term will indicate to which of these two groups a particular singular term belongs.

If we had chosen as our model a language in which we should

have only singular terms that designate individuals in the world to which predicates are attached to yield true or false propositions, there would have been no need within this language for a semantic index of the sort I am now proposing, since it would be true of every singular term that it possesses an extralinguistic referent in the world. Since in fact we are adopting a language in which there are both types of singular terms, those that are referential in this sense and those that are not, we need some way of differentiating them. And in order to accomplish this we shall make use of a semantic index. One of these will be symbolized by the letter 'E' (for 'exist-ent') and is to be attached as a superscript to the appropriate singular term; for example, 'Socrates$^{(E)}$'. The other index is 'F' (for 'fictional') and will be written as a superscript attached to the appropriate individual name; for example, 'Pegasus$^{(F)}$'. Let us now consider what lies behind these assignments of the semantic indices. The analysis of the warrant for the use of the semantic index 'existent' will, in particular, provide the way we should understand the import of a sentence of the form 'S exists' (e.g., 'Socrates exists'.)

As previously remarked, we might have chosen a language in which we should have used only singular terms that make reference in each case to a particular extralinguistic entity or constituent of the world. It would have been entirely legitimate to do so for the purposes of discussing by means of such a language the philosophic problem of existence. And it is true that within such a language we should not have needed semantic indices of the type we have been discussing. Yet we should still have been obliged to analyze in what the referen-tial character of all individual names would consist and in particular what it means to say for any object designated by any singular term that *it exists*. In other words, we should not have escaped the philosophic obligation to examine the sentence type 'S exists' even though that sentence type would be connected in some way with every sentence formed in the language in which some particular singular term replaces the letter 'S' and in which predicates other than 'exist' are concatenated with such singular terms. Instead of such an austerely restricted language we are adopting a language in which singular terms may be either referential in this strict sense or not, and it is in the context of drawing this distinction that we need to analyze 'S exists' and how the semantic index 'E' ('existent') can be used to symbolize and encapsulate this analysis.

7.4   *The Analysis of 'Socrates Exists'*

What analysis, then, are we to give to the sentence 'Socrates exists' within the framework of the language we have chosen? Since in setting up the language we have already presumed that (1) there are extralinguistic individuals to which some individual names correspond, whereas (2) there are other individual names that have no such extralinguistic reference, our immediate problem is obviously focused on the use of the name 'Socrates': we need to determine to which of these two classes of terms we are to assign that name. It is trivially clear that it belongs to the first class rather than to the second. It need not always be the case that confronted by a name in natural language—and where such language is to be reconstructed in accordance with the requirements of the artificial language we are adopting as our guide—that the determination of which of the two types of individual names a particular individual name is to be assigned to is trivially clear; but I am not here concerned with problem or controversial cases; and in any case, in the use of natural language various extraneous clues and aids are normally forthcoming, for example, the context, the intentions of the speaker, and so on, to help us make a reasonably secure assignment when there is some initial doubt or controversy. The name 'Socrates', at any rate, in the examples of its use we have been examining, is not a name devoid of extralinguistic reference; it is not a name for a fictional "individual". The name 'Socrates' has as its designatum the extralinguistic entity in the person Socrates.

In the first place, then, the use of the word 'exists' in the sentence 'Socrates exists' may be regarded as making a *semantic* assignment of the sort we have just engaged in to the *name* 'Socrates'. In this case the use of the word 'exists' functions in a semantic way. It is not an object-language predication about Socrates. It is rather a metalinguistic assignment to the name 'Socrates'. It says, in effect: "The name 'Socrates' as we are using it in other, object-language sentences, for example 'Socrates is wise', 'Socrates is the husband of Xantippe', 'Socrates drank the hemlock', and so on, is an individual name that has a designatum in the person Socrates." What the word 'exists' accomplishes here, and on this level of analysis, is not to describe in any way the person Socrates. It rather classifies or marks the name 'Socrates' as one of the types of individual names we are allowed to use in our language, as that type which in fact has an extralinguistic referent. The explanation of '*S* exists' as meaning in part "The name '*S*' has as its referent a constituent of the world is to *mention* '*S*' in this sentence; it is not to *use* '*S*' referringly in this type of sentence. What is predicated of *the name* '*S*' (the logical subject of the semantic statement) is a semantic description, namely, '. . . is an individual name that designates an individual constituent of the world'. And *this* predicate is a genuine descriptive functor that has "the name '*S*' " as its argument (logical subject); it shows the entire statement to be a semantic statement. The semantic statement stands in a metalinguistic relation to the original statement (e.g., 'Socrates is wise' etc.). Its subject—*the name* '*S*'—is used referringly, though to be distinguished from '*S*' used referringly as subject in the original statement (in 'Socrates is wise'). Is the semantic statement true or false? Yes, its truth or falsity is determined in accordance with whether it is or is not the case that '*S*' designates something extralinguistically in the world. However, if the semantic statement is true, what it is *true of* is *the name* '*S*', not what '*S*' refers to, not, in our example, the man Socrates, the extralinguistic object.

But this is not the end of the matter. We can take the sentence 'Socrates exists' as functioning in another way, in a way, moreover, which is not at all incompatible with the first type of analysis we have given. In saying that we can give *another* equally sound analysis of '*S* exists' we are pointing out, of course, that '*S* exists' is an *ambiguously* formulated sentence. In the first place it can be given the analysis we have just offered, that is, as meaning; "The name 'Socrates' ('*S*') is an individual name that has an extralinguistic reference." However, the sentence 'Socrates exists' can also be given another analysis as well. For we ask: "How or Where are we to find the extralinguistic referent to the name 'Socrates'?" And the sentence 'Socrates exists', in its use of the word 'exists', answers our question. For 'exists' means *being part of the world*. To say '*S* exists' means '*S* is part of the world.' And we may use the expression 'existent' as having this precise sense, namely, 'part of the world'.

The word 'exists' (as well as the word 'existent') does not *describe* the individual referent to which this term is applied. For *all* individuals that are the designata of singular terms in our language which are not fictitious are such that we can say of each and every one that it is a part of the world, that it is an existent. To use the expressions 'exist' or 'existent' therefore with respect to those individuals does not in any way contribute to *describing* them. For to *describe* an individual that is part of the world (an existent) is to assign it to a resemblance class *within* the totality of such objects (the world). Descriptive terms such as 'lion', 'red', 'building', 'philosopher', and so on can and do function predicatively to give us some definite information, if the sentence in which they figure is true, about the individual object which is part of the world, and referred to by some singular term. To give information, to function fruitfully as a description, an ordinary descriptive predicate must indicate the resemblance class to which the individual belongs, and in so doing it must also differentiate that individual from those individuals that fall outside that resemblance class. Terms such as 'red', 'philosopher', 'building', and the like do this, when they function as descriptive predicates. *But the term 'exists' does not function in this way at all.* To say that something exists because it is part of the world, is not to assign it some particular property or properties, not even temporal properties. It is not like saying it weighs five pounds, is dark brown, is made of wood, was made in 1910, or the like. To utter the statement '*S* is an existent' or '*S* exists' does not suffice to characterize *S*. To do that we need some descriptive characteristics that are applicable to the individual designated by '*S*'.

Nor does the term 'existent', even when used in conjunction with a demonstrative pronoun, but apart from the implicit or explicit use of some genuinely descriptive classificatory term, suffice to *identify* or *pick out* some particular individual. Individuation is accomplished by the use of some associated or implied descriptive terms, not by the pseudo-descriptive term 'existent' alone. We cannot say, in other words, 'this existent' and by that alone pick out some particular individual. For in order to know *which* individual is intended, we need to know something genuinely descriptive about the individual over and above the fact that 'it' exists. The term 'exists' or 'existent' does not differentiate an individual from any other individuals that are also parts of the world. Qua parts of the world, all existents are on the same footing. One might be inclined to say 'existent' gives us the basis of similarity, the resemblance class to which *S* belongs, namely, the class of all other parts of the world. But since it doesn't also differentiate this particular object or individual from the others, by itself it is noninformative; it is not helpful in the way normal descriptive predicates are. Normal descriptive terms function both to classify an individual with others with which it has strong enough resemblances, and they set that individual apart (along with others of the class to which it belongs) from all those individuals that do not belong to a particular resemblance class. But the predicate 'exists' and the quasi-sortal nominative 'existent' do not perform this latter function at all.

In collecting the foregoing points, we have shown that '*S* exists' is a sentence that can be treated as saying:

1. " '*S*' is an individual name that has an extralinguistic reference";
2. "*S* is part of the world" (= "*S* is an existent").

Let us agree now that wherever, in connection with the use of 'exists' as a predicate, as in the original sentence we started with ('Socrates exists'), we can give an analysis that allows that sentence to be explicated as saying *both* 1 and 2, we shall use the term '*existent*' as a *semantic index* attached to the singular term that accompanied the use of the verb 'exists'. By writing 'Socrates$^{(E)}$ is wise', 'Socrates $^{(E)}$ is the husband of Xantippe', and so on, we indicate by the use of the semantic index 'E' something of the role of the individual name 'Socrates' and something of the ontological status of the referent of that name, that it is a part of the world, an existent.

7.5   *The Analysis of 'Pegasus Does Not Exist'*

Now consider the sentence 'Pegasus does not exist'. This sentence contains the individual name 'Pegasus' and the predicate 'does not exist'. The analysis to be given of the logical structure of this sentence would be the following. In using the sentence 'Pegasus does not exist' we are to be understood as saying: "*The name* 'Pegasus' does not have any extralinguistic reference to a constituent of the world." This is to make the claim that the name 'Pegasus' is one whose reference coincides with its sense, but is not to be identified with any referent in the world. It is to make a semantic statement about the referential status of the name 'Pegasus'. It is to predicate the semantic property of being nonreferential in the strict sense. Insofar as we accept this semantic statement about the name 'Pegasus' as true, we should then use this as a warrant for writing the superscript 'F' next to the name 'Pegasus' in a sentence in which this expression serves as logical subject and in which the predicate is other than 'exists'. Thus, we should write 'Pegasus$^{(F)}$ is a flying horse'.

The difference between the two sentences 'Socrates exists' and 'Pegasus does not exist' considered from a semantic point of view may be summarized by saying that in both cases the use of the term 'exists' functions to indicate something about the semantic role of the individual name: in the one case to point out that the name has a referent which is a constituent of the world; in the other case that it has no such referent, but at best a referent which is identical with its sense. The term 'exists' ('existent') can also, however, be understood in an *ontological* and not simply in a *semantic* way. In this case the term 'exists' ('existent') means 'part of the world'; in this ontological meaning it applies to Socrates but not to Pegasus.

Chapter 8

The World as a Whole and Existence

8.1 *Individual Existents*

I have described what it is to be an *individual*, that is, what it is to be an *existent*, by saying it is any fragment, part, or real constituent of the world. One way of regarding this formula is to say that whatever is a fragment, part, or real constituent of the world *is* what we mean by 'an individual'. Anything is an individual existent, however large or complex, or scattered in space, or discontinuous in time, provided it is a proper part of the world. It is true that my own typical example of a singular existence statement namely 'Socrates exists' took as an example of 'individual' a person, but this concession to our normal tendency to appeal to ordinary objects or persons as our favorite examples of individuals should not be taken as militating against regarding, for ontological purposes, anything which is a constituent of the world, even other than a single thing, as a perfectly good example of what it is to be an individual and hence as serving as the referent of a logical subject of a singular existence statement.

What, however, are we to understand by the use of the expressions 'part', 'fragment', 'constituent of the world'? Furthermore, if we say an individual existent is *part* of the *world*, does this not imply that the world is in some sense *a whole*? And how shall we understand that? Or is it possible that something can be a 'fragment' or 'part' without its being a fragment or part of a whole? If we do speak of the world as a whole, is it too an individual? And would the characterization of the world as an individual be similar to, or different from, the way

170

we speak of constituents of the world as being individuals? And what of 'existence'? Is the world *an existent*? If not, how, or in what way, can we introduce and use the term 'existence' or 'exists' or any related expression in connection with it? Further, we have used the expression 'the world'; but what differences or similarities does it have in its use to the use of such expressions as 'The Universe', 'Nature', 'Being', Reality'? And is there some special reason for preferring the expression 'the world' to any of these? These are some obvious questions we shall have to consider if we are going to make any headway in clarifying the philosophic problem of existence as we initially sketched it. Our dealings heretofore have been with the analysis of singular existence sentences of the sort 'Socrates exists'. It is time now to turn to the other pole of our problem, namely what we mean by 'the world'. For the philosophic problem of existence consists in an attempt to come to some understanding of what the relation is between individual existence and the world. And to accomplish this we need to deal not only with a sentence of the type 'Socrates exists', but to clarify what our notion of the world is as that to which individual existents are related.

8.2 Wholes and Parts

A necessary first step in the analysis of the phrase 'the world as a whole' is to examine the term 'whole' separately. For this purpose we shall turn to the theory of wholes and parts which goes by the name 'Mereology', a theory whose major ideas were worked out by the Polish logician Leśniewski. Mereology, for Leśniewski, was in turn but one of three interrelated disciplines, the other two being Protothetic and Ontology, which he also developed. The first of these (Protothetic) corresponds roughly to what we should nowadays call the propositional (or sentential) calculus, a branch of logic that is fundamental to all the others; the second (Ontology) corresponds (again, roughly) to what nowadays falls within the scope of the predicate calculus. An alternative characterization of Ontology, in Leśniewski's sense, is that it is a calculus of names. Unlike Protothetic and Ontology, which deal with propositions and names, respectively, and are logical systems that have linguistic expressions as their primary subject matter, Mereology is to be thought of as an account of the basic relations of whole and part for objects in the world (and of the world itself insofar as it too may be considered as an individual whole).[1] Mereology is thus a 'factual' discipline and is intended to describe in very general terms the world in which we live, though exclusively in terms of, or under the perspective of, the whole-part relationship as this holds for complex objects. Mereology, in Leśniewski's conception and account of it, is a systematic, deductive theory. It makes use of symbols for names, propositions, and functors and accordingly employs throughout the results and rules of Protothetic and Ontology.

I shall, for our purposes, adapt some of the characteristic theses of Mereology for use in connection with our special concern with the philosophic problem of existence, and also further adapt these theses to formulation within the relatively simple artificial language we are adopting as our guide, as previously described. Leśniewski's own language, which he uses in the development of his Ontology, and which therefore also reappears in his formulation of Mereology, was a much richer language than the one to which we are appealing. It considered both common nouns and adjectives as well as individual names as falling within the same semantic category, with only one elementary functor (symbolized as 'ε' and roughly translated as 'is') to link names within a proposition. However, in the language we are adopting as our guide the only names are 'individual names'; what are called 'common nouns' and 'adjectives' are assimilated to descriptive functors (verbs, predicates).[2]

By 'whole' we shall understand, with Leśniewski, a class in the *collective* sense, that is, a collective class. This use of the word 'class' is to be sharply differentiated from other uses of this term, for example, in the theory of sets, or also in connection with what are sometimes called 'distributive classes'. For Leśniewski a class is always to be understood in the 'collective' sense, and is indeed therefore something which is itself *an individual* or *an object*.

Leśniewski came to the construction of his views under the impetus of trying to deal with the Russell paradox in the foundations of mathematics. Leśniewski argued that the Russell paradox rests on a faulty conception of what it is to be a 'class' and that Russell's own solution therefore becomes otiose once the initial presuppositions of the statement of the paradox are challenged and overcome. However, in developing his own theory of what it is to be a class, Leśniewski formulated a theory of what the relation of whole and part is that would be applicable to, and in general harmony with, our experience of the world. It is only with this latter relevance of his Mereology, rather than with the controversial question of its suitability as a conceptual foundation for mathematics, that I am here concerned.

Leśniewski developed his ideas in Mereology over a period of many years, beginning with his first publication in 1916 ("Foundations of General Theory of Manifolds or Collective Sets," Part I). The fruits of this early research are summarized and extended in his most important publication, "On Foundations of Mathematics," which appeared from 1927 to 1931. He himself provided a number of different simplifications of the deductive theory, recasting the axioms, choosing different primitive terms, and so on. And the works of Sobocinski, Tarski, Lejewski and others have built upon these researches and continued the refinement and elaboration of these ideas. The basic concepts of Leśniewski's approach to Mereology are already formulated in 1916 as summarized in his "The Foundations of Mathematics." They rest on the following Axioms and Definitions, with the term '*part*' as the only primitive, undefined term of the theory. (Note: phrases in square brackets are my own.)

Axiom I.   If P is part of the object Q, then Q is not part of the object P.

Axiom II.   If P is part of the object Q, and Q is part of the object R, then P is part of the object R.

Definition I. [definition of 'ingredient']: P is an ingredient of the object Q if and only if P is the same object as Q or is part of the object Q.

Definition II.[definition of 'class', i.e., *collective class*]: P is the class of objects *a* if and only if the following conditions are satisfied:

α) P is an object;

β) every *a* is an ingredient of the object P;

γ) for all Q, if Q is an ingredient of object P, then some ingredient of object Q is an ingredient of some *a*.

[By 'objects *a*' or 'an object *a*', we shall understand Leśniewski to mean an object or objects of which a certain description '*a*' holds true.]

    Axiom III. If P is the [collective] class of objects *a*, and Q is the
                [collective] class of objects *a*, then P is Q.
    Axiom IV. If some object is *a*, then some object is the [collective]
                class of objects *a*.

From these axioms various theorems can be deduced. I list (without proofs) a number of these:

Theorems:

1. If P is an object, then P is not a part of object P.
2. If P is an object, then P is an ingredient of object P.
3. If some object is a part of object P, and Q is an ingredient of object P, then some ingredient of object Q is an ingredient of some part of object P.
4. If P is an ingredient of object Q, and Q is an ingredient of object R, then P is an ingredient of object R.
5. If (for all S, if S is an ingredient of object P, then some ingredient of object S is an ingredient of object R), and Q is an ingredient of object P, then some ingredient of object Q is an ingredient of that ingredient R, which is an ingredient of object P.
6. If P is the [collective] class of objects *a*, and Q is an ingredient of object P, then some ingredient of object Q is an ingredient of some *a*, *a* being an ingredient of object P.
7. If P is an object, then P is the class of ingredients of object P.
8. If P is an object, then P is the class of objects P.
9. If some object is a part of object P, then P is the class of parts of object P.
10. If P is an ingredient of object Q, then Q is the class of ingredients of object Q.

By a *whole* we shall understand a collective class in the sense given in the foregoing system of ideas. A collective class is itself an *individual* (or object). We can accordingly speak of an *individual whole*, although the phrase is a redundant one. Further, we shall take individual wholes to correspond to those individuals that are the *designata* of individual names. In this sense empty or fictitious individual names do *not* designate individual wholes. Henceforward, therefore, we shall be concerned with individual wholes, and it is of individual wholes that we can say that they *exist*.

By way of further clarification of what is to be understood by 'an individual whole' ('collective class'), let us note the following points:

The sense in which we speak of an individual whole as a collective class is not to be confused with, or in any way identified with, the use of the term 'class' as designating an abstract entity.

The sense in which we speak of an individual whole as a collective class is not to be confused with, or in any way identified with, what some authors describe as the meaning of the term 'class' in a 'distributive' sense, or with a 'distributive class'. The notion of a distributive class derives from thinking that one can form a class of the so-called multiple denotations of a general term (for example, common noun or adjective). That is, it is thought the individuals that belong to and constitute a particular class do so because they share in the property represented by a general term. This idea is sometimes linked or identified with the *extension* of a concept or general term. Leśniewski writes: "The concept of Frege which treats classes as extensions of ideas I cannot subject to a merited analysis, because I have not been able so far, despite sincere efforts, to understand what various authors are really talking about when they use the expression 'extension of an idea.' If extension of idea *a* is not to be a class of *a* in agreement with my concept of classes and consisting of *a*'s, then, not knowing the answer to the question what the extension of [an] idea might be, when and where one could become acquainted with such an extension and if in general if something like that really exists, I am tempted to suppose that one is concerned here with some sort of objects, 'contrived' by logicians to torment many generations." [3] But this notion of (distributive) 'class' is an eliminable one. For, to begin with, it is misleading to speak of *denotation* (even the 'multiple denotation') of a general term. No more than a general term designates an abstract entity, does a general term multiply-denote, or designate a class of entities. Rather, a general term is best understood in its *predicative* role as 'holding true of' or 'applying to' an individual. It is only individual names that are capable of an extralinguistic referential or designative relation to an independently existing entity. And the function of the predicative general term is to *describe* that individual. Hence we can replace the terminology of 'distributive classes' with the terminology of individual reference and predication. Rather than say 'Socrates is wise' means 'Socrates belongs to, or is a member of, the distributive class of wise persons' or 'Socrates belongs to the denotation of the class of wise persons' it is best to say simply 'Socrates is wise', where 'wise' now is a general term in predicative position that either applies or does not apply to the individual Socrates. All we need therefore in our logical apparatus are linguistic devices for referring to individuals and for functors which are descriptive of those individuals.

A collective class or individual whole need not be continuous, and there may be spatial or temporal gaps among some of its elements (parts, ingredients). Thus not only is the table on which I write an individual whole, but we may regard the United States of America as also a mereological individual whole in the same sense of 'whole', even though the United States of America consists of discontinuous parts, for example the forty-eight states between the borders of Canada and Mexico as well as Alaska and Hawaii. Similarly there is no reason, if it suits our convenience and purposes, not to treat as an individual whole (in the present sense) not only any individual dog, as ordinarily identified, but all dogs in the world both past and present, however scattered in space and time they may be.

We can distinguish, further, a collective class which has as its parts all *a*'s (for example, *all* dogs) from a collective class which, as an individual whole, is comprised, as to its parts, of some selection, some portion of the *a*'s. We may use the term *collection* in the special sense of being the latter type of individual whole. Thus a collection of *a*'s, as an individual whole or object, unlike the collective class of *all a*'s, need not comprise all *a*'s.[4] Thus the dogs owned by a certain family over a limited period of time could also be thought of as comprising an individual whole.

To be an individual whole does not require that it be comprised of parts of only one kind (of only *a*'s, or only *b*'s, and so on). Here again there is a departure from certain standard ways of thinking of 'classes' and as regulated for example in such use by a theory of types. Take our earlier example of the United States of America. From a mereological point of view, the United States of America as a whole does not consist simply of *states*. To be sure it includes New York,

Iowa, Maryland, and so on. But it also includes, as parts, the cities which are elements of these states, as well as villages, mountain chains, rivers, and so on; these too are parts or ingredients of this whole. If our use of the term 'class' were in the 'distributive' sense, the only correct constituents of a given class—for example, of the class 'state'—would be specific states, not, for example, specific cities or villages. But not so in the mereological use of 'class' as a collective whole, because cities and villages *are* parts of states. In brief: a mereological whole can be composed of the most heterogeneous kinds of things, of parts or ingredients to which predicates of the most diverse sorts apply.

There is no mereological null-class: there is no empty, nonexistent collective class or individual whole. (Although Leśniewski's Mereology has certain important analogies with classical Boolean algebra, it differs from it in this important respect that it has no null-class.[5])

There is no predetermined or uniquely correct way in which an individual whole is to be 'taken apart' or discriminated with respect to its parts. Such discrimination can be accomplished in many different ways, each of which may be warranted by some particular interest. Yet each of these, if it is to be correct, needs to be supported, of course, by relevant evidence, that is, by considerations of truth.

Any collective class of individuals is itself an individual. There is no distinction of 'type' as between what it is to be a 'collective class' or 'collective totality', as contrasted with what it is to be *an* individual. We can therefore speak of an 'individual whole' or an 'individual totality' or an 'individual collective class' without contradiction or incoherence.

If and only if at least one individual *a* exists (that is, an individual to which the description '*a*' truly applies), then at least one collective class (individual whole) exists to which that *same* description '*a*' also applies.

Nothing in the account given thus far of what it is to be a whole and the relation of a whole to its parts, requires any special presupposition as to the number or kinds of individuals there are in existence.

Nothing in the foregoing account is to be taken as entering the claim that the notions of 'part', 'collective class', or 'individual whole' are *all* that one needs on the conceptual side for carrying out an analysis of the distinctive qualities or relational structures among individual objects. Mereological notions of 'part' and 'whole' provide a fundamental orientation for ontology; they are not by themselves all-sufficing for carrying out a detailed analysis of the special characteristics of individuals. To accomplish such more detailed analyses, the notions of 'part' and 'whole' require supplementation by conceptual tools and distinctions appropriate to different subject matters. To work out the details of an ontology of individual existents would require a far more extensive series of analyses than is undertaken here. To this extent my own discussion has only been programmatic, pointing in the general direction of a mereological orientation to ontology.

8.3 *A Terminological Question*

Now that we have examined the sense in which we shall be using the term 'whole', we must turn next to bring this analysis to bear in giving meaning to the phrase 'the world as a whole'. And here we meet at the very outset a terminological question: Why fasten on the use of the term 'world'? Could we equally well have used the term 'universe' or the term 'existence' itself? And what of still other terms such as 'Nature', 'Reality', 'The One', 'Being' (among others) that philosophers have used? Is there any rationale for preferring some one or some selection from among these expressions rather than others?

I shall, in what follows, focus on the use of three terms specifically, namely, 'The Universe', 'The World', and 'Existence', and shall seek to bring out, for purposes of ontological analysis, the important connections among them, as well as the important differences in their meanings. Once we have been able to accomplish this analysis, it will be possible to use this analysis as a foil against which to consider the use of other terms. And we might then find that indeed *some* of the uses of these other terms might readily coincide with one or another of the terms 'The Universe', 'The World', 'Existence' as we shall have fixed their meanings. (I have in mind in this connection the use of such expressions as 'Nature', 'Being', 'The One', '*Brahman*', '*Tao*', 'God', 'Reality', '*Sein*', '*To Eon*', as well as others.) At that point we shall no longer need to be anxious, dogmatic, or insistent on the exclusive use of the terms to which we have chosen to devote our attention. Nevertheless, I choose to begin with the terms I have selected ('The Universe', 'The World', 'Existence') because I believe we can fix their uses for our purposes in a way which is relatively free of some of the unwanted associations and entanglements that attend the use of the other terms I have listed.

Consider, by way of brief example, the use of the terms 'Nature' and 'Reality'. The term 'Nature' has had a certain vogue among some American philosophers of the first half of the twentieth century (e.g., among Dewey, Woodbridge, Randall, and others). For these philosophers, Nature is ultimate and self-sufficient. This terminology is best understood, however, as part of an effort to counter the central claims of a supernaturalist or theistic philosophy. Again, the term 'Reality' was much in vogue among the Idealist philosophers of the late nineteenth and early twentieth centuries (e.g., among Bradley, Royce, and others). The choice of this term is associated with a central epistemological contrast between 'Appearance' and 'Reality', as well as with a special sense given to the notion of Reality as an Absolute Whole (one with which the ideas of 'Absolute Truth', 'Absolute Goodness', and 'Absolute Mind' are characteristically linked). In avoiding in my own discussion the use of the terms 'Nature' and 'Reality' as technical terms for ontology, and fastening instead on the use of terms 'The Universe', 'The World', and 'Existence', the intent is to disengage the use of the latter terms from the special contexts of controversy (e.g., of the Naturalists against supernaturalism, or of the Absolute Idealists against empiricistic pluralism and materialism) that lies behind the use of these other expressions, and to dwell simply on those meanings that would give us the opportunity to deal in a coherent way with the philosophic problem of existence as described earlier.

We must acknowledge at the outset, of course, that there is no standard, that is, universally accepted terminological use of the expressions, 'The Universe', 'The World', 'Existence'. For many writers, as indeed in colloquial speech, these three expressions may be used interchangeably. And further, some writers might prefer to use one rather than the other of these expressions, or to give the term thus selected some special or technical meaning. In the face of this situation all that one can reasonably do is to declare what one's own choices are, either from within the existing range of meanings or, if necessary, to introduce a new meaning altogether. I shall, accordingly, indicate how I propose to use the expressions 'The Universe', 'The World', and 'Existence'.

It will be one of the aims of my discussion to show why (for purposes of ontology and its eventual goal of understanding the meaning of the term 'existence') it is best to proceed by considering *first* the use of the term 'The Universe', *then* the use of the term 'The World', and *finally* the use of the term 'Existence'. There is an important point to be made in following this particular sequence. It represents a particular order of increasing abstraction. It would destroy our understanding of these terms if we reversed the sequence or took it in any other combination of steps.

Further, there is the question of whether, or to what extent, the notions of 'part' and 'whole' are to be understood in connection with each of these terms ('The Universe', 'The World', 'Existence'). I phrased our main question as "What does it mean to speak of 'The World as a whole'?" But we shall need to ask whether, or to what extent, we can speak of 'The Universe as a whole' or 'Existence as a whole'. Does it follow that if we can give a particular answer to one of these questions, that the same answer or type of answer can be given to the other questions? If not, why not?

8.4   *The Universe*

First, then, as to the expression 'The Universe'.

(a) This term is in use in astronomy, astrophysics, and cosmology. These sciences distinguish various types of bodies or physical systems, concerning which various types of empirical data are available. These bodies and physical systems are grouped according to different principles of classification and systematic interrelationships, including spatial groupings of wider and wider inclusiveness. Our own planet Earth is a member of a planetary system deployed about a central body, our Sun, itself a star among a very large number of stars (of various sorts) that together constitute our Galaxy. Our Galaxy, however, is in turn but one member of a local cluster of galaxies. And this cluster, in turn, belongs to an indeterminately large collection of individual galaxies and clusters of galaxies. It is to this last, and, as far as is known, this most inclusive collection of galaxies that in current use the term 'The Universe' is attached. The Universe, as far as the astronomer and cosmologist are concerned, is spatially and temporally the most inclusive system of bodies and material systems of which available instruments can obtain empirical data, which are now or have been at some point in physical and causal interconnection with one another, and concerning which inferences can be made in accordance with acceptable physical theory.

The term 'The Universe' is reserved, thus, for the collection of the galaxies, leaving other lesser, subordinate systems (for example, individual stars, planets, local intragalactic bodies of gas, and so on) outside the immediate concern of the cosmologist when he deals with The Universe on a cosmological scale of distances, a cosmological time scale, and with regard to the material composition and spatial distribution of its principal constituents. The observational astronomer, of course, is limited in his observational range by the limits of his actually available instruments as well as by the inherent limits of observability. In this last connection, there are—if certain recently elaborated theoretical considerations are accepted—cosmological horizons which establish limits of observability no matter how refined and technologically perfected our instruments may become.

In any case, the observable domain, at the present time, however vast, is itself but a fragment, a part of some wider, more inclusive domain. We can, then, distinguish the observable universe from this wider domain. In this usage, the phrase 'the observable universe' does *not* designate The Universe, not even The Universe observed, or as available or open for observational exploration, since it is but a *part* of some wider domain. The term 'The Universe' will commonly be employed in cosmology to designate the all-inclusive whole to which the observable universe (i.e., the observable region of galaxies and clusters of galaxies) belongs.

In constructing *models* of The Universe, the cosmologist will be guided, in the first place, by empirical considerations of extrapolation from the observable region. He will take The Universe to be constituted—as far as we know—of the same types of basic units (bodies and physical systems) as are already detected and known in the observable region: these will consist principally of galaxies and the intragalactic and extragalactic physico-chemical primordial elementary materials out of which the galaxies are fashioned and from which they are derived, genetically. In developing his models of The Universe, in addition to the guidance and constraints provided by the empirical materials of observational astronomy, the cosmologist will employ the resources of mathematical physics and mathematics to give to his constructions conceptual unity, clarity, and systematic coherence with established results in other domains. At the present time, despite the lively proliferation of models and the subtle refinement, in general, of the discipline of theoretic cosmology, there is no single, preferred model of The Universe on which the specialists are themselves agreed.

In any case, it is presumed that there is something to which the already developed, or yet-to-be-developed models can be applied and of which one or another might give us an acceptable descriptive account. That of which these various models aspire to give us an account is *The Universe*. This phrase, then, serves the astronomer and cosmologist as a designation of what it taken to be the independently existing individual whole possessed of the most inclusive spatial and temporal scope and that embraces within itself all subordinate bodies and systems. A provisional description of what The Universe is, is that it is a system of galaxies. However, the spatial extent and evolutionary pattern (the spatial and temporal structure) of that system, along with the precise physical principles that govern the interaction of its principal constituent parts, is not anything of which the cosmologist can give, as yet, a precise or secure account. So much, then, for a brief sketch of what the cosmologist and astronomer understand by 'The Universe'.[6]

Let us now bring to bear our earlier analysis of the terms 'part' and 'whole' in clarifying and making more precise these current usages of the terms 'observable universe' and 'Universe' as employed by the cosmologist.

In accordance with our previous analysis of the terms 'part' and 'whole', we can say that *the observable universe*, in the sense this term is used in astronomical cosmology, is itself both a part and also a whole. There is nothing in the use of the term 'whole' which precludes the fact that what is an individual whole (collective class, object) with respect to which we can discriminate parts $a, b, c \ldots$, should itself be a part with respect to some more inclusive whole (individual, collective class). Thus the observable universe is a whole with respect to its observationally identifiable parts—the galaxies observable at a given time with available instrumental resources—and is also a part of some wider, more inclusive whole.

Now suppose we take this 'wider, more inclusive whole' to be an observable region (volume of space) that would be observable were more refined observational resources to become available. We could then ask with respect to this still wider, more inclusive whole whether it, in turn, might be taken as part of some still more inclusive whole. At this point the question naturally arises whether there is some inclusive whole such that either it itself is wholly observable, or all observable regions would be parts of it, and such that it itself is not part of any still more inclusive whole. One way of defining what 'The Universe' is for cosmology is to give an affirmative answer to this question. The Universe then would be that individual whole such that anything that is at any given time taken to be 'the observable universe' is either co-extensively identical with The Universe, or is a part of The Universe, and such that The Universe is not, and cannot be part of some wider, more inclusive whole. In order to leave room for the possible validity of those theories that claim there are cosmological horizons of observability, it would be necessary to define what 'The Universe' is to allow for this. This may be done by saying that The Universe is the single *spatially and temporally* unified, all-inclusive whole all of whose parts are, or at some time have been, within the range of observability or within the range of causal interaction with one another.

In this sense one could say The Universe is an *absolute* whole, since by definition it is not and cannot be part of some more inclusive whole. Should it turn out that what is taken to be The Universe (i.e., what is described as 'The Universe') as an absolute whole is in fact only a part of some still more inclusive whole, it would be a misuse of terminology to continue to describe what is now recognized as being only a part, as 'The Universe'.[7] It is necessary here to make a distinction between a terminological question and factual considerations.

Terminologically, it is a mistake to think of (to define, to conceive) 'The Universe' in any other way but as 'the most inclusive whole'; nor, for the same reason, would it be correct to speak of '*many* Universes'. Nevertheless one may be factually mistaken, at some stage of inquiry, in believing that some identifiable collection of objects and physical systems is, genuinely, The Universe, that is, is appropriately so *called* or *named*. For some fresh factual discoveries or conceptual revisions in cosmological theory itself may involve the introduction of some entirely new way of construing what the special physical and space-time properties of The Universe are, and thus what was formerly thought to be The Universe turns out to be only part of The Universe as now conceived. In short, the term 'The Universe' needs to be reserved for what, at a given stage of inquiry, is taken to be (is defined as being) spatially and temporally the absolute, most inclusive whole.

Suppose one were to ask: "Does The Universe exist?" In the light of the foregoing analysis, it would appear that this question is really *two* questions: (1) Does there exist an individual whole such that we can apply to it the description 'absolute, all-inclusive whole'? (2) Does there exist an individual all-inclusive whole that has the character (astronomical composition, physical, space-time properties) as formulated in some particular cosmological model? For the science of cosmology the answer to the *first* question is idle unless one also includes along with it the asking of the *second* question. And to this compound question scientific cosmology could never, by its very nature qua science, give a final and conclusive answer, since the answer to the second question is in principle always open to revision. The realization of this point lends some support to a reformulated version of the Kantian thesis that the notion of a cosmological whole serves in an important way as a regulative notion for cosmology.[8]

If one insisted, however, on an answer to the first question alone, namely, "Does there exist an absolute all-inclusive whole?" then one would have to say that the decision with respect to *this* question is at any rate *not* a scientific, empirical question. For until and unless one supplies a further description, it is irresolvable scientifically. In short, for scientific cosmology the situation is this. We define 'The Universe' to include the conjunction of the following two components: (i) an invariable, *a priori* component consisting of the statement that 'The Universe is spatially and temporally an absolute, all-inclusive whole'; (ii) an empirical mathematical-physical component consisting of a statement of the particular space-time, physical character of The Universe. (The statement of this second component is variable, changing for different models.) Then for scientific cosmology 'The Universe' is the conjunction of (i) and (ii). And it is impossible (that is, scientifically futile) to try to determine whether anything answers to the description 'The Universe' without including *both* components. It is for this reason, too, that we should have to say that, for scientific cosmology, knowledge about The Universe is open-ended, that is, not finally and irrevocably determinable.

(b) Now there is another use of the term 'The Universe' we must also take note of, which is in some ways a natural extension of the meaning given to this expression in astronomy and cosmology. We said that for the astronomer-cosmologist 'The Universe' is a term usually reserved for that level of interest—in terms of distances, time-stretches, and material composition—in which he neglects, as beyond his immediate concern, any lesser systems or stretches of time and space that are not on a cosmological scale, that is, on a scale appropriate for the galaxies and *their* spatial distribution and evolutionary (temporal) development. But, after all, The Universe in this sense is only the outer frame on the grossest scale of spatial, temporal, and material magnitude that includes, however, within itself all manner of lesser bodies and systems. And when we turn our attention to these, it is necessary to reintroduce not only the astronomical bodies previously 'neglected' when dealing with cosmological matters (such bodies as individual stars within the galaxies, our own solar system with its Sun, the several planets, and our own Earth and its Moon) but also, of course, a great variety of other types of bodies, systems, and phenomena of still more restricted scales of magnitude and of varying material composition, structure, functional roles, and levels of evolutionary development.

These would include such matters as geologic formations (rivers, mountains, continents, oceans), biological phenomena of all sorts, the whole range and multifariousness of human behavior, and the enormous complexity of atomic and subatomic physical phenomena. The Universe surely includes all of these as well, from the galaxies to the grains of sand on the beach and the generations of men and animals, and the lives of individual men in their 'endless' succession, diversity, and multiplicity. In this use of the term 'The Universe' we should need to muster for its description all the descriptive resources of our language, of our ordinary experience, and of our scientific knowledge in order to be able to give an account of its parts, fragments, ingredients, and constituents, as well as what it might be said to be as a 'whole'. We can sum it up by saying that

The Universe is "the heavens, the earth, the seas and all that in them is", or we could, if pressed, be far more specific, detailed, and encyclopedic in our descriptions, enumerations, classifications, and systematizations.

Let us understand, then, by 'The Universe' in this broadened and extended sense, the individual whole or collective class of all the *a*'s, *b*'s, *c*'s ... we are able to (or choose to) discriminate and list as belonging to, and as being parts of, this whole. Finally, let us note and stress again, that the term 'The Universe' in the wider meaning just briefly indicated (just as in the narrower meaning of the astronomer-cosmologist) is a name that designates an individual whole of which we might undertake to give a *description* or *descriptions*, and whose parts, too, are to be discriminated through the use of *descriptive* terms.

So much for what we may understand, in a general and rough way, by 'The Universe' when this term is extended beyond its more restricted use in scientific cosmology and made to encompass matters normally bypassed in cosmology. But once again it will be of some interest and importance, in order to refine these ideas, to bring in our earlier analysis of 'whole' and 'part'. And just as we undertook earlier to fix the precise sense in which, in the cosmologist's use, we may speak of The Universe as a 'whole', so now too we shall need to examine in what sense and to what extent we may speak of The Universe in the extended sense as itself a *whole*.

In considering to what extent we may say The Universe, from the vantage point of cosmology, is a whole, we saw the value of introducing the notion of 'an *absolute* whole'. We applied this notion exclusively to The Universe, since although lesser systems (for example, an individual galaxy, cluster of galaxies, or even the observable region of galaxies) may be characterized as being wholes, each may also be recognized as being parts of some more inclusive whole. And in characterizing an absolute whole as one which, though it itself has parts, is not in turn part of some more inclusive whole, we found this latter characterization uniquely suited to what we should wish to call 'The Universe'.

Now *this* feature of what we mean by 'an absolute whole' that we found applicable to The Universe, when approached cosmologically, is also to be retained in the meaning of 'The Universe' in its *extended* sense. Surely too in this extended meaning The

Universe would need to be thought of as an absolute whole. This is to say it includes, as parts, not only galaxies but all and any sorts of objects, systems, phenomena of whatever magnitude, scale, material composition, evolutionary development, or temporal duration. Moreover, while it includes in this way everything as parts, it itself is not part of some more inclusive whole; it is for this reason that we speak of it as an *absolute* whole.

There is, however, an important *difference* in the reason for saying The Universe from a cosmological perspective is an absolute whole and the reason for saying The Universe in its extended meaning is an absolute whole. It is this. The primary consideration in determining whether, for cosmological purposes, a whole is a *relative* whole (one which may be part of some more inclusive whole) or an *absolute* whole is the matter of the *space and time dimensions* of the whole under consideration. The matter of *inclusiveness* is essentially a matter of *how extensive spatially and temporally* a whole is. The Universe in cosmological perspective is an absolute whole because it is not possible, definitionally, for it to be *exceeded* with respect to its *spatial and temporal extent* by some other whole.

When we turn to the sense in which we wish to think of The Universe in the extended sense as an absolute whole, the spatial and temporal extent of The Universe, though not to be exceeded, is only *one* of the reasons we wish to characterize it as absolute. This time, however, the matter of its being 'the most inclusive' is not just a matter of its spatial and temporal dimension. It also has to do with the *contents*, whatever these may be. To be an absolute whole, in this extended sense, requires that no part—that is, no individual of whatever character, dimension, structure, type of evolutionary development, and so on—be *left out* in any enumeration or identification of the parts of this absolute whole. Thus whereas in the identification and enumeration of the parts of any relative whole we should leave out objects, phenomena, qualities, and the like that are not genuine parts of it, this could not be done in the case of The Universe as an absolute whole. Thus we should say our Solar system (as a relative whole) includes as parts, for example, the Earth and our Sun, but it does *not* include, say, the star Sirius or the Andromeda nebula. Again, the United States of America as a relative whole includes as parts, for example, New York City and Los Angeles, but not Paris or Tokyo. Or again, my body as a relative whole includes, as parts, my heart and lungs but not yours. And so on. In the case of The Universe, however, as an absolute whole, *nothing is to be excluded*. The Universe includes everything as a part within itself, and with nothing left out.

I have just used the word 'everything'. In trying to explicate what lies behind the use of this term, another consideration presents itself. And here, once again, it will be useful to remind ourselves of what we said earlier in connection with The Universe when considered merely from a cosmological point of view. We said that the use of the term 'The Universe' in cosmology included two components: (a) an invariant '*a priori*' (definitional) component, that is, a requirement that The Universe be conceived as spatially and temporally the most inclusive whole, and (b) the empirical requirement that its particular character as an absolutely all-inclusive spatio-temporal whole be specified by some model or other. And we also pointed out in this connection that if one were to ask, therefore, "Does The Universe exist?", for *scientific cosmology* the answer to this question depends on taking into account *both* components in the meaning of 'The Universe'. Further, because of the uneliminable corrigibility in any knowledge-claim that makes use of the second (empirical) component, we could never give a final answer to this question.

Now in turning to our enlarged sense of 'The Universe' and the way in which we said of it that it, too, is an absolute whole, we shall need to make a series of analogous remarks. For once more it would be helpful to say that in this (enlarged) sense of 'The Universe' there are *two* components. The first is the one we stated earlier—'that it include everything, that nothing be excluded'. This too is an invariant *a priori* definitional demand, and would have to be included in *any* adequate characterization of what we *mean* by 'The Universe'. However, its effective meaning is *negative*: 'nothing is to be excluded'. But we should need to add to it a second, this time an empirical or descriptive component. And upon this component falls the burden of giving some *positive* descriptive account of the parts of The Universe. Such a descriptive component would need to consist, at the very least, of an enumeration or listing of the component parts. But here we face at once a crucial fact. We can give a list—a very long list—of *some* of the parts of The Universe. But however long that list may be (and some lists will be longer than others), we should need to break off at some point and admit that the list is incomplete, that it could be made longer, since no actual list could exhaust everything that is a genuine part of The Universe.

There are several reasons for this inevitable incompleteness of any *descriptive* listing of the parts of The Universe. There are, first of all, actual limits, at any given time, for any given person or group of persons (however large the latter may be), in their memory, experience, and knowledge of the actual individuals in The Universe, to which descriptive characterizations '*a*', '*b*', '*c*', and so on may be assigned. Let us remember that however many individuals we collect to which we assign, say, the descriptive characterization '*a*' by virtue of their resemblances to one another, it is the *individuals* thus collected that are ultimately the *parts* of The Universe. Yet the knowledge any one person or group of persons has at any time of actual individuals to which a common descriptive predicate may be applied, is limited, however extensive that knowledge may be.

Not only do we never have anything like a complete, direct knowledge of all the individuals in the present or the past to which a common description '*a*' may be attached, but we also lack, even more fundamentally, any direct knowledge of such *actual individuals* that will emerge in the future, and that are *also* to be included in any presumptively complete listing of the contents or individual parts of The Universe. For example, the innumerably large number of persons that will be born on the Earth for as long as individual men continue to procreate and for as long as the Earth is able to sustain life are also therefore to be included as parts of The Universe, although we have no way *now* of identifying those individuals.

Moreover, the open texture of The Universe as far as its individual parts are concerned is not simply to be assigned to the fact that we do not know, at any given time, what are all the individuals to which a given description '*a*' may be assigned. For in addition we can never be sure that the range of descriptive predicates we do already have available will suffice to describe all the individuals there are in fact in The Universe. The origin of new biological species, the discovery of new types of objects and phenomena hitherto unsuspected (e.g., the quasars) and the possibility, too, that in the far reaches of time and space altogether novel types of individuals are to be found or will be found, remind us surely of how naïve it would be to claim that one could, in practice, exhaustively identify and enumerate all individual parts of The Universe.

Finally, let us remember that what counts as an individual to which the descriptive label '*a*' will be attached, is a function of human powers of discrimination and interest. Since these may and do vary, what lists of 'individuals' one person or group of persons may draw up of the individual parts of The Universe need not be the same as what another does. There is, therefore, an inescapable relativity to criteria or standards of choice and discrimination in identifying what is called 'an individual' that makes any listing of the individual contents of The Universe something for which no unanimity or 'objective' completeness *could* be reached. So much, then, for the reasons one might give for saying that as far as giving an empirical *listing* of the parts of The Universe goes, there is an inherent incompleteness, flexibility, and openness that accompanies all such putative listings.

It follows from all of this of course, too, that precisely because there is no finality that can be claimed for any empirical listing of the parts of The Universe, that any presumption to give an empirically sound account of The Universe as an absolute whole qua *Individual whole* is also therefore doomed to failure. That there may be important and useful unifications and systematizations of regions, segments, parts of The Universe need in no way, of course, be denied. After all, science thrives upon and is inspired by the hope of achieving, and does in fact increasingly achieve, such partial unifications all the time. But what one might be legitimately skeptical of is the possibility of achieving a *total* unification and systematization that would hold for The Universe as an absolute whole. The attempt to formulate such total unifications in terms of the notions of 'mechanism', 'atomism', 'creative evolution', and so on, strew the pages of intellectual history. Whatever the imaginative appeal of such grandiose speculative syntheses, they must not only be set down as 'premature', but—more seriously—as incapable of attracting to themselves any serious empirical acceptability and warrant.

What all this comes down to, then, is that with respect to the idea of The Universe in the extended sense as an absolute whole, there is an ineluctable openness and uncompletability in it, because of the 'positive' empirical component. The idea of The Universe as an absolute whole functions nevertheless—to adopt the Kantian terminology—as an important *regulative* one. And here, in terms of the distinction we have made between the invariable '*a priori*' and 'empirical' components in the notion of The Universe as an absolute whole, we might say it is the invariable *a priori* component (that The Universe includes everything, that nothing be excluded) that continually drives on any presumed empirical synthesis or listing with the reminder that it is not and cannot be final.

8.5   *The World*

As to the expression 'The World', as previously remarked, there are some who would use the term interchangeably with 'The Universe', while some would prefer one expression to the other, even though giving roughly the same account of what they mean. There are also some who use the term 'The Universe' in a quite different sense from those we ourselves have just examined, and for our purposes, settled on. Among the uses of the term 'The Universe' that some writers employ is one which I shall in fact adopt, but instead of using the expression 'The Universe' for this, I shall use the expression 'The World'. I propose now, and shall henceforward use the expression 'The World' to mean 'The individual whole (or collective class) whose parts are all existents whatsoever'. This meaning of 'The World' corresponds to the definition given in Mereology to the expression 'Universe' (symbolized '*Un*') and concerning which various theorems have been established. Sobocinski expresses the matter as follows: "*A* is the Universe if *A* is the mereological class of all existing objects." [9]

It will be asked immediately, of course, what the difference is between the meaning of 'The World' and 'The Universe'. To this I should reply that if by 'meaning' is meant 'reference' or 'designation' and thereby we intend to ask "What is the difference in the *designation* of the expressions 'The World' and 'The Universe'?"—the answer is: "There is none!" Both expressions refer to identically the same individual whole. The World is identical with The Universe. There is nevertheless a difference in what Frege would have called the 'sense' as distinguished from the 'reference', since the formulas or analyses we give to explicate their sense *do* differ. The sense of 'The Universe' (in its broader employment, of the two we described) is given in part by the descriptive terminology taken from the empirical sciences of cosmology, astronomy, geology, biology, and so on. The formula for describing the composition and structure of the Individual Whole that is The Universe is, in effect, an indeterminately large number of sentences, each of which would undertake to describe the cosmological structure of The Universe as a whole or some part of The Universe. Anything that exists is a part of The Universe—in the mereological sense—however arbitrarily demarcated this may be, and whether described in ordinary language or in scientific terminology. Not only is the listing of the parts an inherently arbitrary matter (there is no uniquely correct way of doing this), but also because of the changing and growing character of human knowledge, there is no final list or description of structural arrangements that *can* be given of the parts. In a sense, therefore, giving a *description* (or descriptions) of The Universe is an enterprise that is not only not finished now, but that, for the reasons given, cannot in principle ever be completed in some final, irrevocable, and uniquely correct way. Yet an appreciation of this point does not in any way lessen the utility of the expression 'The Universe', provided we understand its open-ended character and the inherent limitations and relativities connected with its use.

But when we turn to the sense to be given to the expression 'The World', the situation is different. For here, unlike the *open-ended, descriptive* character of the expression 'The Universe', there is a certain finality and closed character—one is tempted to say an *a priori* character—to the use of the expression 'The World'. It has, we might say, a quasi-formal character. (I use the expression 'quasi-formal' because, after all, in talking about The World, even though we use the descriptively empty and neutral expression 'existent', nevertheless we are, by these means, talking ontologically about what *does* exist. Each and every existent, and the whole these compose, is not a formal matter; it is not merely a symbolic or linguistic matter, which it would be if the formulas were altogether *purely* formal.)

In using the formula 'the whole which has all individual existents as its parts' to explicate what we mean by 'The World', we make no attempt to go beyond this and give an actual *descriptive* account of either the whole or its parts. It is sufficient for the account of The World to talk simply of individual existents and the whole which they compose. We need not, for this purpose, specify or describe what these existents or individuals are. To be sure, there cannot be—and I am not claiming for one moment that there can be—individuals that are *just* or *only* existents. On the contrary, we have seen in our earlier discussion how the term 'existent', though not itself a descriptive term, is attached to the use of an individual name that does explicitly or implicitly involve descriptive terms as part of its meaning. (There cannot be—to put it in linguistic terms for the moment—just the semantic index 'existent' as *taking the place* of an individual name or definite description in a true *empirical* statement.) Our understanding of what it is to exist is always accompanied by, and embedded in, a subject that possesses specific qualities and relations. Nevertheless, one may separate out, for purposes of philosophic analysis, their existence-aspect, and it is this existence-aspect *alone* that is of relevance in considering what is essential to the nature of The World and its parts. In short, the term 'The World' serves the purposes of ontology by prescinding from The Universe just its existence-aspect, and the term 'individual existent' similarly serves the purposes of ontology in prescinding from the parts of The Universe, whatever they may be, *their* existence-aspect.

In discussing The Universe and its parts (whether on a cosmological level or in the 'extended' sense), we stressed the need to include in any explication of the meaning of 'The Universe' a variable empirical component in addition to an invariable *a priori* one. What 'The Universe' means cannot be brought out without including *both* components. Now, in talking about The World and its parts, we are able to give an account that does not explicitly contain any empirical component. We do not need to know in detail, or by making particular descriptive specifications of the structure of the whole or its parts, anything at all about those details or that character in order to have an understanding of what it is to exist, whether as the whole or as a part. Whatever specifications of a descriptive sort one may give of the particular character of The Universe or its parts, or whatever changes or modifications one may be obliged to make as a result of fresh discoveries in those specifications, will not affect in the slightest our comprehension of what we mean by 'The World' or by 'individual existent'. For any new or different empirical account of The Universe as a whole or any of its parts will only provide the *same kind* of material for ontologic discourse about existence. And *any* examples—however limited and open to modification on an empirical level these are—are adequate for this conceptual purpose of ontology. Despite our always-present, relative ignorance and uncertainty about the makeup and extent of The Universe we can say that insofar as our conception of The World is an invariant quasi-formal one, no further or deeper experience need affect our *conception* of The World. No matter what changes and discoveries will be made with respect to The Universe by the various sciences, the ontologic account of The World will not be affected. The *philosophic* understanding of 'exists' ('existent', 'existence') need not change as a result of any growth or change in empirical knowledge.

Is The World an absolute whole? Yes—in the specific sense that it includes, without exception, anything that is an individual existent as one of its parts. To qualify as being an individual existent it is necessary that something be part of The Universe, and if something is part of The Universe that already makes that something an individual existent. It is not the other way around. This is the point of starting with The Universe and its parts in undertaking a discussion of existence in ontology.

If to 'qualify' as an existent it is necessary and sufficient to be *part of The Universe*, why should we not say that *this* is the meaning (the definition) of what it is to be *an individual existent*? Is not, therefore, the expression 'individual existent' replaceable by the expression 'part of The Universe'? To this our answer has to be a (qualified) "Yes!" "But, then," it will be said, "we don't need the term 'existent' at all!" And the answer to this is that, strictly speaking, we don't! But normally, in characterizing what it is to be a 'part of The Universe', we require the use of *descriptive* terms in saying what the character of the part is. We describe its properties, for example, its space-time locus (its size, its duration, its location in the past, present, or future), its qualities and relations (for example, its color, its chemical composition, etc.). All of this, however, is unnecessary as far as being simply an *existent* is concerned, although it is necessary in being the particular propertied kind of individual part it is. As a particular part, therefore, we should label it an '*a*' or a '*b*' or a '*c*' and so on (e.g., a 'city', a 'bird', a 'star', etc.) However, in order to be an individual *existent* we need none of these descriptive terms. However important they are for being the particular kinds of parts they are, such descriptive characterizations are unimportant and irrelevant when it comes to considering them simply as existents, that is, simply insofar as they are *parts* of The Universe. Therefore, in this sense *all* parts are equal, *qua* parts, and we only need therefore the term 'existent' to 'describe' them. Except, of course, that the term 'existent' is *not* a description in the sense in which the particular terms '*a*', '*b*', '*c*' *are* descriptive terms. The term 'existent' or 'part' simply indicates *the ontological status* of what we are talking about: that it is a part of The Universe, *and nothing more.* Hence if we use terms like '*a*', '*b*', '*c*', and so on to describe particular parts of The Universe, we cannot include among these terms the term 'existent' itself.

The expression 'individual existent' is thus a 'formal' concept in Wittgenstein's sense of this expression. Wittgenstein, building on a point introduced by Frege, points out that it is necessary to distinguish what he calls 'formal concepts' (or sometimes also 'pseudo-concepts') from ordinary or 'proper' concepts. An ordinary or proper concept, such as 'cat' or 'star', can be represented by means of a descriptive predicate. When we apply a proper or ordinary concept to some individual and say of it that it is a such-and-such, say a cat or a star, we are saying something informative, and what we are saying is either true or false; it either fits or does not fit that to which we are applying this concept. In contrast with such concepts, however, Wittgenstein calls attention to what he calls 'formal concepts'; these concepts cannot be identified with descriptive predicates. Nor can they be used informatively about something. They have to do rather with the way in which certain signs are used. Thus for Wittgenstein the concepts 'thing', 'object', 'fact', 'concept', 'function', 'number', 'complex' are all formal concepts. They have to do with special types of variables and the way in which these are used in our language. The way of characterizing a formal concept is to show its distinctive use, that which distinguishes it from other formal concepts.[10]

What I am calling 'an individual existent' exemplifies what Wittgenstein calls a 'formal' or 'pseudo-concept'. He points out, for example, that since the expression 'object' is, according to this terminology, a formal concept: "it is nonsensical to speak of the *total number* of objects" (*Tractatus*, 4.1272.) *For the same reason it would also be nonsensical to speak of the total number of individual existents as such.*

It also follows from the above that if 'existent' is not a descriptive term, then there is no *kind* of objects we call 'existent' ones. Hence it makes no sense, strictly speaking, to talk of a *collective class* or *Individual Whole of existents as such*. What then, it may be asked, becomes of our statement that The World is the Individual Whole whose parts are existents? And why should we not treat the expression 'The World' as having the same meaning as 'The Universe'? To this latter question the answer is: "We can!—*provided*, however, we separate out as necessary and sufficient the invariant and purely 'formal' part of the meaning of 'The Universe', namely, that it is an absolute whole from which nothing is to be excluded, and that is itself not part of any more inclusive whole." Just as we retain the term 'individual existent' as a shorthand for 'any part of The Universe', so we can retain the term 'The World' to stand for just that part of the meaning of 'The Universe' which consists in its purely formal component, leaving out, *for this purpose*, any further descriptive specification of the particular character of either the cosmological (space-time) structure of The Universe or any enumeration, in descriptive terms, of its contents.

Just as to speak of individual existents, qua individual existents, as *parts*, is to use the term 'part' in a stretched or deviant way as compared to the sense in which it is used when exemplified descriptively (as '*a*', '*b*', '*c*', etc.), so too the term '*individual whole*' when used to characterize The World is also to use the term 'individual whole' in a stretched or deviant way. For if the 'parts' (individual existents) are not parts in any ordinary way, then neither can the Individual Whole which is 'composed' of these 'parts' be a 'whole' in any ordinary way. Yet for all that there is value in using this terminology of 'whole' and 'part' in connection with The World and individual existents. For it does remind us of their essential connection with, and derivability from, The Universe (in the full sense) and *its* parts (in the full sense). And such attenuated use of the terms 'whole' and 'part' in connection with The World and individual existents has a certain value, for it permits the use of these terms, now *analogically* rather than *literally*, for ontological purposes.

8.6 *Existence*

What now of 'existence'? Is this a term we need *at all*? We said that with properly understood qualifications we can define 'individual existent' as meaning 'part of The Universe'. And similarly we pointed out that with appropriate restrictions in the meaning of 'The Universe' we could use the expression 'The World' as its equivalent or synonym. Yet where, or how, with respect to the latter pair of terms ('The Universe' and 'The World') does the expression 'existence' come into *their* analysis as Individual Wholes? If the expression 'existent' or 'existence' is either replaceable or perhaps not needed at all, are we not facing, apparently, the thoroughly deflating outcome that the whole subject of ontology (since it has allegedly the analysis of 'existence' as its core problem) is itself about to disappear—like the grin on the Cheshire cat—leaving us with no subject matter at all!?

We must turn then finally to examine what we can say of existence itself in the light of our previous discussion of 'The Universe' and 'The World'. Far from evaporating, I shall argue that we are now in a better position to come to a genuine understanding of the import of this term, and that its retention is not only of fundamental importance, but what it signifies *cannot* be eliminated. We should delude ourselves if we thought that we could dispense entirely with this 'concept'. For while, to be sure, the *word* 'existence' is easily replaceable, we should not have succeeded in getting rid of *some expression* that now carries the burden of what *it* signifies. In short, the expression 'existence' is philosophically a 'rock-bottom' one such that—try as we may—we should not avoid appealing to it in some form, or in some new (and perhaps unsuspected) terminological guise.

The thesis I shall argue for may be summed up briefly as follows: Existence is what it is *to be* The Universe itself. This is a tautology. The expression '*to be' as here used means the same as 'Existence*'. What Existence is cannot be grasped conceptually and is transcendent of all that is conceptually intelligible. It is that which remains when all particularity, differentiation, and predicative (conceptual, descriptive) distinctions have been left behind.

There is a preliminary point worth making to avoid misunderstanding. I wish to direct our attention to what is the '*referent*' of our use of the word 'Existence'. I shall not be using the capitalized expression 'Existence' to refer to something about our language, or the use of linguistic expressions, or about 'semantic indices' for this or that expression. I shall be talking about what we may try to convey by means of language; but what Existence is, is not essentially linguistic, not even partly or ambiguously linguistic. It is what is 'out there'—whether we are aware of it or not, whether we manage to capture and articulate it (in some way) in language or not. I return to our primitive, preanalytic intuitions (which I take to be sound) and which assure us that *The World* (The Universe) exists, that *this table* exists, that *I* exist, and so on. I wish to consider *Existence* in connection with what we are talking about when we use these sentences. And I wish, specifically, to see what it means to say it is *Existence* about which in some way we *can* have an awareness, and concerning which we can attempt to direct the use of our language in order to refer to *it*.

I proceed to develop the foregoing points. And to begin with let me examine, first, the use of the capitalized expression 'Existence' as I intend to employ it. I wish to consider it as it arises in the context of considering The World as an Individual Whole.

Thus far, in reaching our conception of how to characterize The World as an Individual Whole whose constituent parts are individual existents, we have relied for the purposes of describing it *as* 'a whole' (in an attenuated sense) on the fact that it is 'composed' of a mul tiplicity of 'parts' (again in an attenuated sense). Let us now carry this process of attenuation one step further. The parts of The World, though we continue to speak of them in the plural as individual existen*t*s, are, however, *qua* existents, *not different* from one another. Their plural differentiation stems from the use of descriptive predicates and such individuating descriptions (e.g., space-time locations) as we may find relevant. However, these are no longer operative when we characterize something as simply 'an individual existent'. Because of this we shall be further prepared to relinquish all differentiation of individuals. For the use of the expression '*individual* existent' on this level of discourse is by courtesy only—by virtue of our remembrance of the way in which we originally came to identify such and such *as* an individual, that is, through its being a part of The Universe, and through its being described in an individuating way. Since these criteria of differentiation are not now operative, there is, in effect, no longer any distinction between *one* individual *existent* and *another* individual *existent*. The 'existent'-aspect of each now blends with the 'existent'-aspect of any other individual existent. The result-ant of this process of 'blending' is *one* way of coming upon what I intend by the use of the term 'Existence'.

But instead of starting with the 'multiplicity' of individual exist-ents, we may start at the other end, and reach the same conclusion, the same awareness of Existence. We spoke of The World as an Individual Whole, as a unique, all-inclusive absolute whole of all individual existents. Let us focus now on this matter of its being an absolute unique Individual, *qua Individual*, neglecting for the moment the consideration that it is composed of a multiplicity of parts. That it is not an individual in the ordinary sense in which we speak of parts of The Universe—for example, Socrates, this table, that lightning flash —as individuals, we have already brought out. *They* are individuals in the full sense because (1) they are proper parts of The Universe, and (2) they can be described (e.g., located). The World is neither of these. *It* is not a proper part of any more inclusive individual whole. And, qua 'whole' it is not open to the use of descriptive predicates (e.g., it has no shape, color, size, location, duration, numerical magnitude of any sort, chemical composition, etc.). If we continue to speak of The World as an 'individual' it is so only in a very special sense. It is properly speaking an Individual only insofar as it is *absolutely unique*. There are no other Worlds. Nevertheless, The World exists. The 'Individual' which The World is, exists.

Since we may, on the one hand, continue to speak of The World as an *Individual*, and yet, on the other hand, we have spoken of the individual parts of The World (when we regard it as a 'Whole' of 'parts') as being *existents*, it would be inadvisable (because misleading) to characterize The World as an utterly unique Individual as itself *an existent*. If we use the expression 'existent' to designate any individual (proper) part of The World (to the extent that we think of The World as a 'whole' of 'parts'), then the word 'existent' cannot also be used to stand for the utterly unique 'Individual' which The World is. If we keep the expression 'individual existent' to mean (proper) *part* of The World, insofar as The World is thought of as a 'whole' of 'parts', then we shall need another expression to designate and differentiate the utterly unique existence of The World as an 'Individual'. For surely if there is anything at all which has a primary lien on our use of the word 'existence' it is The World itself. It is an inexpungeable truth that The World exists. This is the merest tautology. And one way of bringing this out is to drop the use of the grammatical predicate 'exists' and to use its nominalized counterpart. Because we wish to signalize the sense in which The World as an utterly unique 'Individual' exists, we capitalize the word 'existence'. *The World (as an utterly unique 'Individual') is (iden-*

tically) *Existence*. The two expressions that flank the (identity) use of 'is' here have *the same* 'referent' as their target. To be The World as an absolutely unique 'Individual' *is* Existence.

When we combine these two routes, that through 'blending' the multiplicity of individual existents, and that through reflecting on the utterly unique character which The World as an 'Individual' is, we arrive at the same result: The World as undifferentiated and as utterly unique *is* Existence.

Is Existence a Whole? The question now answers itself. If 'whole' (whether relative or absolute) is defined relatively to 'part', then in the sense we have tried to make clear, Existence cannot be said to be a Whole because it does not have any parts *at all*, even in an attenuated way. The use of the term 'whole', just as the use of any other term to *analyze* it, is totally inappropriate and ultimately futile. It is so utterly unique that any attempt to explicate what it is in *simpler* terms, or by finding what it shares by way of resemblance with something else we are already (independently) familiar with, *must fail*. We have used the analysis of 'whole' and 'part' as a ladder to climb to our awareness of Existence. But once we reach it, we can "throw the ladder away." Existence is the supreme ontological fact for which a discussion of even the discrete ontological character of individual existents, let alone the discussion of the parts of The Universe in their full-blown qualitative particularity, were only preliminary steps and halfway houses toward its final disclosure.

If there is any paradox in saying individual existents are parts of The World as a Whole, though Existence is not a 'whole' and has no 'parts', the clue to dissolving the paradox is at hand in terms of the distinctions we have drawn. We need not be troubled to acknowledge that it makes perfectly good sense to say that while Existence is itself not diversified, not a complex whole, nevertheless in another way of regarding the matter, The World is constituted of individual existents. Again it would be perfectly correct (though sounding paradoxical) to say that The Universe, The World, and Existence are one and the same, though utterly different! The key to dissolving the 'paradox' is in recognizing the order of 'abstraction' and awareness on which we base the use of these terms and what they represent.

What Existence is, in itself, is ultimate, irreducible, and unassimilable to any conceptual, that is to say, explanatory or descriptive, characterization whatsoever. The presupposition that if something exists it must yield to some positive description, that it must be possible to assimilate it in some fashion to what we already know, to that which in some way is already familiar, is one that we commonly employ in our everyday dealing with objects, persons, events, and situations. It is a presupposition that is deeply embedded in our use of language, and in the processes of thought that such language serves to express.

We inevitably use general terms in giving descriptions, whether for example these consist of definitions of the meaning of a general term or in giving definite descriptions of individuals. General terms by their very nature are founded in their meaning and use on the possibility of establishing resemblances of some degree or other among individuals we encounter in our experience, whether these individuals are things, occurrences, persons, or situations. However distinctive any individual is, there is always some respect in which we find it comparable to some other individual; and the fact of such resemblance-associations is the basis of our varied efforts to assimilate, that is, to classify and describe anything whatsoever by reference to other cases with which it is compared, and with which it is brought into connection.

It follows therefore that if anything were absolutely unique, that is, wholly incomparable and incapable of assimilation to resemblance-classes of one sort or another, we should not be able to give a description of it, since we should not be able to use general terms at all. All we could do, if there were such an 'entity', would be to say over and over again, "not this," "not that". Our account would be completely negative, and this of course would raise the question whether under these conditions we could be said to have given an 'account' at all, since in our normal use of this term we mean our ability to say something positive about whatever it is to which we are referring; and such positive descriptions are always available or possible because, as we have pointed out, the use of general terms is always feasible. If something were absolutely and wholly unique, however, it would not be possible to say anything positive at all about it because it could not be brought into comparison with, or possess some degree of, resemblance to anything else; we should not be able to describe it by the use of a general descriptive term, since it would not be *like* anything else whatever.

In the case of Existence our 'account' (so called for the moment) must always be of this negative sort, because Existence cannot be assimilated to anything else. Existence is not a member of a resemblance-class, that is, it cannot be described by a general term or set of general terms. It is in this respect utterly unique: we can use, therefore, the traditional terms 'The One' (not of course in a numerical sense) or 'The Wholly Other' as synonymous with 'Existence'. In this respect the expression 'Existence' cannot, strictly speaking, even be called an individual name, in the sense in which we should ordinarily use an individual name for something that can in some fashion, be described. This not the case with Existence. It is wholly futile to think of 'Existence' as a term that might function as a referring phrase in a predicational statement and the reason is that whenever we use a referring phrase we do so normally in a context in which we wish to *say* something about that which is so being referred to. And even where, as in abortive cases of making a statement—that is, where we manage to pick out something but do not go on to say anything about what is thus picked out—we have at least managed with some degree of success (for example through the use of token indexical expressions, demonstratives, or proper names) to mention or to point to something about which we *might have* gone on to say something. However, the term 'Existence' does not function in any of these ways. For Existence is not anything that can be *described* or *picked out*. And for this reason we face a wholly different situation from what we ordinarily face when asked to give the meaning of a term. We come armed, as it were, with criteria of meaningful reference and meaningful descriptions that are appropriate to all those individuals with which we ordinarily have commerce. All our ordinary language and the logic that specifies the criteria for the effective use of this language have to do with these normal uses. When we seek to apply these criteria, however, to Existence we find they are wholly inappropriate. Strictly speaking, therefore, the term 'Existence' is not a name at all. We should be obliged to give altogether negative accounts of it, if pressed, or else resort to synonyms that are just as unenlightening as the term 'Existence' itself.

The point then that we need to stress in connection with the 'wholly other' use of the term 'Existence' is that its use is not to be found in a propositional context of a predicational sort. We are not to look at it, for example, as a referring expression that might occupy the subject role in a proposition. Nor indeed could it fruitfully serve in a predicate role, for to what could such a putative predicate apply except to Existence itself? And in this case we should have nothing more than a trivial identity or a degenerative proposition. For the term 'Existence' functions neither as a subject nor as a predicate. It is thus perhaps best to think of it not as a term in a proposition at all. It is a 'term' only in an extended and special sense, whose role, if it has one at all, is not to be found in any part of a propositional assertion.

It follows from this that ontology, in the sense of a body of propositional discourse purporting to give us some reasoned conclusions about Existence as the subject of our knowledge, is impossible. For not only is there no such thing as an ontological theory about Existence, whether of a rigorously demonstrative kind or even of a more loosely probabilistic sort, there are not, even more stringently, single ontological propositions at all, let alone propositions that form parts of more complex argument-structures. For to have an ontological proposition is to be able to say something about something. And if the subject of our would-be ontological assertion is Existence, what is there we can say about it? Anything we can say about Existence, if it is to be taken literally, would be a tautology such as "Existence is Existence", or "Existence exists". Any other statement would be at best metaphorical, borrowing its terms of description from some segmental domain of The Universe, yet not literally applicable to Existence itself.

One might sum all this up by saying it is a plea for a 'negative ontology'. Just as in the theistic tradition, 'negative theology' proclaimed the total impossibility of saying anything literal and informative about God, so, for us, 'negative ontology' asserts a parallel ultimacy and cognitive inaccessibility of Existence.

It emerges from this that Existence, in its 'wholly other' aspect, is not a proper subject matter for *study* by philosophy, although in another sense it is perhaps the most important *topic* for philosophy to consider. At the point where this paradox takes hold, religion enters—or rather religious experience. Existence, as a *mysterium tremendum et fascinans*, needs to be recognized as the principal target of religious experience, and not as the subject for either conceptual analysis or scientific exploration. Moreover, philosophy—in one direction of its cultivation—can have no higher ambition or more fruitful outcome than, by means of conceptual analysis and argument, preparing the ground and making the way clear for this culminating religious awareness.

One way of summing up the differences that have engaged our attention in distinguishing The Universe, The World, and Existence from one another is to characterize the type of human response appropriate to each. For knowing about *The Universe* we rely on ordinary commonsense experience and science. To deal with *The World* we employ ontology as a positive, discursive, philosophic discipline. On the other hand, the only response appropriate to *Existence* would seem to be negative ontology and a mystical or religious type of human experience. Confusion, intellectual rivalry, and controversies as to 'competence' and 'meaningfulness' result from a failure to keep these separate and operative each in its proper domain and on its own level. One outcome of our investigation, it is to be hoped, is an ecumenical awareness of the conjoint harmony that could prevail among these several human interests when each is allowed to perform its own distinctive role.

The chief problem of ontology, as I have argued, is to give a satisfactory account of existence, and this amounts to giving an analysis of the relation of the domain of plural existents to the transcendent One that is Existence. In traditional 'religious' terms, it is to give an account of the relation of the finite to the Infinite. In the history of thought there have been, among others, two main types of 'solutions' to this problem, each in its own way highly influential. One, whose chief example is theism, takes the relation to be that modeled on causality: The One (God) creates the world (the domain of the Many). In other terminology, the Infinite is the 'ground', 'source', 'cause' of the finite Many. The other view takes the domain of the Many as a domain of illusion, of appearances that screen the True Reality which is The One, and where only the eventual disclosure of The One brings genuine enlightenment. I shall refer to the first type of view as that of *Creationism*, that of the second as *Illusionism*. My own attempt at showing how both the domain of existents (The World) as well as transcendent Existence itself is, each in its own way, an abstractive ontologic aspect of The Universe would involve a rejection of both Creationism and Illusionism.

I would argue against the first view that there is for ontology no relation of production, causation, derivation, or creation holding between the One Existence and the many existents. Both the One and the Many are equally real and primary, different sides or aspects of what exists. Causality however applies only *within* the domain of existents, when these are in turn filled out in all their descriptive richness in order for causal relations to be suitably expressed and embedded. Causality does not, however, cut across and hold as a linkage between Existence and existents.

The second view, the illusionistic one, has been the dominant view in some Indian religious philosophies. For this type of outlook the world, as a realm of plural existents does not have a *subordinate* status as in creationism; in creationism plural existents though subordinate to the ultimate reality of God, are nevertheless real. For Illusionism, rather, the world is a domain of illusion and unreality, preoccupation with which shields us from coming to know the *only* genuine reality, and that some would call 'Brahman'.

Now this ontological disparagement of the realm of plural existents is a thesis with which the ontology developed in this book has no sympathy. To ignore the reality of existents is to ignore that aspect of existence which derives in the first place from seeing that The Universe is a whole of many parts: and these parts, however we come to identify, enumerate, and classify them, *do* belong to The Universe: without them it could not be a Universe at all. Indeed therefore Existence, as the other aspect of The Universe—its aspect of being indescribable and conceptually inaccessible (what we become aware of when all multiplicity drops out of view but not out of existence)—cannot itself be real unless there were also a multiplicity of parts. To deny reality to the domain of existents is tantamount to removing the very ontological base for Existence itself.

I think it is important to keep separate these two things: (1) the extent to which concepts, judgments, and the exercise of human faculties of perception, imagination, and intelligence are relevant and ineradicably important for dealing with the domain of finite existents; and (2) the inappropriateness and irrelevancy of these same faculties and methods when dealing with Existence. The great mistake is to select one of these as all-sufficient and to ignore or condemn the other. This would be a mistake not only for ontology which undertakes to determine the nature of existence; it would also be a mistake for any *value* considerations that would counsel us in what directions we are to look in order to exercise to the fullest our human faculties. In this respect the pragmatists, materialists, nominalists, and various species of moral idealists, are guilty of ignoring the extent to which we must also dwell upon and acknowledge the Transcendent.

On the other hand, those who condemn intellect, judgment, conceptual analysis, because they have, through meditative exercise, succeeded in ridding the mind of these and any regard for the private self, the social scene, or the natural world, are just as guilty of philosophic and human inadequacy. Having found tranquility in their awareness of Brahman or a state of Nirvana, they relegate the domain of ordinary human affairs, and the exercise of reason and conceptual understanding, to the status of illusion. On a practical level this only paves the way for disaster, and on a philosophic level it shows a failure to do equal justice to the finite as it would to the Infinite.

What is called for is not a preference for The One over the Many, an exclusive mystical absorption in the former as the sole ultimate reality, but an awareness of the *coordinate* ontologic status of the realm of the many existents and Existence. The task of elaborating in adequate detail the lineaments of such a coordinative analysis of the two sides or dimensions of existence, of existents and Existence, is the major task of philosophy. It would seek to bring to a harmonious integration the best available insights of the rich heritage of the East and West, and thereby provide the philosophic support and matrix in which both a serious regard for science and an equally serious regard for the rewards of a transcendental spirituality can be realized.

Notes

Preface

1. M. K. Munitz, *Space, Time, and Creation* (Glencoe, Illinois: Free Press, 1957; reprinted, New York: Crowell-Collier, 1961).
2. M. K. Munitz, *The Mystery of Existence* (New York: Appleton-Century-Crofts, 1965; reprinted, New York: Dell Publishing Co., 1968; New York University Press, 1974).

Chapter Two

1. The challenge to this position has been effectively made by G. E. L. Owen, "Eleatic Questions," *Classical Quarterly*, X (1960), 84-102.
2. "... No one with a live religious sense will refuse to count his pure ontology as a genuine mystery and revelation; nor will he fail to be deeply stirred when he sees how much it meant to Parmenides to experience the nature of Being." W. Jaeger, *Theology of the Early Greek Philosophers* (Oxford: Clarendon Press, 1947), 107. Cf. F. M. Cornford, *Plato and Parmenides* (London: Routledge and Kegan Paul, 1939), 28; W. K. C. Guthrie, *A History of Greek Philosophy* (Cambridge: Cambridge University Press, 1962), II, 13.
3. Here I use the translation of C. H. Kahn, "The Thesis of Parmenides," *Review of Metaphysics*, XXII (1969), 703, 711, 713.
4. The term νοῆσαι should be translated as 'for knowing'. Many interpretations go wrong in trying to make sense of Parmenides by translating the verb νοειν and its various forms as having to do with *thought*. "... as von Fritz has shown, the sense of νοειν in early Greek is not some vaguely psychological notion of 'thinking,' not even the pseudo-logical concept of conceiving or imagining consistently (as in a speculative 'thought-

experiment'), but rather one of *noticing, observing, realizing, gaining insight* into the identity of a person, into the facts of a situation and their true implications; νοειν is 'a kind of mental perception . . . a kind of sixth sense which penetrates deeper into the nature of the object.' . . . The proper translation for the verb in Parmenides is a term like 'cognition' or 'knowledge'; it is paraphrased by γνῶναι, 'to recognize, be acquainted with,' at 2.7." (Kahn, *loc.cit.*, 703, footnote.)

5. Parmenides's term is one which describes this course or route as one which "turns back on itself" (B 7.9 παλίντροπος); cf. A. P. D. Mourelatos, *The Route of Parmenides* (New Haven: Yale University Press, 1970), 77.

6. A useful summary and codification of these is to be found in Mourelatos, *op.cit.*, 269-76.

7. Mourelatos, *op.cit.*; G. E. L. Owen, "Eleatic Questions," *loc. cit.*; M. Furth, "Elements of Eleatic Ontology," *Journal of the History of Philosophy*, VI (1968), 111-32.

8. I use Kahn's translations, *loc. cit.*, 721.

9. See C. H. Kahn, *The Verb 'Be' in Ancient Greek* (Dordrecht: D. Reidel, 1973); same author, "On the Theory of the Verb 'To Be' " in M. K. Munitz (ed.), *Logic and Ontology* (New York: New York University Press, 1973), 1-20.

10. Cf., e.g.: "Parmenides himself was unconscious [of the ambiguity] between the predicative and the existential uses of the Greek word εστι. . . . Parmenides is attacking those who believe, as all men always had believed, that it is possible to make a significant negative predication; but he is enabled to attack them only because of his own confusion between a negative predication and a negative existential judgment." G. S. Kirk and J. E. Raven, *The Presocratic Philosophers* (Cambridge: Cambridge University Press, 1957), 269-70.

11. ". . . the rejection of the negative route is not a rejection of negative predication in general." (Mourelatos, *op. cit.*, 75).

12. Cf. Kahn, *The Verb 'Be' in Ancient Greek*, Ch. VII, sec.2.

13. B 27; Mourelatos's translation, *op. cit.*, 75.

14. "It is remarkable that so many of the metaphors *we* are inclined to use as vehicles for the concept of 'ultimate reality' are found in B8. We say 'in itself' or 'self-contained'; Parmenides says ταυτον τ'εν ταυτω, 'the same and in the same' (8.29), and οι . . . ισον, 'equal to itself' (8.49). We say 'self-sufficient'; Parmenides says ουκ επιδευες, 'not in need' (8.33). We say 'in a strict sense'; Parmenides projects this as a personified Constraint who binds with 'fetters' and 'shackles'. We speak of being 'in the fullest sense'; Parmenides says παν εμπλεον . . . εοντος, 'all of it full of what-is' (8.26). We speak of being 'in its own right'; Parmenides

anticipates the metaphor with the mythical projection of Justice and Right Ordinance as guarantors of the identity of what-is. We speak of 'absolute' being; Parmenides emphasizes that the what-is has been gathered apart as a result of κρισις, 'decision' or 'separation' (cf. 8.16), and adds that it abides καθ εαυτο, 'by itself' (8.29). The very idea of 'ultimate' is implicit in his assignment of the τελος attribute to the real." (Mourelatos, *Route*, 135.)

15. As, e.g., Kahn argues in "Thesis," *Review of Metaphysics, loc. cit.,* 715.

16. Kirk and Raven put it thus: "Truth is described as well-rounded because, presumably, wherever you pick up the chain of Parmenides' reasoning, you can follow it round in a circle, passing through each of its links in turn, back to your starting point. . . . Every attribute of reality can be deduced from every other." (*Presocratic Philosophers*, 268.)

17. B8.7-10; Mourelatos's translation, 98.

18. Kahn's translation, "Thesis," *loc. cit.,* 717.

19. Mourelatos's translation, 105.

20. Cf. G. E. L. Owen, "Plato and Parmenides on the Timeless Present," *The Monist*, L (1966), 319. Plato echoes this use of the tenseless 'is' in his own philosophy (in connection with the timeless Forms)—as, e.g., in the following passage: "Days, nights, months, years . . . are all parts of time, and 'was' and 'will be' have come about as forms of time. We are wrong to apply them unthinkingly to what is eternal. Of this we say that it was and is and will be, but strictly only 'is' belongs to it. 'Was' and 'will be' should be spoken of the process that goes on in time, for they are changes." (*Timaeus*, 37e-38a.)

21. Cf. Mourelatos, *Route*, 108: "Even if the terms αναρχον απαυστον of B8.27 are to be understood as excluding a temporal beginning and end . . . this in no way presupposes duration. It is characteristic of Parmenidean negations that they are unrestricted. And so αναρχον απαυστον would carry the strong sense: '*not* the *sort* of thing that can have a beginning, or end'. If the application of these words presupposes duration, then, by the same argument, the application of αγενητον presupposes the possibility of generation: or the application of ακινητον the possibility of motion. For in these cases too we can distinguish between 'unborn' and 'ungener*able*', or 'unmoving' and 'unmov*able*'. We can be confident that Parmenides understands all these negative attributes (double negatives, according to his own account) with the force of the negative prefix unrestricted. The sense in each case corresponds to the English '____able' version (for example, 'immovable' rather than 'unmoving')." Cf. W. Kneale, "Time and Eternity in Theology," *Proceedings of the Aristotelian Society* (1960-61), 87-88.

22. Cf. Mourelatos, *Route*, 113.

23. "Plato and Parmenides," 321.
24. I use G. E. L. Owen's translation, "Eleatic Questions," *loc. cit.*, 88.

Chapter Three

1. For a recent statement, see P. Merlan, "On the Terms 'Metaphysics' and 'Being-qua-Being'," *The Monist*, LII (1968) 174-94. An extensive historical summary of the views of other thinkers, ancient and modern, will be found in J. Owens, *The Doctrine of Being in the Aristotelian Metaphysics* (Toronto: Pontifical Institute of Mediaeval Studies, 1957), Ch.1.
2. R. G. Collingwood, *Metaphysics* (Oxford: Clarendon Press, 1940), 6-10.
3. In connection with this last form of the question, it would be an error to interpret Aristotle's concern as having to do with one and only one such entity, 'That which is' (τὸ ον). Cf. C. Kirwan, *Aristotle's Metaphysics Books* Γ, Δ and E (Oxford: Clarendon Press, 1971), ch. i,1003ᵉ21, Notes,77.
4. My discussion is much indebted to C. H. Kahn's *The Verb 'Be' in Ancient Greek*, Ch. II.
5. Cf. Ackrill's comments on Aristotle's discussion in *Categories*, Ch. 2, on the distinction between 'said of a subject' and 'in a subject', and the fourfold classification that results from combining these with their negatives: "It is often held that 'said of' and 'in' introduce notions of radically different types, the former being linguistic or grammatical, the latter metaphysical or ontological; and that, correspondingly, the word translated 'subject' (literally, 'what underlies') means 'grammatical subject' in the phrase 'said of a subject' and 'substrate' in 'in a subject'. In fact, however, it is perfectly clear that Aristotle's fourfold classification is a classification of things and not names, and that what is 'said of' something as subject is itself a thing (a species or genus) and not a name. Sometimes, indeed, Aristotle will speak of 'saying' or 'predicating' a *name* of a subject; but it is not linguistic items but the things they signify which are 'said of a subject' in the sense in which this expression is used in Chapter 2. Thus at 2a19ff. Aristotle sharply distinguishes things said of subjects from the names of those things: if *A* is said of *B* it follows that the name of *A*, '*A*', can be predicated of *B*, though from the fact that '*A*' is predicable of something it does not follow that *A* is said of that thing. . . . Being said of a subject is no more a linguistic property than is being in a subject—though Aristotle's adoption of the phrase 'said of' to express the relation of genus to species and of species to individual may have been due to the fact that if *A* is the genus or species of *B* it follows that '*A*' can be predicated of *B*." J. L.

Ackrill, *Aristotle's* Categories *and* De Interpretatione (Oxford: Clarendon Press, 1963), 75-76.

6. See C. Lejewski, "Proper Names," *Proceedings of the Aristotelian Society*
   (1958), 229-30.

7. In trying to understand and assess Aristotle's use of ontologic predication, it would be necessary to get clear about the precise ontologic status
   of what grammatical predicates stand for. Are they in some sense
   'universals' that are, qua universals, independent of the particulars that
   instantiate them? How then do such universals differ from Plato's
   conception of the Forms? If they have no being independently of
   particulars altogether, how nevertheless is the being of such universals
   to be conceived as independent of this or that particular? On the other
   hand, if the ontological counterparts of predicate terms have some
   extensional being only in the individuals that instantiate them, as
   individuated, how can they still continue to be thought of as predicates,
   as *general*, that is as something 'common' and 'shareable' among a
   plurality of individuals? Moreover, if the form exists only as individual,
   then on Aristotle's own view an individual, a *this*-such, can *never* be a
   predicate. These questions have no clear and definite answers. Yet
   despite their relevance and importance, we need not hesitate to continue to speak of Aristotle's view as supporting the notion of ontologic
   predication; to say that for him the predicate in *some sense* is 'out there'
   and 'belongs to' the subject, and where, of course, the subject too is 'out
   there' in the world.

8. Cf. S. Mansion, "Notes sur la doctrine des catégories dans les *Topiques*"
   in G. E. L. Owen (ed.), *Aristotle on Dialectic* (Oxford: Clarendon Press,
   1968), 198 ff.

9. Cf. G. E. L. Owen, "Aristotle on the Snares of Ontology," in R.
   Bambrough (ed.), *New Essays on Plato and Aristotle* (London: Routledge
   and Kegan Paul, 1965). "There are passages where Aristotle does seem
   to assign the *copulative* 'is' a different sense in different categories: a text
   such as *Prior Analytics* A 48b 2-9 (cf. 49a 6-9) suggests the explanation. 'A
   is B' can be turned into 'B belongs to A', and 'belongs to' has a different
   sense in different categories: why? Because for *red* to exist is for it to be a
   quality, so for *red* to belong to A is for it to be a quality of A; and the
   analysis would be different with predicates of substance or quantity,
   etc." p. 82.

10. See *Topics* 144a 36-b 3; cf. W. D. Ross, *Commentary on Aristotle's Meta-
    physics* (Oxford: Clarendon Press, 1924), I, 235.

11. Thus, let

    (1)   if anything is a *man* (A, species) it is an *animal* (B, genus)
    (2)   if anything is a *man* it is *rational* (C, differentia)

represent what are the normal relations among genus, species, differentia. If we were to allow a genus to be 'predicated of a differentia', we should have the following for the above example:

(3)   if anything is *rational* it is an *animal*.

But then by combining (3) and (2) we could derive (1), and therefore since we have already established (1) without benefit of derivation, simply as a normal relationship between species and genus, to assert (3) is to say more than is required: it is redundant with respect to (1). It yields (1) as a conclusion, whereas it has already been asserted independently.

12. As G. E. L. Owen points out, "Philosophers who remark that existence is not a predicate sometimes find support in Aristotle's argument that being is not a genus. But what Aristotle says is that 'to be' means 'to be so-and-so', and that the values of 'so-and-so' vary with the sort of subject we assign the verb. So it seems that if Aristotle does not treat existence as a predicate this is only because he treats it as a disjunctive set of predicates." "Aristotle on the Snares of Ontology," in R. Bambrough (ed.), *New Essays on Plato and Aristotle* (*op. cit.*), p. 78.

13. Cf. L. Wittgenstein, *Tractatus*, 4.1272 and 4.12721.

14. *Anal. Post.* 92b 13-14; Geach's translation in G. E. M. Anscombe and P. T. Geach, *Three Philosophers* (Oxford: Basil Blackwell, 1961), 89.

15. Cf. A. Kosman, "Aristotle's First Predicament," *Review of Metaphysics*, XXI (1967), 483 ff.

16. Cf. J. L. Ackrill, *Aristotle's* Categories *and* De Interpretatione (*op.cit.*), "Notes," 74, 80, 83.

17. *Met.* Z,Ch. 13; M. J. Woods, "Problems in *Metaphysics Z*, Chapter 13," in J. M. E. Moravcsik (ed.), *Aristotle* (New York: Doubleday [Anchor Books], 1967), 215-38; R. Albritton, "Forms of Particular Substances in Aristotle's Metaphysics," *Journal of Philosophy*, LIV (1957), 699-708.

18. Cf. Anscombe and Geach, *Three Philosophers*, 16-39; G. E. L. Owen, "Inherence," *Phronesis*, X (1965), 97ff.; R. E. Allen, "Individual Properties in Aristotle's Categories," *Phronesis*, XIV (1969), 31 ff.; J. Duerlinger, "Predication and Inherence in Aristotle's Categories," *Phronesis*, XV (1970), 179 ff.

19. It would be helpful to distinguish two different senses of 'accident' (or 'accidentally') involved in these examples: where 'white' or 'musical' is, let us assume, predicated of a man, separately and veridically, we can, as we have pointed out, form the compound 'musical man' or 'white man' and each, when accompanied by a demonstrative (as 'this'), will serve to refer to a single *per accidens* existent. Since 'white' or 'musical' are not part of the definition ('essence') of 'man', each is an 'accident'.

The first meaning of 'accident', then, as brought out by these examples, is 'not part of the definition, not essential'. On the other hand, if from the statement 'this white man is musical' the expression 'this white man' is formed, 'this musical' would be a case of a *per accidens existent* in the sense that 'white' and 'musical' are *coincidentally present* in the same subject (man). 'Coincidental co-presence' might then serve to distinguish a second sense of 'accidental'; and a second type of *per accidens* existent would be one in which this second sense of 'accidental predication' were involved (cf. Ackrill, Notes to *De Interp.* 21a7, pp. 147-8).

Chapter Four

1. See M. Dummett, *Frege: Philosophy of Language* (London: Duckworth, 1973), chs. 2,3.
2. B. Russell, *Logic and Knowledge* (London: Allen and Unwin, 1956), 232.
3. W. V. Quine, *Ontological Relativity and Other Essays* (New York: Columbia University Press, 1969), 97.
4. Cf. T. Hailperin and H. Leblanc, "Non-designating Singular Terms," *Philosophical Review*, 68 (1959), 129-36; J. Hintikka, *Models for Modalities* (Dordrecht: D. Reidel, 1969); C. Lejewski,"Logic and Existence," *British Journal for the Philosophy of Science, 5* (1954), 104-19; K. Lambert, *The Logical Way of Doing Things* (New Haven: Yale University Press, 1969); R. Schock, *Logics Without Existence Assumptions* (Stockholm: Almqvist and Wiksell, 1968); A. Orenstein, "Existence and Quantification" (Ph.D. Thesis, New York University, 1972); J. Dunn and N. D. Belnap, Jr., "The Substitution Interpretation of the Quantifiers," *Nous*, II (1968), 177-85; L. Linsky, "Two Concepts of Quantification," *Nous*, VI (1972), 224-39; R. Marcus, "Quantification and Ontology," *Nous*, VI (1972) 240-50.
5. See Dummett, *op. cit.*, chs. 2, 3, 8, 18.
6. G. Frege, *The Foundations of Arithmetic*, trans. J. L. Austin (Oxford: Basil Blackwell, 1950), 65.
7. *Foundations of Arithmetic*, 64-65.
8. "Concept and Object," in P. Geach and M. Black (eds.), *Translations from the Philosophical Writings of Gottlob Frege* (Oxford: Basil Blackwell, 1952), 49; cf. I. Angelelli, *Studies on Gottlob Frege and Traditional Philosophy* (New York: Humanities Press, 1967), 181.
9. *Translations from the Philosophical Writings. . .* , 50.
10. Cf. Angelelli, *op. cit.*, 225.
11. *Translations from the Philosophical Writings*, 50.
12. *Logic and Knowledge*, 234.

13. "The Existential Import of Propositions," *Mind*, 14 (1905), 398-401; reprinted in B. Russell, *Essays in Analysis* (ed. D. Lackey) (New York: George Braziller, 1974), 98-99.
14. Reprinted in *Logic and Knowledge*.
15. *Ibid.*, 232.
16. *Ibid.*, 234.
17. *Ibid.*, 230.
18. *Ibid.*, 232; cf. *Principia Mathematica*: "The symbol '$(\exists x)$. ϕx' may be read 'there exists an x for which ϕx is true,' or 'there exists an x satisfying ϕx . . .' " (Vol. I, 15).
19. *Logic and Knowledge*, 232-3.
20. *Ibid.*, 231.
21. *Ibid.*, 254.
22. *Ibid.*, 252.
23. *Ibid.*, 233.
24. *Ibid.*, 233.
25. *Ibid.*, 250.
26. G. Ryle, "Systematically Misleading Expressions," in A. Flew (ed.), *Logic and Language*, First Series (Oxford: Basil Blackwell, 1952), 18.
27. P. Geach, *God and Soul* (London: Routledge and Kegan Paul, 1969), 65.
28. G. Ryle, *The Concept of Mind* (London: Hutchinson's University Library, 1949), 23.
29. W. V. Quine, *From a Logical Point of View* (Cambridge, Mass.: Harvard University Press, 1953), 21.
30. Cf. C. A. Hooker, "Quine on the Referential Functions of Bound Variables and Quantifiers," *Mind*, LXXX (1971) 481-96.
31. W. V. Quine, *The Ways of Paradox* (New York: Random House, 1966), 128.
32. W. V. Quine, *Word and Object* (New York: John Wiley, 1960), 179; cf. *Ways of Paradox*, 225.
33. *Word and Object*, 179.
34. *From a Logical Point of View*, 102.
35. *Ibid.*, 103.
36. *Ibid.*, 105.
37. W. V. Quine, "Existence," in W. Yourgrau, *Physics, Logic and History* (New York: Plenum Press, 1970), 91.
38. *Word and Object*, 179, 182.
39. Cf. Quine, "Notes on Existence and Necessity," *Journal of Philosophy*, 40 (1943) 113-27; W. V. Quine, *Mathematical Logic* (New York: Norton, 1940), 150; W. V. Quine, *Methods of Logic* (New York: Henry Holt, 1950), 148; C. Lejewski, "Logic and Existence," *British Journal for the Philosophy of Science, loc. cit.*
40. "Existence," in Yourgrau, *op. cit.*, 90.

41. *Ways of Paradox*, 225; italics mine.
42. See A. Orenstein, "On Explicating Existence in Terms of Quantification," in M. K. Munitz (ed.), *Logic and Ontology*, 59-84.
43. Cf. *Word and Object*, 176.

Chapter Five

1. Geach's account of the philosophic theory we are about to examine is to be found principally in his papers "Form and Existence" and "What Actually Exists" (both reprinted in P. Geach, *God and Soul*) and in P. Geach and G. E. M. Anscombe, *Three Philosophers*, ch. II (Aquinas).
2. *Three Philosophers*, 90.
3. *Ibid.*, 91.
4. *God and Soul*, 58.
5. *Three Philosophers*, 91 ff.
6. *God and Soul*, 60.
7. *Ibid.*, 59.
8. A convenient scheme of classification is offered by Zeno Vendler in his "Verbs and Times," *Philosophical Review*, LXVI (1957), 143-60, to which my own discussion is indebted.
9. *Three Philosophers*, 80.
10. Cf. *God and Soul*, 42.
11. *God and Soul*, 61.
12. *Ibid.*
13. *Ibid.*
14. *Ibid.*, 65. This definition of 'actual' accommodates a sense of 'act' which can be *distinguished* from 'that which undergoes change' and hence which need not itself be characterized as undergoing change, although it may 'initiate' changes in things. Such a characterization of 'act' allows the use of the term as applying to God. But the sense of 'actuality' with which I am at present concerned is to be understood in a sufficiently broad sense as *including* change. In this respect I shall follow the account of the word 'actual' given by Frege who remarks that the world of the actual is "a world in which this acts on that, changes it, and again experiences reactions itself and is changed by them." Thus whereas Geach makes actuality a matter of *either* acting or undergoing change, or both, Frege's account is conjunctive, requiring both. Cf. R. H. Stoothoff, "What Actually Exists," *Proceedings of the Aristotelian Society Supplementary Volume* XLII (1968), 17.
15. For a fuller discussion of what is meant by the phrase "individual fragment, or part, of of the world," see below, Chapter 8.

16. G. E. Moore, *The Commonplace Book 1919-1953* (ed. C. Lewy) (London: Allen and Unwin, 1962), 329; cf. A. N. Prior, *Past, Present, and Future* (Oxford: Clarendon Press, 1967), 151.

Chapter Six

1. Cf. P. F. Strawson, "Identifying Reference and Truth-values," *Logico-Linguistic Papers* (London: Methuen, 1971), 75.
2. Cf. P. F. Strawson, *Introduction to Logical Theory* (London: Methuen, 1952), 175; "Reply to Sellars," *Philosophical Review*, LXIII (1954), 216.
3. P. F. Strawson, *Introduction to Logical Theory*, 175; cf. Bas C. van Fraassen, "Presupposition, Implication and Self-Reference," *Journal of Philosophy*, LXV (1968), 136-52.
4. These have been critically examined in G. Nerlich, "Presupposition and Entailment," *American Philosophical Quarterly*, 2 (1965), 33-42 and in G. Nerlich, "Presupposition and Classical Logical Relations," *Analysis*, XXVII (1967), 104-6.
5. *Loc. cit.*, Nerlich, "Presupposition and Entailment," 34.
6. For example, he writes: "Thus, that there exists a particular item to which the name or description is applicable and which, if not unique in this respect, satisfies some uniqueness-condition known to the hearer (*and* satisfies some uniqueness condition known to the speaker) is no part of what the speaker *asserts* in an utterance in which the name or description is used to perform the function of identifying reference; it is, rather, a *presupposition* of his asserting what he asserts." ("Identifying Reference and Truth Values," *Logico-Linguistic Papers*, 80.)
7. P. F. Strawson, "Is Existence Never a Predicate?", *Critica*, 1 (1967), 5.
8. P. F. Strawson (ed.), *Philosophical Logic* (London: Oxford University Press, 1967), "Introduction," 3.
9. "Is Existence Never a Predicate?", *loc. cit.*, 12.
10. "Introduction," *loc. cit.*, 3.
11. P. F. Strawson, *Individuals* (London: Methuen, 1959), 239.
12. *Ibid.*, 227.
13. *Introduction to Logical Theory*, 191.
14. *Individuals*, 239 f.
15. "Is Existence Never a Predicate?," *loc. cit.*
16. *Ibid.*, 12.
17. *Ibid.*, 13.
18. *Ibid.*, 14-15.
19. *Ibid.*, 14; my italics.
20. *Ibid.*, 14-15; my italics.

Chapter Seven

1. See Dummett, *op. cit.*, 198-203, 427-429.
2. My analysis is indebted to C. Lejewski's "The Problem of Ontological Commitment," *Fragmenty Filozoficzne Seria Trzecia Ksiega Pamiatkowa Ku Czi Porfesora Tadeusza Kotarbinskiego* (Warsaw: Panstwowe Wydawnietwo, Nankowe, 1967), 147-64.
3. See Lejewski, *op. cit.*

Chapter Eight

1. The principal sources on Mereology are the following: Leśniewski, Stanislaw, 'O podstawach matematyki' *Przeglad Filzoficzny*, vols. 30-34, 1927-1931. (Vol. 30, pp. 164-69; 169-81, 182-89, 190-206; vol. 31, pp. 261-91; vol. 32, pp. 60-101; vol. 33, pp. 77-81, 82-86, 87-90, 90-105; vol. 34, pp. 142-53, 153-70.) Of these vol. 31, pp. 261-91, deals with the "Foundations of general theory of manifolds" (later renamed Mereology) and recapitulates the 1916 article *Podstawy ogognej teoryi mnogosci* I., Moscow (Foundations of general theory of manifolds, or collective sets). A useful summary of Leśniewski's theory is to be found in B. Sobocinski, "Studies in Leśniewski's mereology," *Polish Society of Arts and Sciences Abroad, Yearbook for 1954-55* (Rocznik V, pp. 34-43); cf. Eugene C. Luschei, *The Logical Systems of Leśniewski*, North Holland Publishing Co., 1962; B. Sobocinski, "L'Analyse de l'antinomie russellienne par Leśniewski," *Methodos*, vols. I, II, 1949-50; B. Sobocinski, "Atomistic Mereology," *Notre Dame Journal of Formal Logic*, XII (January 1971), 89-103 (April, 1971), 203-13; C. Lejewski, "A single axiom for the mereological notion of proper part," *Notre Dame Journal of Formal Logic*, VII (1967), 279-85.
2. Cf. Lejewski, "The Problem of Ontological Commitment," *loc. cit.*
3. "Foundations. . . ," *30* (1927), Sec. III.
4. Cf. B. Sobocinski, "Studies in Leśniewski's Mereology," *loc. cit.*, 4, D6.
5. Cf. A. Tarski, *Logic, Semantics and Metamathematics* (Oxford: Clarendon Press, 1956), 333, footnote.
6. Cf. M. K. Munitz (ed.), *Theories of the Universe* (Glencoe, Illinois: Free Press, 1957); M. K. Munitz, *Space, Time, and Creation*; M. K. Munitz, *The Mystery of Existence*, Ch. 4; M. K. Munitz, article on 'Cosmology' in *Encyclopedia of Philosophy* (ed. P. Edwards, New York: Macmillan, 1967); M. K. Munitz, article on 'Universe' in *Encyclopedia Americana*; M. K. Munitz, "The Use of 'The Universe'," *Monist, 48* (1964), 185-94.

7. Cf. M. K. Munitz, "One Universe or Many?" *Journal of the History of Ideas*, XII (1951), 231-55.

8. Cf. M. K. Munitz, "Kantian Dialectic and Modern Scientific Cosmology," *Journal of Philosophy*, XLVIII (1951), 325-38.

9. B. Sobocinski, "Atomistic Mereology," *Notre Dame Journal of Formal Logic*, XII (1971), 93; cf. Sobocinski, "Studies in Mereology," *loc. cit.*, 5; A. Tarski, "Appendix E" to J. H. Woodger, *Axiomatic Method in Biology* (Cambridge: Cambridge University Press, 1937), 162.

10. Cf. L. Wittgenstein, *Tractatus Logico-Philosophicus*, 4.1272; M. K. Munitz, "The Concept of the World," in H. Kiefer and M. K. Munitz (eds.), *Language, Belief, and Metaphysics* (Volume I, *Contemporary Philosophic Thought*) (Albany, New York: State University of New York Press, 1970), 190-235.

Index

219